The Praesidium

by

Paul Georgiou

Published by Panarc International 2018
Copyright © Paul Georgiou, 2016

First Edition

The author asserts the moral right under the Copyright, Designs and Patents Act 1988 to be identified as the author of this work.

All rights reserved. No part of this publication may be reproduced, stored in a retrieval system or transmitted, in any form or by any means without the prior consent of the author, nor be otherwise circulated in any form of binding or cover other than that in which it is published and without a similar condition being imposed on the subsequent purchaser.

www.panarcpublishing.com

Panarc International Ltd
www.panarc.com

Paperback: 978-0-9931103-9-9
Epub: 978-0-9954637-0-7
Kindle: 978-0-9954637-1-4

Contents

Author's introduction		1
1.	R & R	4
2.	Westminster	8
3.	Noble schemes and Minofel machinations	16
4.	Harrovian stirrings	22
5.	Adam meets the Praesidium	25
6.	Kit's mission	31
7.	Ground rules	35
8.	The first lesson	39
9.	What's wrong with religion	41
10.	Excursion 1 – Edgar Exton	46
11.	Regrouping	51
12.	Excursion 2 – Lotte Axelrod	55
13.	Communication established	64
14.	Excursion 3 – Oliver Nates	67
15.	Chinks	77
16.	Action	80
17.	Excursion 4 – Charlie Cornick	84
18.	Aletheia	91
19.	Gloating	96
20.	Alarm bells	99
21.	Remission	102
22.	Excursion 5 – Charlie Cornick	105
23.	Swordplay	110
24.	Excursion 6 – Charlie Cornick	112
25.	Prepping Adam	115
26.	The coup	118
27.	Teleportation	129
28.	The breath of death	135
29.	First move	139
30.	Murder most foul	143
31.	An act of kindness	145
32.	Best laid plans	149
33.	Confusion	152
34.	A pre-trial consultation	157

35.	Technical speculations and practical plans	160
36.	Appointment of the defence counsel	164
37.	Serious words	168
38.	The long spoon	171
39.	Preliminary trial proceedings	174
40.	A death in the family	178
41.	Client relations	187
42.	The trial begins in earnest	191
43.	Good news, bad news	196
44.	The trial resumes	199
45.	The trial concludes	207
46.	The sentence	211
47.	Thoughts that do lie too deep	212
48.	A surprising reaction	217
49.	Preparing for the endgame	221
50.	The day of execution	224
51.	Diabolical discussion	233
52.	Problem resolution	236
53.	Meeting of the board	240
54.	"I would some god …"	243
55.	The brutal truth	248
56.	Job done	255

Author's introduction

In the first book, *The Fourth Beginning*, the Smiths, together with their dog, Luke, set out on an epic adventure to find answers to some of life's most challenging questions. Eve desperately wants to know why her daughter had to die; Adam is looking for reasons to live.

The questors' guide on the journey is the Storyteller. Their mode of transport is a camper van, equipped with an exponential drive and a paradox device, inventions of a couple of brilliant Irish engineers, the wizened Prune Leach and the long-legged Andrew Rimzil.

As soon as the journey begins, Adam and Eve are warned by the Breaker, Nick Peters, and his shapeshifter sidekick, Grimrose, that their quest is hopeless. Breakers argue that there is no truth out there to be found. If you want to understand anything, you have to take it apart. Undeterred, Adam and Eve persist, picking up an odd couple of hitch-hikers, the ever-curious Uncle Rambler and his willing pupil, Nephew Numpty, on the way.

The questors visit the God of the Old Testament in the Garden of Eden, near Hook, off the M3. The interview with God produces no answers to the questors' questions and, indeed, turns rather nasty when Eve gives God the sharp edge of her tongue. They escape a bloody end with the help of the enigmatic blind man, Kit.

Next, employing the exponential drive and the paradox device, the questors travel back in time to the Caucasus, where they are greeted by Prometheus who has always looked favourably on man. The Titan wishes to help but has no answers, other than to encourage the Smiths in their search for the truth and their hopes for the future.

The Storyteller then decides to give Adam and Eve a unique opportunity to witness the three great beginnings: the creation of the universe, the birth of life, and the emergence of human consciousness. None of these extraordinary events provides the Smiths with answers, but they do provide a feast for thought.

When the travellers return, they find themselves in a mysland, a virtual replica of a part of the New Forest. The mysland is entirely under the control of the Breakers, who have a regional office at Cadnam. The questors are arrested; Adam is imprisoned. The Breakers fear that the questors will initiate a fourth beginning.

After a violent and vicissitudinal struggle with Nick Peters and the Breakers, the questors, aided by the military might of the Metaphorce, seem to be victorious, and the Fourth Beginning is set in motion.

At this point, *The Devil's Truth*, the second book in the Truth quartet, begins.

After the abrupt termination of the Fourth Beginning, Adam and Eve Smith reluctantly settle back into their old lives until, unexpectedly, Adam is approached by the business consultancy firm Slievins. David Minofel, a partner in Slievins, makes an appointment to discuss Adam's future.

On the evening Minofel visits the Smiths' home in Harrow to offer Adam a job, a couple of burglars burst into the Smiths' home, and beat up Adam and Eve. Just as one of the burglars is about to rape Eve, Minofel arrives for his appointment with Adam. When he rings the bell, one of the burglars sends him away but, realising something is wrong, Minofel returns, bursting into the house and killing both burglars.

Adam and Eve are both inexpressibly grateful to Minofel, who reveals that he spent years in the SAS and, later, worked as a mercenary, before joining Slievins.

Adam's first Slievins posting is in Geneva, as Marketing Director of ZeD, a major Swiss pharmaceutical company. Adam's mentor in Geneva is the beautiful and highly intelligent Miss Gorgeous Tomic, personal assistant to the Managing Director of ZeD and another Slievins protégée. Adam quickly learns the Slievins philosophy. Define your goals, devise the most efficient way of achieving them regardless of moral considerations, and act, uninhibited by any scruples.

Meanwhile, at the Smiths' house in Harrow, the other questors, including Kit, the enigmatic blind man from *The Fourth Beginning*, have joined Eve. Kit is keen to reactivate the Fourth Beginning, but Eve and the other questors are less enthusiastic, fearful of swift retribution from whatever aborted it.

Undeterred, Kit visits Adam in Geneva, to enlist his support but meets with a cool reception.

Adam feels challenged but fulfilled by the demands of his new job. He enjoys the power he has to get things done and the extraordinary financial incentives he is given to succeed. His main task is to oversee the successful introduction of ZeD's new drug, Angeloma. All seems to be going well until a patient on the drug dies in a clinical trial in Basel.

Adam soon discovers that the application of Slievins' modus operandi involves him in bribery, blackmail and, finally, murder.

While Adam is in Geneva, Eve discovers she is pregnant. She misses Adam and becomes increasingly concerned that his work for ZeD is taking him over. As the weeks pass, their relationship deteriorates until she confides to Kit that she thinks she has lost Adam and that their marriage may be dying.

Although Adam does not fully understand Slievins' objectives, he enjoys tremendous success. Despite the collapse of ZeD in a maelstrom of corruption, his career, guided by Slievins, seems assured and his financial future secure. Indeed, the prospect of real wealth beckons. Perhaps even more importantly, Adam feels he has found a kind of truth, not the abstract truth he had sought in the Fourth Beginning, but a practical, pragmatic truth about the nature of man – and his own true nature.

Adam has no idea that Slievins is preparing him for the Praesidium, a secret organisation that for thousands of years, with the assistance of the Breakers, has been guiding man and directing history. The goal of the Praesidium is to enable man to be true to his own nature, and to reject at all costs any exhortations by what they call Emergents for man to aspire to be in any way better than he is. To this end, the Monitaurs, agents of the Praesidium, promote depravity, extremism, corruption, obfuscation and negativity.

Minofel is grooming Adam. He knows that Adam and Eve had set out with the Storyteller to find the truth. Minofel is going to provide Adam with a different kind of truth, one which will satisfy him and ensure that he and Eve are never again tempted to set out on another quest.

1. R & R

After the successful destruction of the pharmaceutical company ZeD, David Minofel, senior consultant, accomplished practitioner and effectively deputy CEO of the Slievins Consultancy, felt he was entitled to a few days rest and recuperation.

All the arrangements for the delivery of Adam to the Praesidium were in hand. Within a week, he would fly with Adam and Miss Gorgeous Tomic to London. In the meantime, he decided to recharge his batteries by returning to his house in Geneva and resuming work on his current literary project, a biography of Vlad the Impaler. He settled down in his study and prepared to write. He was determined to give the next few days to Vlad. For various reasons, the composition of the biography was taking far longer than he had intended.

Vlad the Impaler, or Dracula, had been a hero of Minofel's from his earliest years. Some of the stories about Vlad's brutality had been exaggerated, but even so the man had shown a talent for cruelty that few others could match. For committed sadists, there is an inherent problem in the exercise of their craft. Minofel knew well enough that after a while each act of cruelty loses its edge, not so much for the victim who generally expires before ennui can set in, but for the perpetrator. The first time you break a man's finger, you feel a frisson of pleasure more or less commensurate with the victim's pain. After the third or fourth finger, it becomes routine, boring, banal for the sadist.

Vlad fascinated Minofel not so much for his cruelty as for his apparent ability to continue to derive pleasure from the endless repetition of similar acts. His passion for impaling his victims was a case in point. The number of people (men, women and children) impaled by Vlad is disputed, but it is beyond question that he indulged this particular penchant with remarkable frequency.

To be fair, Vlad did turn the impaling of people into an art form. At its crudest, the victim would die immediately or, at best, within minutes. But with skill and admittedly some luck, the agony could be prolonged for hours or, in exceptional circumstances, for days. The trick was to avoid the vital organs. Impaling a person by driving the stake through the chest or stomach, though simple, was generally fatal immediately or, at most, after an hour or so. No, the art lay in driving the stake up through the body from below, through the anus and then following as closely as possible the path of the spine. If the point of the stake missed the vital organs, the victim could endure indescribable agony for days.

Minofel was particularly intrigued by the story of the two Catholic monks who inadvisedly visited Vlad in his palace at Targoviste, at that time the capital of Wallachia. Vlad invited them to survey his courtyard in which, as was often the case, there were rows of impaled corpses, the rotting bodies of those who had committed some crime or offended their prince in some way. Vlad asked the priests their opinion of his penal system. One priest answered that it was God's work to punish evildoers; the other priest condemned Vlad for his cruelty. What happened next is disputed, and the two versions fascinated David Minofel. According to one tradition, Vlad had the critical monk impaled for his impudence. But in the other tradition, Vlad had the sycophantic monk impaled for his cowardice. The first version suggested Vlad approved discretion; the second, moral courage and integrity. Minofel favoured the first version. After all, Vlad was certainly not a man to take impudence lightly. But in his own account of the incident, he decided it was far more likely that Vlad had both monks impaled.

Minofel's ruminations on Vlad prompted him to consider the long history of cruelty in human affairs. He conceded that the modern world had a much more refined sense of human rights than in Vlad's time. We have come a long way from the days when tyrants had the power of life and death over others. Now such power lay with democratic governments who, at the press of a button, could shower down in one minute more death and destruction, more pain and anguish on humanity than had been achieved by all the tyrants over millennia. But such modern acts of indiscriminate annihilation were not executed on the whim of a despot motivated by sadistic drives; rather they were acts of impersonal cruelty initiated and performed at a much higher, more bureaucratic, level on behalf of whole nations – and, therefore, in many ways more satisfying to the Praesidium and Slievins.

The sole purpose of the Praesidium and the Slievins Consultancy was to help man be true to his own nature. Aided by man's existential fear and proclivity for all forms of corruption, combined with an innate human capacity for hypocrisy, they had done rather well.

"One shouldn't underestimate hypocrisy," Minofel mused. He was thinking of the utterly absurd UN Declaration of Human Rights. How did it begin?

"We are all born free and equal in dignity and rights. We are endowed with reason and conscience, and should act towards one another in a spirit of brotherhood."

Pernicious, Emergent drivel!

If it was intended to be a statement of fact, it was false from start to finish.

Most people were not born free. They were not born free from even the most basic forms of repression – poverty and hunger – much less from the other political and economic constraints society imposed on them. They were not "equal in dignity and rights". A starving child has no dignity, unless there is dignity in hopeless and helpless submission to the inevitability of death. An innocent mother has no rights when a random bomb or mine blows her child to pieces.

"We are endowed with reason," Minofel scoffed out loud. Really! Most people are incapable of following the simplest logic. Nowadays, people happily hold completely inconsistent views, so long as they feel comfortable with them. Conscience! What conscience? We can, and do, excuse any form of behaviour in our secular, relativist, non-judgmental world. As for a spirit of brotherhood, that only exists when we have another group of brothers to hate.

"Of course, you could read that first article of the UN Declaration as a wish list," Minofel conceded to no one in particular, unless it was the spirit of Vlad, "an example of the 'apple pie, world peace, be happy' school of thought, in which case it is harmless but irrelevant to the real world."

That's where the hypocrisy came in. Many countries happily signed up to the Declaration of Human Rights knowing it was untrue and irrelevant simply because it looked good and was harmless.

No, the real world was the world of human nature, the world that the Praesidium promoted and protected, the world that the Praesidium would reveal to Adam.

And that was why David Minofel's biography of his hero Vlad the Impaler was taking longer than it should. Whenever he started to write, he found his mind inevitably drawn to consideration of man's true nature, of Adam's true nature, and the nature of whatever it was that bound them together – and that was a very deep well which, if not entirely dry, drew its sustenance from the rivers of fire in hell.

2. Westminster

Through the windows of his penthouse apartment Adam could see the Houses of Parliament. Although the sun was shining through a clear blue sky, the buildings appeared just a little hazy. Adam assumed it was a feature of the triple-glazing, which provided perfect sound-proofing against the hubbub of the crowded streets of central London.

The apartment exceeded Adam's wildest expectations. It was not quite the size of a football pitch, but it was a good deal more spacious than any apartment in a capital city should be. It had a carpeted reception hall that was sparsely furnished, but larger on its own than most London flats, even those at the top end of the price range. There was an enormous fully equipped kitchen, with an eating area furnished with a table and seating for eight; a large, separate dining room, with a white oak dining table for twenty diners; an even larger sitting room furnished with comfortable settees and armchairs where up to twenty guests could relax and converse, and a huge television screen with access to hundreds of channels from all around the world; five double bedrooms with en suite bathrooms, all beautifully appointed; a well-furnished library; and a games room/gymnasium about the same size as the reception hall. Outside the apartment was a balcony with access to a private roof-top garden, adorned with lawns, flower-beds and, at its centre, a finely wrought iron pergola with seating for two.

Adam scratched his head. He knew Westminster well enough to be fairly confident that there was nowhere close to the Houses of Parliament that offered such extraordinarily lavish accommodation. And yet there was no denying the grandeur of his apartment, or its central location.

He was also puzzled about his journey from Geneva to London. The first leg of the trip was perfectly comprehensible, albeit very impressive. He had flown with David Minofel and Miss Tomic from Geneva airport in a private jet, a private jet bearing the Slievins name. They had landed at a private airport on the outskirts of London, somewhere to the northwest. From the private jet, the three travellers had transferred to something that Adam at first took to be a helicopter, except that it was of an entirely unfamiliar design. The body was the shape of a conventional helicopter, but the craft had no rotor blade, and it operated in almost complete silence. Once the passengers had boarded, the craft rose effortlessly and flew towards the centre of London. Adam had two questions: who was piloting the craft? and how could you travel the twenty-odd miles from the private airport to central London in less than two minutes?

"You're in for a lot of surprises," David Minofel had confided. "Most, if not all, will be pleasant."

And now, on his own in this extraordinary apartment, Adam sat down in one of the armchairs in the sitting room and began to take stock. He desperately needed to understand what had happened in the last few weeks.

His uppermost thought was that he had been misled, duped by the Slievins consultancy. That rankled with him. David Minofel had placed him in a position of trust with ZeD with the express purpose of abusing that trust. Adam had thought his task had been to help ZeD. In reality, his entire purpose had been to implement Minofel's plan to bring the company to its knees. And as Adam unwittingly played his part in Minofel's scheme, he had found himself doing things of which he had never thought himself capable.

He pondered that last point. What was he capable of? Was there a limit to what a person would do? Or did you know your limits only once you'd been tested by circumstances? Some lines of Pope came to mind:

> Know then thyself, presume not God to scan;
> The proper study of mankind is man.

"Know then thyself." Not so easy. Adam had lived a pretty ordinary, comfortable life until the death of his daughter. When the lightning had struck, and the bough had fallen and crushed the life out of Bella, the world had changed for him. His grief and his rage had been without limit. After months, he had looked into himself and found nothing but the grief and the rage. He began to think that he was holding on to those two emotions simply because if he let them go, there would be nothing left. There was no Adam; only the memories and the emotions they provoked. In the end, he decided he could no longer bear the emotions, so he let them go. And he found there was an Adam. It was a body with a brain that had to spend its days living, breathing, eating and excreting – and, of course, thinking and doing things. But it was all pointless.

Then he'd met Terence Torrance, the Storyteller. He had told Tel – short for Terence – how he felt. Tel had made him an offer.

"You want to know if life has any meaning," he had said.

"Not really," Adam had replied. "I'm pretty clear on that. It doesn't. When Bella died, it was obvious there was no point."

"And yet here you are," the Storyteller had observed. "Morose, depressed, but still alive. You always have a choice. Have you considered suicide?"

"Thanks for that," Adam had answered. "I was hoping you might cheer me up, not suggest I slit my wrists."

"I wasn't suggesting wrist-slitting. I was just demonstrating that you're not completely convinced that there is no point. I have a suggestion. I can take you on a journey – you and Eve, if she's up for it. It's a journey with a difference – more a quest than a journey. Together, we can look for the truth. It will be a dangerous journey. The risks are great, but the possible rewards are greater."

So Adam had told Eve of his meeting with the Storyteller. He had thought she would dismiss the Storyteller's offer as the ramblings of a lunatic, but she hadn't. She had said she would undertake any journey, take any risk, to find an answer to one simple question: why had Bella died?

And so they had set off on the quest.

And now, courtesy of the Slievins consultancy, Adam had been on another journey, a very different journey, but one which had its own risks and rewards.

At this point, David Minofel entered Adam's apartment.

"What do you think of it? Isn't it everything I promised?"

"Everything and more! I had no idea there were places like this in Westminster. In fact, I was pretty sure there weren't. It's ridiculously big. If I'm the only one living here, I'm going to rattle around like a pea in a bell jar."

"In a bell jar! Do you see yourself as part of an experiment? How interesting!"

"I just meant the apartment is a good deal bigger than I need."

"Good or bad, no deal is bigger than you need," quipped Minofel, moving the conversation on. "And you won't be here on your own. Miss Tomic will be living in the guest section of the apartment. I know, it's amazing that a London apartment should have a guest wing. Fortunately, space here is less expensive than you think."

Adam wondered why Miss Tomic was to share the apartment. He had no objections, but was surprised that she would be joining him from Geneva.

"Like you, Miss Tomic needs to be away from Geneva for a while," said Minofel, answering Adam's unasked question. "You two seem to get along well enough. You'll be good company for each other."

Adam nodded his assent.

"Now, to more serious matters," said Minofel, settling down into one of the many armchairs in the sitting room. "Slievins has plans for you, believe me. When I spot potential, I am rarely wrong, and, in your case, I'm absolutely certain I'm right. Your assignment in Geneva has been a great success. Pharma BioSolex has put in an absurdly low offer for ZeD, and the board of ZeD has recommended that shareholders accept it. They're afraid that if they don't take the PBS offer, the share price will actually drop below the offer, which is a bit of a stretch, but just about possible. We're still hitting ZeD with titbits of scandal, and we've found a few more dubious clinical trials in some of their other submissions to the EMA. As for you, you're a hero."

"Not with ZeD I'm not. I wouldn't be surprised if they put a price on my head."

"That's the spirit." Minofel laughed. "Don't worry. They haven't hired a hit squad. They're far too cautious and mediocre to have you killed. But I'm so proud of you to think of it. If the roles were reversed, I'm sure you'd have had the traitor executed before he could do any more damage. And even if he couldn't do any more damage, you'd have him taken out as a matter of justice, or revenge – or both."

Adam didn't know whether to be pleased or shocked. Clearly he had Minofel's approval. Indeed, this extraordinarily powerful headhunter, who'd summarily executed the two burglars that had attacked him and Eve – this superman, ex-SAS, ex-mercenary – admired him.

"You are learning so much about yourself," Minofel continued. "And while you're here you will learn so much more. Tomorrow you will meet John Noble and his team. Today, I will tell you a little about where you are and how the Praesidium operates.

"As you can see through the windows, you are in the heart of London but, as you must have already worked out, you're in a building that does not exist. The explanation is simple, and as someone who participated in one of the Storyteller's idiotic quests you should find it easier to understand than most. You are in a PCC, a Parallel Coincident Construct – what your Andrew Rimzil has termed an anomalous construct. I'm not very keen on 'anomalous', but he's caught the essence of the fact with 'construct'. You are in a fully functioning patch of space and time, anchored to, and coincident with, what you would call the real world. You can see your real world through the glass of the windows. But they can't see us."

"So who or what is the Praesidium? And why are they here? And why am I here?" Minofel's explanation raised more questions than it answered.

"Take it easy," urged Minofel. "We have plenty of time. I will answer as many questions as I can today. Tomorrow, John Noble will be able to deal with any remaining areas of obscurity.

"So, the Praesidium first. The Praesidium is an organisation of elite human beings who guide man and human society in those directions that provide maximum fulfilment. The Praesidium has existed for thousands of years. It draws its power from the Crucible of Eternal Light. Don't ask me what that is or where it came from – John Noble is better placed to answer such questions. It's sufficient to say that the Crucible provides all the energy necessary to maintain this PCC, and all the other PCCs around the world.

"Why are you here? Well, from time to time, an exceptional human being appears, an individual who stands out from the crowd, who has the courage to fulfil his full potential and who seeks the truth. You are such an individual. When the Praesidium becomes aware of such individuals they are brought here. They are shown how the world of man really functions. And they are given the opportunity to work for the Praesidium, either here or back in your 'real' world."

Adam shook his head. "Are you sure I'm one of the chosen? Why me? I'm not given to undue modesty, but I really can't see why I'm so exceptional."

"You have proved yourself. In the last few weeks you've handled a difficult assignment with considerable skill and ingenuity. You've taken the decisions that needed to be taken. You've kept focused."

Minofel paused and smiled before going on. "There's something else. You seek the truth. Here at the Praesidium you will find it. You will find out how things work and why. And at last you will find the meaning you have been seeking."

Adam shrugged. What could he say? There was no denying he was remarkable in one sense. He had set out with the Storyteller on the quest that had initiated the subsequently aborted Fourth Beginning. In the course of that quest he had witnessed events that few, if any, had seen before. There was no doubt that he had earned his spurs as a questor. And now David Minofel was offering him a new quest – not much like the Storyteller's quest, but a quest nonetheless, and a quest that promised the answers that had so far eluded him.

"We should also take this opportunity," Minofel continued, "to sort out your finances. Before Dr Dubois departed for Northern Cyprus, happily for him a territory with no extradition agreements with Switzerland, I was able to persuade him to arrange your severance pay."

"My severance pay?" Adam laughed. "I'd have thought they'd prefer to sue me."

"Not at all," Minofel replied. "When I explained to Dr Dubois that his departure, with all his funds, to Northern Cyprus was entirely dependent on tying up any loose ends at ZeD, he was more than happy to comply. Anyway, he agreed a payment of five million euros. That's roughly three and a half million in pounds. I thought that was reasonable, given that your career in the pharmaceutical industry is effectively over."

Adam was stunned. "What pharmaceutical career?" was all he could manage.

"You may not have spent very long in the industry, but you went in at a very senior level, and you had excellent prospects. I assure you, £3.5 million is perfectly reasonable, and will be honoured by PBS."

"My God!"

"You will have to pay Slievins fifteen per cent, a sum of £525,000, as our commission."

"Of course."

"Now for some really good news," Minofel continued. "Slievins has made quite a lot of money from its contract with PBS – £50 million, to be precise. Given the benefits they will gain from acquiring ZeD and its pipeline of products at a ridiculous price, I think we probably undercharged, but no matter. Normally, the fee would be retained in its entirety by Slievins, but on this occasion, following representations by me to my colleagues on your behalf, we have decided to give you an *ex gratia* reward of ten per cent. We all felt you had gone above and beyond the call of duty in making the project a success. So as soon as the money is through, you will find yourself £8,075,000 to the good. That includes the €100,000 I owe you for the bet we had. You certainly sorted out the Dr Reed problem. And I always pay my debts."

Adam tried to absorb what David Minofel was telling him. Within just a few weeks, he had made enough money to retire.

"I'm in a different world," he said, meaning he was in a world where large sums of money seemed to be available for very little effort.

Minofel laughed. "You're certainly in a different world, my friend. You're in a Parallel Coincident Construct. But if you're referring to the money, I thought you understood by now that there is no necessary connection, no direct correlation, between work and wealth. Indeed, if you work you simply don't have time to make money. You still have much to learn."

"I need to tell Eve what I'm doing," said Adam. He wanted to talk to her, to explain that his career with Slievins was going to change their lives, that they were now financially secure, that they could afford to do anything they liked. In any case, he felt uneasy about the way he had ended their last telephone conversation.

"Bit of a problem there," said Minofel. "Communications between the PCC and your world are strictly regulated. They have to be – the success of the Praesidium depends on absolute secrecy. I will arrange for you to talk to Eve. Indeed, when your induction here is complete you can go and see her. But in the meantime contact is impossible."

Adam frowned. He didn't like to be told when he could and couldn't see his wife. On the other hand, it seemed that co-operation with David did have its rewards – more than eight million of them in total. It wasn't worth making an issue of it. After all, in a few days he would be back in the real world, and then he and Eve could catch up at their leisure.

"I hope you won't mind me saying this," Minofel continued, "but

I think you need to rebalance your relationship with Eve just a little. You are a Slievins man now. More than that – you are one of the Praesidium's chosen ones. That means, above everything else, that you are your own man. There's no limit to how far you can go, so long as you're not dragging too much baggage from your past life along with you."

"I don't think Eve would take kindly to being described as baggage from my past life. She's not baggage, and she's not from my past life. She's pregnant. We're going to have a child. She and the child are my future life."

"Of course," Minofel said soothingly. "Don't misunderstand me. Eve is your wife. Slievins would never come between a man and his wife. It's just that you can't allow Eve to hold you back. I'm not saying she will. I'm not saying she would want to. It's not her I'm worried about – it's you. You're going to be doing things – indeed, you may already have done things – of which Eve would disapprove. But that's only because she doesn't see the big picture. In fact, if you're honest she never has. When you set off with that scoundrel Tel, the Storyteller, you were seeking the truth. Eve just wanted to know why Bella had died. Do you see what I mean? When she looked up, she wanted to know why a particular raindrop had hit her in the eye. When you looked up, you wanted to know why there was a storm."

Adam's frown deepened. "So, what exactly will I be doing?" he asked.

"You will be making sure all's well with the world. If at any point it isn't, you will eliminate the problems. In return, you will be richly rewarded, and you will learn the truth. Deal?"

Adam shrugged, and then said, "Deal."

3. Noble schemes and Minofel machinations

John Noble, Praesidium Chairman, was feeling rather pleased. He relaxed his tall frame in the chair at the head of the boardroom table, stroked his neatly cut grey moustache and beamed at the empty room.

He had spent the previous evening with Kathrin, Manfred Bloch's wife. She had given him the names of those members of the board who would side with Simon Goodfellow when the Deputy Chairman made his move. Most of the names fell into the "usual suspects" category, but there were one or two surprises.

"You have done well," he had said to Kathrin.

She had looked at him with total commitment in her blue eyes. "Your wish is my command." She laughed. "Ever and always."

The relationship between John Noble and Kathrin was complicated. She was young enough to be his daughter. Had she been his daughter, he might well have been distressed by her promiscuity; but she wasn't, so the issue didn't arise. With her blonde hair, blue eyes and voluptuous figure, she was intensely desirable to any warm-blooded heterosexual man or lesbian woman. She knew it, and had decided to use it. She had mastered the art of giving and taking pleasure, and saw it as an accomplishment to be enjoyed and exploited. As a result, in addition to a number of affairs she had undertaken purely for pleasure, she had married Manfred Bloch, the chief engineer who doted on her, and bedded Simon Goodfellow, the Deputy Chairman who planned to oust John Noble from the presidency.

Many saw Kathrin as a wanton, empty-headed, if not simple-minded, woman, but such people seriously underestimated her. In her late teens, she had embarked upon an acting career. She had some talent and was moderately successful, a success most put down to her willingness to sleep with any male or female who could further her career. But such a judgement was unfair for two reasons. First, she had a natural aptitude for entering the mind of the characters she played. Secondly, her ambitions lay not in the theatre, nor in the bedroom, but in the boardroom of the Praesidium.

Pursuing her acting career afforded her the opportunity to meet the many distinguished guests who attended her performances. Although she rarely played a leading role, her sexual appeal and stage presence enabled her to outshine most leading ladies. Certainly, access to her dressing room was always a prize most energetically contested. In her early twenties, she had become the essential female guest at any social gathering of the Praesidium. Through these events she had met Manfred Bloch, whose bovine features and powerful, thickset body – not to mention his generous income and substantial wealth – appealed to Kathrin.

Married to Bloch, Kathrin had been able to learn much about the workings of the Praesidium, albeit only from the rather jaundiced, technically orientated perspective of the chief engineer. An early confidence that Manfred shared with his wife was his opinion of Simon Goodfellow. Her husband had described the Deputy Chairman as "a self-centred, sadistic, scheming, philandering turd". Contrary to Manfred's expectations, his description aroused, rather than subdued, Kathrin's interest, but she decided to hold back from exploring the possibilities Simon Goodfellow might offer until she had more securely acquired her political bearings.

Then, at a dinner given to celebrate the elimination of a young revolutionary wrongly suspected of being an Emergent, Kathrin had met John Noble. She was twenty-five; he was in his late forties. When he took her hand for the first time to welcome her, as Bloch's wife, to a seat at the top table of such social gatherings, she had known at once that this was the man who would be more important than any other in her life. John Noble had felt something extraordinary too. It was not sexual attraction, although he did indeed feel that. No, it was a conviction that, together, they would form a bond that would constitute a central part of their lives. She would not be his mistress or his wife, and she was not his daughter, but he knew that they were soulmates and that their destinies were entwined.

In the five years since that first meeting, Kathrin and John Noble had worked together. At the start, after their first meeting, she had helped him unofficially with simple administrative matters. However simple the tasks were, Noble had always taken the time to explain their purpose and how they fitted in with the Praesidium's wider goals. She had been a quick learner, and it was not long before they were discussing quite important issues as equals. Noble valued her input, her common sense, her empathic abilities. After two or three years, there was nothing that Kathrin didn't know about the workings and the politics of the Praesidium.

It was in the course of one of Kathrin's purely recreational assignations that she had caught wind of moves to oust the Chairman. When she told John Noble what she had heard, he had smiled and said, "That will be Simon allowing his ambition to edge ahead of his patience."

Kathrin had needed no instructions. It was time to satisfy her curiosity about Goodfellow, while serving the interests of the man she loved. Within days she was in Goodfellow's bed, taming, for the moment, his darker sexual drives. With consummate skill she set about educating him in the refinements of pure physical pleasure which, in pursuit of his sadistic tendencies, he had previously overlooked. Within weeks, she – and John Noble, of course – knew almost as much about his business and his machinations as he did.

While John Noble was happily pondering how best to frustrate the impending coup attempt, David Minofel was making his way along the Praesidium corridors towards the boardroom. The practitioner, too, was in a good mood.

"Come in, come in," said Noble. "What a lovely day!"

The weather inside the Praesidium bubble was set to match the weather in the real world, and the sun was shining on Westminster.

Minofel settled into a chair. "Adam Smith is happily ensconced in one of your better apartments in the accommodation block. Miss Tomic is with him, to keep an eye on him and to keep us informed of progress."

"Are you sure he's ready?"

"Oh yes, he's ready. I don't in any way wish to diminish my extraordinary expertise in readying subjects for enlightenment, but I have to admit he has proved easier to prepare than most – an apt and willing pupil."

"And Kit Turner, the suspected Emergent?" queried Noble. He didn't want the meeting to turn into a Minofelian self-congratulatory eulogy.

David Minofel paused before answering, then said, "The blind man's fate is entwined with that of Adam Smith. Your original commission required me to ensure that Adam, Eve and the other questors would never attempt to reactivate a Beginning, an anomaly. Adam is a key element in the group. Without him, the risk of a reactivation is eliminated."

"Yes, yes, as you've already said." The Praesidium Chairman

invariably found his dealings with practitioners difficult. There was always too much complacency and arrogance. "We can take it that Adam has been neutralised. His presence here confirms the progress he has made, and after the experiences we will now provide for him we can be sure his transformation will be irreversible. But what about the Emergent? If he is truly an Emergent, he poses a far graver threat than Adam."

"My point," Minofel replied, with just a hint of condescension, "is that Kit Turner is much less likely to create problems if the frontman in the group of questors has been neutered. It was always my intention to deal with Adam first, before tackling the Emergent. I'm sure you can see it will be easier to destroy Kit Turner if the man he had pinned his hopes on has changed sides, so to speak."

John Noble grunted. Practitioners always had an answer for everything. "So, what exactly is your plan now for dealing with the blind man?"

Minofel laughed. "If only it were that simple." He could see that the Chairman of the Praesidium was becoming irritated and he couldn't resist giving him another prod. "If it were that simple, you would scarcely need the expertise of a practitioner."

John Noble glared at Minofel. In two short sentences the practitioner had implied that the Chairman of the Praesidium, the man who effectively controlled all major events in his region, was stupid and inadequate. He glared at him, then smiled and said, "Let me rephrase my question. If, despite your expertise, you are unable to be precise, perhaps you could give me a broad outline of how you intend to proceed. I will then be better able to judge when we should be ready to release your fees. I assume you have a plan, even if you cannot tell me exactly what it is?"

Minofel bridled at the suggestion that the Praesidium would use release of his fees as leverage, but given they already owed him so much he had to be careful. He changed tack; he would use shock tactics.

"I propose to bring the Emergent here, to Praesidium headquarters."

John Noble could not believe his ears. "Say that again," was all he could manage.

"I propose to bring the Emergent, and Andrew Rimzil, here – to the Praesidium PCC," Minofel replied.

"Have you taken leave of your senses?"

"I sincerely hope not. It would be tragic if the Praesidium had retained the services of a lunatic or imbecile."

"You cannot bring a suspected Emergent here. You know that."

"You have asked me to annihilate the blind man. By that, you mean literally – erase him as though he had never existed, to fill the spaces he occupied in life with nothing – no substance, no memory, no trace. I have undertaken this task, but if he is an Emergent, I will need all my skills and the resources of the Praesidium. I propose to bring Kit Turner here and to provide him with a training programme to run in parallel with the one I have in mind for Adam. While Adam grows and matures, Kit Turner will age and decay. While Adam's strength grows, Turner's will diminish. In the end, Adam will experience a form of life so powerful that it would destroy most men. Meanwhile, Kit Turner will find his mind, his body and his essence fading away into nothingness. I need Adam here, I need the blind man here, and I need to have the Praesidium's resources at my disposal. These are my terms."

John Noble could see some sense in what Minofel said. Emergents were rare and previous attempts by practitioners to subvert them had been only partially successful. Sometimes they had used vanity to drive the Emergent off course and to distort his message; on other occasions, they had relied on the inferiority of the Emergent's followers to corrupt any truth the Emergent had purveyed. But in no case known to the Praesidium had they successfully erased all traces of an Emergent from human consciousness. Some successes had been claimed, but all had been of doubtful authenticity. Not a single proven Emergent had been completely annihilated.

One thing was certain. The Praesidium was heavily reliant on practitioners to deal with the Emergents. And there was another certainty: practitioners always got their way. The Emergent had to be destroyed, and only a practitioner could do it. This particular practitioner had set his terms, so why argue. In any case, if the operation was performed within the Praesidium bubble, Internal Discipline and Security would be better able to monitor progress, and to take remedial action if things started to go awry.

In the end, he said, "And why do you need Andrew Rimzil here? I thought you had him confined in your house in Geneva. How does his presence help to solve the Emergent problem?"

"I need Andrew Rimzil here to solve a rather different problem.

You know he has used the paradox device to scan your headquarters here. I am holding him in Geneva but allowing him to use the facilities in my laboratory to pursue his studies. He's a very clever man and has already invented a device that has enormous potential. I honestly believe there is no limit to what the device can do – and I mean 'no limit'. I believe that when it is fully developed, and we understand how to operate it, it could create or destroy universes."

"That's a little over the top," Noble grunted. "Create and destroy universes?" he scoffed. "He has used the device for observation only. Admittedly, he created that improbable lay-by at the beginning of time to allow the questors to observe the start of the universe. And it's also true that he's penetrated the cloaking to scan our PCC. But there's no evidence it can do anything else, certainly not on a grand scale. It's a worry, but surely there's no need to bring him here."

"We need to find out what he knows and what he's capable of doing. We need to know how a device powered by a car battery can break through your PCC cloak that is powered by the Crucible. And we need to persuade Rimzil to build us a paradox device."

Once again, Noble could see the sense in Minofel's argument, with the added bonus, in this instance, that the Praesidium could end up with its own fully operational paradox device. "You understand that if Rimzil and Kit Turner are brought here, neither of them will be allowed to leave alive."

"Really?" Minofel responded. "Oh my word! You're quite right, of course. The thought hadn't crossed my mind. I really must learn to think things through." Then he winked. He knew exactly how to provoke the Praesidium Chairman.

4. Harrovian stirrings

Kit was now so familiar with the house in Harrow that he could move around it and use all its facilities as well as any sighted person. He had long ago developed an ability to create, in his head, a three-dimensional image of any space that he had already explored using his other senses. He then needed only to touch any part of his environment – a door knob, the corner of a table, a kitchen cupboard – to lock his three-dimensional image on to the real world, and then, to all intents and purposes, he could see it.

He was in the middle of preparing a scrambled egg and toast breakfast for everyone when Eve joined him in the kitchen.

"You don't need to do the cooking," Eve objected. "I can do that."

"You are putting up with me, as well as Prune, Rambler and Numpty. The least we can do in return is help around the house. In any case, I like cooking. Feeding people is one of the few things I can do that I know pleases people and does no harm."

"Well, it's true – we all love your breakfasts," Eve conceded and then fell silent.

Several minutes passed; then Kit said, "We have to do something, don't we?"

"What can we do? I've lost contact with Adam. I don't even know where he is – in Geneva, London or somewhere else. No, I haven't lost contact – he's severed contact, he's blocked me out. He doesn't want me to reach him. And if that's the case, I'm not going to pursue him."

"Eve, Eve, what are you saying? Adam is your husband. He's the father of the child you lost, and he's the father of the child you are carrying. You've loved Adam for years and he's loved you. We can't just write him off."

"Love is a two-way street," said Eve. "You can't love someone who won't love you."

Kit frowned and said, "Yes, you can. 'Love is not love that alters when it alteration finds.' But that's not the point. Of course Adam still loves you. This David Minofel is exerting some kind of malign influence over him."

"Yes," Eve interrupted. "Money. I've checked our joint account.

I was worried that if Adam has left me, I might run short of money. But there are thousands of pounds, tens of thousands of pounds, pouring in. I don't know how he's doing it. It can't be just from his salary and the odd bonus."

"Well, there you are," said Kit. "If he's pouring money into your joint account, obviously he is concerned about you."

"Salving his conscience, more likely," said Eve, a mixture of sadness and bitterness in her voice.

"That's a word you don't often hear," observed Rambler, who had overheard Eve's last remark as he joined them in the kitchen. "I suppose the noun form "salve", meaning ointment, remains in use. In general, as a verb the only thing that gets salved is a conscience."

Neither Eve nor Kit responded.

"Oh dear, I've interrupted a serious conversation. I do apologise. I shall withdraw immediately."

"No, stay," Kit said. "We need your input. What are we going to do about Adam? We all need to agree a plan of action."

"A plan of action for what?" asked Rambler, a little nervously. They had discussed the possibility of attempting to reactivate the Fourth Beginning, but there had been no agreement. Clearly, there were risks in taking on whatever had aborted the Fourth Beginning, and they had all agreed that without Adam's support, attempting reactivation was out of the question. As it was fairly obvious Adam wasn't interested, why did they need a plan?

"We need to rescue Adam," Kit explained.

"Rescue him from what?" asked Rambler.

"You can't rescue someone if he's not held prisoner," said Eve. "He's said little enough to me in the last few weeks, but from that little I gather he's completely committed to his new life with Slievins. Minofel promised him an exciting and rewarding career, and he certainly seems to be enjoying both."

"Are we talking about the same Adam?" asked Kit. "The Adam who was willing to risk everything to find the truth – or even *a* truth, who survived a spell in hell at Cadnam, who was prepared to go to the ends of the earth and the start of time to understand the here and now?"

"We have reached a fork in the road," said the Storyteller. He had come in after helping Numpty with some digging and planting in the back garden of Eve's house, and had been listening at the door for the last minute or so. "There are two paths and we now have to make a choice. Kit is right: whether he is happy about it or not, whether he knows it or not, Adam is in mortal danger. We can leave him to work his way through these new challenges on his own or we can stand by him and face these challenges by his side.

"Before you make up your minds, I need to explain the risks you will be taking if you decide to help Adam. I cannot tell you everything because the path you choose affects the journey and the journey's end, but I can reveal that this time you will be dealing with an altogether more sinister and powerful adversary. The battle will be complicated by Adam himself because both we and those we are fighting will have a hold on him. The odds against us, if we accept this challenge, are high. You might think defeat is certain and that the choice is simple. But you are stronger than you know. The Fourth Beginning was aborted, but some of its effects persisted. Numpty, who at this moment is digging earth and planting seeds, has acquired levels of intelligence and, indeed, mental powers that exceed his uncle's wildest hopes for his nephew. Luke, the dog, always a remarkable animal, has undergone a step change in canine evolution. And then there is you, Kit. You have been singled out by our enemies as a special case, a real threat to their success, perhaps even their survival. Whether or not we as a group decide to take up the challenge, our enemies will not let Kit be. They fear him."

"What are our chances?" asked Rambler.

"As things stand, not very good! But we have not taken the decision yet. Each decision we take, each battle we fight, affects the story and the odds. But I will say this – this and no more – if we take up the challenge, we will once again be seeking the truth, both in the conflict and within ourselves, just as Adam has been told he will find truth, a different truth, with Slievins, and through the work he does for them."

The Storyteller turned away from the door and made his way back to the garden where he found Numpty leaning on his spade, sweating.

"So you've told them?" Numpty said.

"Yes, I've told them. Now it's up to them, and to you. Together, you have to decide."

"They have decided," said Numpty quietly. "And so have I. We are going to make a fight of it."

5. Adam meets the Praesidium

At the end of his meeting with John Noble, David Minofel collected Adam from the Praesidium's large, well-lit reception area where he had left him, and escorted him to the boardroom.

Seated at the head of the table was John Noble, who was now joined by Simon Goodfellow and Manfred Bloch. Noble and Minofel had agreed that it would be best if Adam met the senior managers first. Introductions to the heads of the operational divisions, Lotte Axelrod, Edgar Exton, Charlie Cornick and Oliver Nates, would be delayed until Adam had a better grasp of the Praesidium's work.

"Adam," said an ebullient John Noble, "you have no idea how pleased I am to meet you. You're quite a celebrity round here."

Adam was disconcerted. He shook John Noble's hand. It was a firm, warm handshake.

"This is my deputy, Simon Goodfellow," said John Noble, "and this is Manfred Bloch, Doctor Manfred Bloch. He's the Technical Director, the man who makes sure everything works."

When the introductions were completed, Noble added, "And this, as you know full well, is David Minofel, a practitioner. He will be overseeing your introductory programme. Please take a seat."

Adam sat beside Simon Goodfellow and opposite David Minofel.

"Well now," said John Noble, "where should I begin? I think I should perhaps start with a warning. Adam, you are an outstanding talent. You have proved yourself willing to learn and willing to act. David has been most impressed with your progress. Nevertheless …" He paused for a moment to emphasise the importance of what he was going to say before continuing. "… nevertheless, even you will find what I am about to tell you difficult to absorb – perhaps even difficult to believe.

"Up to today you have been living your life on false premises. Your assumptions about human nature, free will and morality have been entirely incorrect. Your pursuit of truth is laudable, but, sadly, you have been looking in the wrong direction and in the wrong places. Minofel here has put you through your paces in Geneva, and we are all mightily impressed with the way you have responded. Yet we know you are still troubled. You have ties to your old life. That is not a problem. But you also have ties to the old ways of relating to your old life, and those ways must change."

Noble paused to see whether Adam had any questions, but Adam had so many questions, he did not know where to begin, so he said nothing.

"We are going to introduce you to some new concepts. For example, conflict as a source of meaning, deconstruction as a pathway to understanding, and what you call evil as the key to true freedom. Yes, I know, this all sounds meaningless or mad, but when you have spent some time here with the heads of our operating divisions you will understand.

"The first truth we will give you, just as a taster, is this. Your governments, your bureaucracies and your establishments do not run human affairs. We do. We operate through all your institutions. We set the parameters within which they manage affairs, and the objectives they seek to fulfil."

Now Adam really did feel the need to ask a question. "Who are you? Are you aliens? Are you human? What are you? What is the Praesidium?"

John Noble laughed. "We're human, don't you worry about that. We are, if you like, the ultimate humans. We are the very essence of humanity. Back in the mists of time, when mankind was young, there was an individual of extraordinary ability and foresight. Little is known of him. He is thought to have come from South America, but even his birthplace is uncertain. He is known by various names, the most common of which is Nastafilu Verdicel, but his name is unimportant. It was his vision that mattered. He realised that if man was to fulfil his potential, he must embrace his own true nature and the true nature of the predicament in which he finds himself. That may sound obvious, but that wasn't what was happening. Man was pretending to be what he wasn't. Man was refusing to accept his predicament, preferring to invent fantasies to provide comfort and to avoid the truth. He pretended to be a moral creature, wrestling throughout his short life with issues of right and wrong. He invented gods and fairies and an afterlife to make the brevity of his life and the certainty of death bearable. As a result, he became a puling weakling, his head filled with the nonsense of prophets and storytellers. Instead of facing his fears and drawing the obvious conclusions from the situation, he tried to hide in nonsense and fantasy. And because he'd betrayed his nature, he decided good was bad and bad was good. He inverted, and thus perverted, all the true values.

"So Nastafilu Verdicel set up the Praesidium. It was a tiny organisation at the start, its influence limited to a few tribes, but as the Praesidium members gained expertise, they began to extend their reach, always keeping their identities and their activities secret. Cells were set up in various regions of the world, but progress was slow.

"Then, on a proselytising expedition in the Carajas mountain caves in the depths of the Amazon rainforest, Nastafilu chanced upon a source of extraordinary power, an inexhaustible source of energy, a phenomenon he called the Eternal Light. Summoning three metal workers and a skilled glass blower, he commissioned them to create a glass globe and an iron casket to hold the Eternal Light. Over time, the original casket decayed, and so the Praesidium commissioned a new one. Each time a casket deteriorates, a new casket, similar in design, is manufactured using the latest technology. The current version, the Crucible, is a work of art. The outer case of the Crucible sphere is made from thousands of very small interlocking triangles, each of which is made from two layers of titanium with a lining of graphene in between. The Crucible of Eternal Light is the source of the power that both maintains and conceals this Parallel Coincident Construct, or PCC, as we call it.

"When Nastafilu had contained the Light, he had enormous power at his disposal. This was long before mankind had harnessed carbon-based fuels to work its machines. The Praesidium recruited the brightest of the bright to work on exploiting the power of the Eternal Light. Some early members of the Praesidium urged Nastafilu to use his power to build an empire. Today, a battle between the Praesidium and a modern-day army would run the risk of destroying the planet, but back then merely revealing the power of the Eternal Light would have forced the empires of Sargon, of Cyrus the Great, of Rome itself, to submit, with very little, if any, environmental damage. But Nastafilu would hear nothing of it. 'I don't want an empire. I want the world,' he'd said. And he was right. If the Praesidium overtly ran an empire, it would provoke competition. Even if it conquered every empire, there would be dissidents. No, Nastafilu knew that the best, and only, way to rule mankind was by seeming not to rule, not even to exist. Hence the PCCs."

Adam had settled back in his comfortable boardroom chair. He had entered a mental state not dissimilar to a child listening to a story. It took almost a minute for him to realise that the Chairman had finished speaking. Finally, he picked up on John Noble's last words.

"So the Praesidium rules the world?"

"Pretty much," Simon Goodfellow answered, feeling his Chairman needed a breather. "Of course, we don't micromanage. But we set the goals and we keep things on track. We do it because we enjoy exercising absolute power, but I like to think it's a win-win situation. We run things for our benefit, but it just so happens that our goals invariably fit in well with mankind's true nature. Mind you, the price for power is eternal vigilance. There are always those who want to persuade people to betray their true nature and to spin off into worlds of illusion. We see it as our duty to explain to the victims of these confidence tricks that we deal in truth, the whole truth and nothing but the truth. Those who tell them otherwise deal in lies, false hopes and empty promises."

"I see," said Adam. "You've given me much to think about. I do have one question, if I may."

"Of course," said John Noble. "Ask whatever you like. You are here to ask, and we are here to answer."

"That's my question. Why am I here?"

John Noble stroked his neatly trimmed moustache with thumb and forefinger. "The answer depends on how well you are able to fit in with our plans. Before you ask what our plans might be, let me say that our plans depend on how well you fit in. I'm not being evasive, but we can offer you many possibilities. As good managers of men, we understand that it is the talent of people like you who can create possibilities. Let's leave it at that for now. I will add only that your prospects here are bright."

oooOooo

When the meeting ended, David Minofel escorted Adam back to his apartment.

"What do you think?" David asked.

"It's funny," Adam replied. "I've always felt there was more to life than the obvious, more than the ordinary person sees. But I'd always thought it might be something spiritual or religious. It had never crossed my mind that the reason why my ordinary life made little sense was because it was being run by someone else. I mean, obviously I knew about government, the law and the police, but they often seemed as lost as I was. They made idiotic mistakes that were apparent to most fairly intelligent people, but seemingly invisible to the establishment. Now I'm beginning to understand. They were being guided, or misguided – I'm not sure which – by a higher power. Not by God, but by a bunch of suits in a Parallel Coincident Construct." Adam laughed. "Of course, it all makes sense. Why didn't I think of it?"

Adam was mildly hysterical. His experiences in Geneva had compelled him to go far beyond his normal boundaries, but it had all happened so quickly that there had been little time to consider what, if anything, it meant. He had nevertheless realised that Slievins was offering him, in addition to pecuniary rewards beyond his wildest dreams, a freedom and a power he had never dreamt he would enjoy. Just once or twice in his Genevan apartment, after a couple of whiskies, he had wondered what gave Slievins its authority, what mandated Slievins' people to pursue their goals in such a direct, almost pure, manner. Towards the end of his time in Geneva, Minofel had mentioned the Praesidium, but Adam had assumed it was a conventional human organisation, located firmly in the real world.

If the Praesidium had turned out to be an entirely alien organisation, staffed by a strange lifeform from Alpha Centauri, rather than a group of humans running everything from a Parallel Coincident Construct, he would have found it easier to grasp. They evidently had at their disposal a unique technology unknown to their fellow men. Having harnessed the power of the Eternal Light, they had taken it upon themselves to run the affairs of men behind humanity's back. They were, it seemed to Adam, a bit like God, an unseen power exercising ultimate control over the lives of men – except, unlike God, they were simply men who happened to hold and exercise absolute power.

David Minofel smiled. "I can almost see the cogs turning in your brain. Don't worry. It's a lot to absorb. I should leave you to think on these things. Tomorrow we will start your induction course. John Noble himself will fill you in on the history of the Praesidium, what its goals are, how it works, and how members are recruited. I don't want to jump the gun, nor do I wish to raise false expectations, but it is only fair to tell you that if you respond well to the induction programme, there's a chance – I might even say a good chance – that you will be invited to become a member of the board. You already have some idea of the scale of the rewards you will enjoy if you decide to work with the Praesidium. If you are a board member, those past rewards will dwindle into insignificance. There's something else. We know you have been searching for answers all your life. Well, let me tell you, the Praesidium will surely reveal the truth to you, and if you become a member, it will certainly give your life meaning."

oooOooo

When Minofel had left, Miss Tomic joined Adam.
"How was your meeting?" she asked.
"You have no idea," he said.
"Well, tell me. We have plenty of time."
So Adam told her what he had learned. Minofel wouldn't have brought her to the PCC if he wanted to keep her ignorant of the Praesidium's existence. And he wouldn't have put her in Adam's apartment if he didn't expect them to talk. So Adam talked. Miss Tomic listened. He couldn't be sure, but when he looked into Miss Tomic's beautiful green eyes he thought he could see the hint of something strange. Precisely what it was remained unclear. Did she already know what he was telling her? Was she smiling? Or was there a hint of sympathy – or perhaps even pity – in her expression?

6. Kit's mission

After the discussion in Eve's house about what the questors should do, and the Storyteller's unexpected intervention, all six of them put their minds to working out a viable plan of action.

"We need to proceed with caution," offered Rambler. "We have very little idea of whom or what we are taking on. We do know they are powerful, and assuming they are connected with the Breakers, who obstructed us at every turn on our recent quest, we know they are utterly ruthless."

"They may be ruthless," Kit responded, "but we had the better of our exchanges with the Breakers. We even initiated the Beginning. Yes, someone stopped it. My guess is that whoever is brainwashing Adam belongs to the organisation that aborted the Beginning. Minofel is either one of those we will be fighting, or he's someone who knows who they are."

"You're making a lot of assumptions," said Eve. "You're assuming Adam is being brainwashed. I'm not so sure he is. It could just be that his head has been turned by an exciting job that offers absurdly generous rewards."

Kit trod carefully. He heard the hurt and anger in Eve's voice. "You know Adam better than all of us," he began, "certainly better than I do, but I find it inconceivable that Adam is willingly cutting himself off from you and the child you are carrying just because he's had a salary hike."

"We need to contact Adam," suggested Numpty.

"Easier said than done," said Kit. "He doesn't answer his mobile. ZeD is in a state of chaos, and in any case Adam's employment with ZeD has been terminated. We don't even know if he's still in Geneva."

"He's back in the UK," Eve interrupted. "I saw him on the television news. He was being interviewed in central London."

"That makes things easier," said Kit. "With all this media attention it must be possible to find out where he is staying."

"Not necessarily," said Prune. "I've been experimenting with the paradox device. I haven't taken any chances, but I have used the scanning system Andrew set up. I can't prove it, but I think Adam is in the London anomalous construct. The monitor shows that the light in the London construct is powerful and pulsating. I can't be sure, because there's still some activity in Geneva, but I've a feeling that's being caused by Andrew, not Adam."

"It would be helpful," commented Rambler, "if the lights carried more detailed information to indicate the type of activity behind the increased light intensity or, better still, a signature to indicate who is causing the heightened activity."

While the six of them were speculating about Adam's whereabouts, and how best to proceed, the doorbell rang.

Eve got up, but Kit said, "It's all right, Eve – I'll answer the door."

Numpty, who had become something of an expert on figures of speech, pondered Kit's "I'll answer the door", and made a mental note to determine whether the expression was an example of metonymy, personification, synecdoche, metaphor, or a combination of several, or all, of them.

When Kit opened the door he was confronted by the square solid form of Jedwell Boon.

"Hello, Jedwell," said Kit with a smile.

Jedwell wondered how the blind Kit knew it was him. "I'm sorry to arrive uninvited, but I come on a matter of some urgency." He used exactly the form of words Minofel had prescribed.

"Come in," Kit responded. "Eve, it's Jedwell. He's here on an important matter." Kit was delighted Jedwell had come to them. He was their best link to Minofel and Adam.

"How is Adam?" Kit asked Jedwell, as soon as Minofel's messenger had settled himself, rather uncomfortably, in one of Eve's armchairs.

"More to the point, where is Adam?" Prune asked. He was in no mood for niceties. "And what's Andrew doing, and where?"

Jedwell was never much at ease with large groups of people, especially when individuals in the group were firing questions at him and the entire group was waiting for his answers. Beads of sweat appeared on the top of his immaculately shaved and polished head.

"Give the man a chance to catch his breath," Eve intervened. "Would you like some tea or coffee?"

Jedwell took a cup of tea. He could see there was no hostility towards him – at least not from Eve or Kit. "Adam is in London and

Andrew Rimzil is to join him. They are both well. I have come here today to take Kit to Adam. They, and Adam, feel another meeting would be helpful at this time."

Kit and Eve exchanged glances.

"They, and Adam?" said Kit. "Who are 'they'?"

"Just Mr Minofel," Jedwell replied nervously. He shouldn't have said "they". The "they" referred to the Praesidium board, but Jedwell had no wish to explain. He hated all this talk, especially when he had been given a set speech to deliver, but without precise guidance on how to deal with any questions. He would have much preferred a brief that simply required abduction by force. Of course, that would have involved logistical problems (knocking out the abductee, keeping the person sedated, sealing them in a packing case, using a small airport with poor security arrangements, chartering a private plane, hiring an unscrupulous freelance pilot, etc.), but to Jedwell all of that seemed far simpler than sitting in an armchair, sipping tea and being grilled by a persistently inquisitive audience.

"Mr Minofel is not a 'they'," observed Numpty, "unless you're saying he has multiple personalities."

"I made a mistake," said Jedwell lamely. "Mr Minofel and Adam think another meeting would be of value, a chance for Kit to understand the place that Adam is in." Jedwell was desperately trying to keep to the expressions Minofel had stipulated.

"Jolly good," said Kit. "I'll be ready to leave with you tomorrow morning. I take it our destination this time is central London."

"That's right," said Jedwell, a little uncertainly.

"Excellent," said Kit, as he ushered Jedwell out of his chair and towards the front door. "Tomorrow morning. Shall we say 10 a.m.?"

When Jedwell had gone, Kit returned to the others. "I suggest we talk about what I should do when I meet Adam. I guess I need to find out whether he's under duress. I'll try to find out more about David Minofel, and his company, Slievins. And I'll also tell him he has to come home and talk to you, Eve."

Eve shrugged, but said nothing.

oooOooo

By noon the next day, Kit found himself in the main reception hall of the Praesidium. Jedwell had been solicitous of Kit's comfort throughout the trip, but had not given his charge any explanation for where they were, or how they had reached their destination. Kit had thought they would take the tube, or perhaps a taxi, into central London, but the journey had been far shorter and smoother than he had expected.

"Where are we?" Kit asked.

"Best if Mr Minofel explains," was all Jedwell said. He had, of course, simply been obeying his master's orders, but if he was honest, he felt embarrassed by his part in Kit's abduction. There was something about the blind man that had touched him.

7. Ground rules

On Minofel's advice, Simon Goodfellow had been put in charge of Kit.

The practitioner had explained the plan. It was simple, yet comprehensive. Kit would be invited to observe Adam throughout his training programme. He would be compelled to watch as Adam made steady progress towards fulfilment. Of course, every advance that Adam made would, in Kit's mind, be a seriously retrograde step. What the Praesidium would see as improvement, Kit would consider corruption; what the Praesidium judged to be growth, Kit would deem decay. And as Adam blossomed, Kit himself would wither. Both Kit and Adam would learn to accept the Praesidium's value system, but while Adam was enriched, Kit would be impoverished. According to David Minofel, this process would utterly destroy Kit. The Emergent would be forced to accept the vacuous nature of the aspirational philosophy that drove all such aberrants. In the end, the blind man would welcome death as a clear and certain release from a life based on false hopes and wilful perversion of the true nature of existence.

Simon had listened to Minofel's exposition. He was rather less certain than the practitioner that the plan would be a success, but that was not his concern. If Kit really was an Emergent, he had to be stopped, and the Praesidium was paying Minofel to stop him. If the plan succeeded, some credit at least would go to the Praesidium manager who had overseen the plan. If it failed, it would be another nail in the coffin of the man who had retained the practitioner and squandered Praesidium resources on a feckless and futile exercise – namely, John Noble.

oooOooo

Kit was taken from the reception area to Simon Goodfellow's apartment in the accommodation block. Simon greeted his guest.

"So you are the blind man Kit," he began. "Please be seated."

Kit sat down. He felt the edge of a table in front of him. Simon walked round to the other side of the table and sat down opposite his visitor.

Kit shivered.

"Are you cold?"

Kit ignored the question. "Where am I?"

"Let me introduce myself," said Simon. "I am Simon Goodfellow, and I am going to look after you while you are here."

"I thought I was to meet David Minofel and Adam."

"You will meet Minofel, and you will certainly observe Adam, but for now you are in my care, and I need to set down some ground rules."

"Ground rules?"

"Yes, ground rules. You know – rules with which, while you are here, you will be expected to comply."

"And if I don't?"

"Let's not get ahead of ourselves. I'm more than happy to explain, and even to demonstrate, what will happen if you fail to comply, but for now let's assume you are sensible and do as you are told."

Kit said nothing. Goodfellow studied Kit to assess his reaction. It was not anger, nor was it fear; it was simple refusal. That's what it was: a straightforward refusal to accept what Simon had said. Simon frowned.

"Let me make the situation clear. You are not a guest, you're a prisoner. You will do as I wish, or you will be punished, and, believe me, I'm very good at punishing. Truth to tell, I rather enjoy it. Adam is to undertake a training programme …"

Kit interrupted. "I'm here to talk to Adam."

"No, you're not. You're here to do as I say. You're here to observe Adam as he passes through our training programme. You will witness every stage of his development, but you will not be able to talk to him or communicate with him in any way."

"I insist that you take me to Adam now."

Simon's frown deepened. "Give me your hand," Simon said.

Kit did not move, so Simon seized his right hand and pulled it across the table so that Kit's whole arm was outstretched.

"One of the ground rules," said Simon, "is that you do what I say. If you don't, then this, sadly, is the type of thing that will happen."

With that, he drove a knife through the back of Kit's hand, nailing it to the table.

Kit gasped but did not cry out.

"Now you can continue to be difficult if you wish," Simon

continued in a matter-of-fact tone, "and I can continue to teach you a lesson – although at some point you will run out of appendages for me to nail to the furniture, and I shall run out of knives. Alternatively, you can be sensible. It's your choice."

Kit leant across the table with his free left hand and pulled the knife from the table, releasing his damaged, bleeding right hand. He laid the knife down. "You and I," he said without any hostility, "have some serious issues to resolve."

"On that, at least, we can agree," Simon replied.

oooOooo

Kit was taken away to one of the holding cells in the basement of the accommodation block. The cell was not uncomfortable. It was arranged like a bedsit, with a bed, kitchen, dining area and partitioned-off bathroom. Only the lock on the door and the absence of windows indicated it was designed to keep its occupant contained.

A nurse attended to Kit, cleaning the wound in his hand, bandaging it carefully. "I guess you have just come from an interview with Simon Goodfellow," said the nurse. "I have some experience of Simon's procedures. The wound is clean, and I don't think the hand is permanently damaged."

"Don't worry," said Kit. "I've felt worse. Fortunately, I'm left-handed. In any case, I'm a good healer."

oooOooo

When Kit had been escorted from the apartment, Simon summoned a house servant. "There's a bit of a mess on the table," he said, indicating Kit's blood. "And there's some damage to the wood. The table has some sentimental value, so I want it repaired. Make sure the cabinet maker does a perfect job, or he – and you – will regret it."

When he was alone, Simon pondered his first encounter with the alleged Emergent. The man was certainly strange, as well as being either highly self-disciplined or gifted with a very high pain threshold. Simon was something of an expert in the infliction of pain. He knew from previous experiments that a nine-inch blade driven through the hand was painful enough to elicit a cry from almost everyone, but the blind man had scarcely gasped. Of course, he might be congenitally insensitive to pain, which from Simon's viewpoint would be deeply disappointing, but he considered it unlikely as he knew congenital analgesia was extremely rare.

The only other unusual feature of their meeting was the blind man's refusal to be cowed. Simon took some pride in his ability to break anyone. He often told other members of the Praesidium board that "there is always a limit to the amount of pain and humiliation a person can take". So far he had been proved correct. There was, of course, a long way to go in employing his repertoire of torture and degradation, but Simon had the feeling that to break this blind man, he might well have to use all the means at his disposal.

Was Kit an Emergent? Simon didn't try to answer the question, leaving it open. The subject had given no sign that he possessed any Emergent powers, but it was far too early to say, one way or the other.

8. The first lesson

Adam spent his first full morning in the London PCC in the company of John Noble, the Praesidium Chairman. John Noble did most of the talking.

"Adam, I need you to open your mind. What I am going to tell you contradicts much of what you believe. It will challenge ideas that you have taken for granted all your life. It will shock you. But hear me through to the end.

"Yesterday, I mentioned our founder, Nastafilu Verdicel. He was a man of great wisdom and humanity. By that I mean he was so wise that he could look into the heart of man and know him for what he is.

"Until now, you have been taught that man is a flawed being, striving but always failing to achieve a high moral standard. This, my friend, is wrong. Not just misleading, but fundamentally wrong. Man is what he is. He is not supposed to aspire to be different from what he is, any more than the lion or the tiger should try to be what they are not. Nastafilu Verdicel said that the noblest aim of every creature is to be what it is, to be true to its own nature. That is the principle on which the Praesidium was founded.

"From earliest times, evil men have tried to persuade man that he should not be true to himself, but that he should strive to be something they called 'better'. But that was a contradiction promulgated by those who sought power, those who knew that they could achieve and maintain power only by convincing those they wished to rule that they were inherently inferior. Flawed! Unenlightened! Sinful! It was a cruel trick. No man can be better than himself, his true self. Was it not Shakespeare who said,

> To thine own self be true
> And it must follow, as the night does day,
> Thou canst not then be false to any man.

"And so, throughout history, man has been burdened with false expectations of himself. It has caused him dreadful anxiety, entirely destructive feelings of guilt and desperation, engendered by a profound sense of inadequacy. We at the Praesidium have always tried to redress the balance, to tell man to be true to himself, to be honest with himself. That is what we do. That, Adam, is the work of the Praesidium.

"Now I know that you have a curious mind. I know that you have always sought the truth. Well here, courtesy of the Praesidium, is the first great truth – man is as he is.

"Tomorrow you will meet the heads of our operating divisions. There are four of them. Together with the top management, the operational heads – Monitaurs, to give them their true title – constitute our Decon committee. I want you to spend time with each of them, to observe what they do, note how at all times they encourage mankind to be true to itself. It will be an eye-opener, but I promise you that by the time your training here is complete, you will never see the world in the same light again."

They chatted for another hour. Adam asked questions and John Noble was frank in all his answers. He shied away from nothing because, as he said, the Praesidium was proud of the work it did and he was happy to stand by its record in human history. Occasionally, the Praesidium had lost ground to those who wished to pervert the nature of man, but in the end the Praesidium had always prevailed because, in the final analysis, it had man on its side.

Adam thought of pointing out that the Shakespearian lines the Praesidium Chairman had quoted were spoken by a pompous, opinionated, self-serving individual who ended up prematurely dead, skewered by the hero of the play – but he didn't. How could he be sure John Noble would be amused?

9. What's wrong with religion

Edgar Exton was the last man you would have expected to be in charge of religious affairs, an area of responsibility that, within the Praesidium, fell under the heading of extremism. Edgar, as he appeared, was a very average man, middle-aged, and of average height, with an average brain inside a head suffering from an average degree of hair loss. The transformation from his natural state into human form had gone smoothly that morning, so for someone engaged in promoting the most violent and destructive of human emotions, Edgar was in a pretty good mood.

It was the morning after his session with John Noble that Adam met Edgar. The Monitaur was wearing a plain grey suit and a bright red tie. The red tie seemed to Adam to jar with Edgar's persona, but Adam had much to learn about Edgar Exton.

After the introductions, Adam asked his mentor what area they would be covering that day.

"We must start, and quite possibly end, with religion. My brief covers all forms of extremism. Here, we see all religions as a form of extremism, so it falls squarely into my area of responsibility.

"Our Chairman has told all the heads of the operational divisions to go back to basics with you, so that's what I plan to do. I hope you won't find it too tedious. I'm sure you will want to engage in some of the hands-on stuff, but we need to set the scene first.

"All religions have one thing in common. They all tell man he is not good enough as he is. They tell him that he has to be redeemed – through reincarnation, through high moral purpose and good deeds, through the generosity or courtesy of God. But there is nothing wrong with man. That's what is wrong with religion. It's essentially an abusive relationship, one in which the senior partner continually undermines the weaker one.

"Now, we could tolerate some of the earlier religions. The Greek gods, the Titans and the Olympians were fine. They were, generally speaking, avaricious, bellicose, deceitful, jealous, lustful, spiteful and vindictive on an industrial scale. They murdered and raped with the best of them. No problem there then. They were a magnification, but nonetheless a fair reflection, of man.

"Nor was the god of the Old Testament a problem. Indeed, in his enthusiasm for genocide and ethnic cleansing he set a pretty good example. Even the god of Islam was tolerable. At least we could work with him. More on that later.

"No, our problem was with Buddhism and Christianity, and any other religion or philosophy that promoted selflessness, and declared love – love of others, love of humanity, love of God – to be the greatest good. They commanded man to deny his self. I mean, just how damaging is that? You can undermine someone by telling them they've got an ugly nose, or a squinty eye, or that they have foul body odour. But when you tell someone they should repudiate their very being, their self – well, in our book, that's just about as malicious and destructive as you can get."

Edgar always became emotionally disturbed when he talked about religion.

"So you see religion as an evil?" Adam queried.

"Absolutely," Edgar replied enthusiastically.

Adam knew well enough the track record of Judaism, Christianity and Islam. After all, he remembered their interview with the God of the Old Testament in the Garden of Eden, near Hook off the M3. There they had met a deeply flawed God, clearly unworthy of worship. Rambler was fond of quoting chapter and verse for God's explicit instructions to the Israelites to commit genocide (Deuteronomy 7).

Adam was also familiar with the history of the Crusades, carried out in the name of Christianity. Crusaders, granted a plenary indulgence by Pope Urban II, had happily raped and murdered their way across Europe into the Middle East, persuaded that whatever sins they committed in the name of Christ would be forgiven by his Father in heaven. "*Deus vult*," the crusaders proclaimed. "God wills it."

As for the Muslim God, Adam knew that in certain circumstances he endorsed violence against women and children within the family and against people of other faiths anywhere in the world. He had seen the following verse quoted from the Quran:

> I will cast terror into the hearts of those who have disbelieved, so smite them over the necks, and smite every fingertip of them.
>
> Verse 8: 12–13

After giving the matter several minutes' thought, Adam said, "Well, I can certainly agree that religion has been used as an excuse for committing the most appalling acts of savagery – genocide in the Old Testament, the Crusades in the eleventh and twelfth centuries, and the violent jihad of modern Islamists."

Edgar seemed confused. "The Praesidium is not against savagery," he said, attempting to clarify. "As I said, we have no problem with the Old Testament, and we can work with Islam. Our difficulty is with religions that ask man to be what he is not. Christianity is a case in point. Jesus made ridiculous demands on man, setting the moral bar so high that you had to be a fanatic to get anywhere close. Turn the other cheek? Really? Give the thief who takes your coat, your shirt also? What is that? SOGOF – steal one, get one free? No one can or should behave like that, not if they want to retain any vestiges of true humanity. Effectively, Jesus condemned everyone to failure, and to an enduring sense of guilt. We at the Praesidium have done our best to minimise the psychological damage caused by the Sermon on the Mount, and, without wishing to brag, we've done a pretty good job. Take Israel today. We're proud of the way they deal with the Palestinians. It took centuries of pogroms and the efforts of Hitler to enable the Jews to strip the humanity away from those they had dispossessed. The Crusades, another great success! It was truly liberating to see thousands of Christians utterly abandoning Christ's high-falutin' esoteric moral precepts as they butchered Christians and Muslims alike. As for Islam, we worked hard with the Quran and the medieval mindset at the heart of the Prophet's revelations to inspire 9/11, Daesh and general jihadery. Result!"

"You approve of all these acts of violence?" asked Adam. Now he was the one who was confused.

"Absolutely," said Edgar. "Don't you see? In all these cases, sometimes against the odds, man's true nature asserted itself, sometimes with, but often against, pressure from the religionists."

"Man's true nature?" mused Adam.

"That's it," said Edgar, excited and relieved. "If you want to understand what we do, why we do it, and why what we do is unquestionably and irrefutably right, all you need to grasp is the truth about human nature. The drives that religion calls sins are simply the natural instincts of man. Someone offends you – you feel angry. Someone insults you – you wish them harm. You see an attractive woman – you want to bed her. You have lustful or perverse desires – you wish to fulfil them. You are told that all men are equal, but you know they are not. You are told to treat others as you would have them treat you, but you are not them and they are not you. You do not feel their pleasure. You do not feel pain when they are hurt. You have been given a separate body. Everything you see and hear and feel comes to you through that body. Your body is yours to command. Its demands are the only authentic demands."

"But wouldn't the world be chaotic if people behaved as you suggest?" Adam asked.

Edgar smiled. Adam noticed a red glow suffusing his face and the top of his head.

Then Edgar said, "Adam, I think you are ready for your first excursion."

oooOooo

Throughout Adam's meeting with Edgar Exton, Kit, accompanied by Simon Goodfellow, had sat in the observation booth, listening to every word.

"Interesting, don't you think?" queried Simon when the session ended.

"If you think it interesting to watch an attempt to excise any sense of decency from a fellow human being, then it's absolutely riveting," Kit replied.

"Oh dear, I think you do Edgar an injustice. This is not an attempt – it is a process. You are being given the privilege of witnessing the birth of a complete, authentic human individual. You will see Adam liberated from the chains of moral inhibition. He is at the start of the process, although all credit to Minofel for having prepared him so well. By the end of the process, Adam will emerge as someone who has fully fulfilled his potential – strong, confident, entirely self-assured. He'll be a new man. You won't recognise him."

"If you succeed, you may well be right. But evidently you're not certain of success. Otherwise, you wouldn't be so desperate to keep Adam and me apart."

Simon laughed. "We are keeping you away from Adam because you have nothing to contribute. You are here not because of what we are doing to Adam. You are here because of what Adam, as he progresses, will do to you. I see no harm in telling you that the practitioner, David Minofel, believes that as Adam strengthens, you will weaken, and that when Adam is, so to speak, completed, you will be destroyed. Personally, I have my doubts. I think you may well be upset by Adam's transformation, but I think it is unlikely to prove fatal – but, hell, who am I? By the way," he added, "how's your hand?"

"It still hurts a little, but the nurse cleaned the wound and I think it is healing well."

Simon winced and turned pale for a moment, then recovered. "I just hope you have learned your lesson," he said, without conviction.

When Kit had been returned to his cell, Simon leant forward in his chair and rubbed his right hand, trying to assess the effect of their first observation exercise. Kit had been attentive throughout. Strangely he had not seemed unduly disturbed by the experience, although clearly he understood what the Praesidium was doing to Adam and was unhappy about it. He desperately wanted to talk to Adam, but following the little lesson with the knife he seemed to have accepted the situation. There were no signs that the blind man would be mentally or physically destroyed by Adam's transformation, nor was there any evidence that Kit was an Emergent. Unless, of course, you attached some significance to the sharp pain Simon had felt when he had asked Kit about his hand. That was puzzling. Simon concluded it was obviously some kind of mental aberration in his own brain that had sent an excruciating pain signal to his right hand. It was Kit's right hand that he had nailed to the table. Certainly the pain had had nothing to do with Kit's supposed Emergent powers, but the possibility that, heaven forbid, it might have been caused by an inexplicable and entirely unacceptable twitch of empathy was still worrying. Simon Goodfellow didn't do empathy.

10. Excursion 1 – Edgar Exton

"Where are we?" asked Adam, as he hid behind what was left of a shattered wall in a bomb-blasted building.

A series of explosions shook the ground; fighters shouted instructions, intermingled with the screams of those injured and the dying. The air was hot and full of dust.

"This, my friend, is Raqqah Province in Syria," said Edgar. "It's February 2015. We are in ISIS territory, and the allies are bombing ISIS ammunition dumps and supply lines."

An explosion nearby sent shrapnel flying everywhere. Edgar's advice to Adam to keep his head down was unnecessary. "As you can see, there's quite a lot of collateral damage." As Edgar spoke, a bomb hit an oil dump. The explosion was deafening, the heat unbearable.

"Why are we here?" Adam managed to gasp.

"You are here to see the true nature of man, and how we help man fulfil his potential."

"Couldn't you have explained all this in your PCC in London?"

"Certainly not," Edgar replied. "You need to take ownership of this lesson by being there – or rather here – and being part of it."

"Part of what? I don't know what is going on. I don't know who's doing what to whom. I just know we're in danger."

"Good. You're getting a feel for it."

The aerial bombardment stopped. The sounds of battle faded away.

"Come on, Adam, we have to walk across town to a place on the outskirts. There's a lull in the fighting, so we will be safe. In any case, no one can see us. We are going to witness what man can do to man."

Adam and Edgar walked across the town. When they reached the outskirts, Adam noticed an increase in the number of Islamic State fighters, all sporting weaponry, standing around in their desert camouflage uniforms as though waiting for a planned event. They reached a ruined building where hundreds of ISIS fighters were standing on the rubble. Then Adam saw it – a cage with a man standing inside.

"Oh no!" said Adam. "I know what this is. I don't want to see it."

"You need to see this, and then we must discuss it," said Edgar firmly. "You have to understand what you are."

Two masked ISIS fighters were throwing flammable liquid all over the man in the cage. He wore an orange jumpsuit and was standing completely still, staring ahead. The ISIS fighters laid a trail of the liquid away from the cage. Then, when they were at a safe distance, one of them knelt down and lit the fuel. The flame trickled across the ground and, when it reached the cage, leapt inside, creating a column of fire in the cage, engulfing the man. The man, now screaming, performed a grotesque dance of agony as the flames consumed him, until, finally overcome, he sank to his knees and succumbed.

oooOooo

"Where are we now?" asked Adam.

"It doesn't matter. We are alone in a desert."

Adam looked up. The black velvet sky twinkled with more stars than Adam had ever seen. The air was cool.

"The man you saw burnt alive was a pilot. He had been shot down while on a bombing mission. You saw what bombs and missiles can do. The captured pilot was tortured by ISIS. They invited their Twitter followers to suggest how they should kill him. There were many suggestions, of which burning alive was only one. He was a Muslim. Those who join ISIS are Muslim. The leaders of ISIS claim their religion endorses such a form of execution.

"Also, bear in mind that the armies of the world accept 'collateral damage', which in more explicit terms means civilian deaths, deaths often as painful and more lingering than that suffered by the pilot. What have you learned?"

Adam shrugged. "I've learned that people can do terrible things to each other."

"You'll have to do better than that," said Edgar.

"I guess both the pilot and those who killed him thought they had right on their side," Adam added.

"Good," said Edgar. "It's in human nature to believe you are justified in what you do. Religion tries to impose a universal moral system, but it fails because it ignores human nature. You, as individuals, have to decide what is right for you. That's how each side in a dispute can insist they are right when, logically, they know that, at best, only one of them can be right. What else? How did you feel when you saw what ISIS did?"

"I felt sickened."

"Anything else?"

"I felt anger at the callous way in which the two masked ISIS fighters lit the fire."

Edgar nodded. "Good. You felt anger. The relatives of the pilot felt anger. The government of the country the pilot was from felt anger. They immediately executed two ISIS prisoners. Then they flew more than fifty bombing missions against ISIS in three days. No doubt a lot more collateral damage. Do you see? All these feeling are natural. The anger of ISIS towards the pilot for bombing them. The anger of the pilot's people when ISIS tortured and burnt their man alive. Your anger. All perfectly natural."

oooOooo

Back in the observation booth in the Westminster PCC, Kit had witnessed both the burning of the pilot and Adam's discussion with Edgar Exton afterwards. Simon, who was at his side, had provided a graphic description of the burning of the pilot, assuming that since Kit was blind, he wouldn't be able to appreciate the full horror of the scene. He was wrong: Kit was perfectly capable of visualising the scene, and the man's screams were more than sufficient to convey the evil that man could do to man.

"It's funny," said Simon Goodfellow when the observation screen was turned off. "But both the pilot and his tormentors believed they were doing God's work. The ISIS fighters sincerely believe that suicide bombing, for example, is a certain passport to the gates of Paradise, and access to dozens of virgins. In many ways, their faith, though manifestly absurd, is our kind of religion. It encourages fanaticism, and fanaticism brings out the best in man, in the sense that it frees him to discover his true nature."

Simon waited for Kit to respond, but he remained silent.

"Don't you think?" Simon prompted.

Still Kit said nothing.

"We're not having a tantrum, are we?" Simon goaded. "I'd really appreciate it if you could be a little more forthcoming," he added.

"I'm a busy man. Chatting here with you is not how I would choose to spend my time, so I'd really like you to put some effort into our sessions together, if only as a matter of courtesy."

Eventually, Kit said, "Those men, when they do evil things, are convinced they are right, but when you do evil things, you know you are wrong. You will both arrive at the Gates of Hell, you can be sure of that, where you and they will have time to consider which of you is worse. My money is on you."

"That's better," said Simon. "I was concerned you'd become dumb, as well as blind."

oooOooo

Simon felt relieved when his session with Kit ended. He didn't want to admit it, but he found it difficult to deal with his charge. So far at least, the blind man seemed impervious to the treatment the practitioner had prescribed. Of course, he was unhappy with what was happening to Adam, but it didn't seem to be breaking, or even shaking, his will. He appeared to be supremely self-confident in a situation that most men would find deeply unnerving. He was a prisoner – he couldn't communicate with Adam or Eve, or any of the other questors – and he was being forced to watch the mind of his friend being recast.

Even driving the knife through the blind man's hand had produced less effect than he had hoped for. It had at least given Simon some satisfaction, and it was always useful to bring those with pretensions to mental or spiritual strength down to earth with a reminder of their essential physical vulnerability. "You're never more than a pair of pliers away from exquisite pain," was one of Goodfellow's many aphorisms. Minofel had not sanctioned physical abuse, but he hadn't explicitly excluded it either. So in Simon's view there was scope for further experimentation in that direction.

That settled, Simon turned his thoughts to more important matters. A substantial number of board members were ready to join him in ousting John Noble. Some of them, Simon had bribed with money or promises of promotion; others bore a grudge against the Chairman for some real or perceived slight in the past.

The number of his supporters was substantial, but still not a majority. More work needed to be done. Kathrin, Manfred Bloch's wife, had offered to help. Simon felt considerable satisfaction in knowing he had the wife of his main rival to succeed John Noble on his side and, better still, in his bed. If he could enlist the support of just two more board members, he would make his move.

11. Regrouping

"Probably slipped his memory," suggested Prune Leach.

Eve had heard nothing from Kit since he had left Harrow with Jedwell. He'd promised to contact her as soon as he arrived in central London to let her know what was going on.

Prune was not in the best of moods. His heavily wrinkled brow had taken on a striking resemblance to an extended noughts and crosses patchwork. He had more or less mastered the scanning function of the paradox device, but he had searched in vain for a means of activating its other functions. He knew it could create temporary bubbles outside, yet still somehow connected to, time and space, but he just couldn't work out how to do it. As for what else the device might be capable of, he could only guess. He needed help.

"I don't suppose anyone has heard from Andrew?" he asked hopefully. "He's probably with Adam and Kit by now."

"No," Eve answered. "We've heard from no one."

"It's as though they're picking us off, one by one," mused Rambler. "First, Adam, then Andrew, now Kit. Perhaps we have underestimated the opposition."

Luke had taken up his favourite position – lying down with his head on Numpty's feet. "You'd better fill them in," he minded to Numpty, "but leave me out of it." Luke had found he could communicate quite easily with Kit and Andrew, but was still meeting a total block when he tried to reach Adam.

"How do I do that?" Numpty minded back to the golden retriever. "How do I explain I can communicate with Kit and Andrew?"

"Well, it's a lot easier for you to explain it than it is for me," minded Luke firmly. "They might swallow a telepathic human, but a dog? Get real."

Numpty considered arguing but realised there was no point. Luke couldn't talk, and in any case the dog was right – ascribing telepathic powers to Luke rather than assuming them himself just made things more complicated, and certainly no more credible.

"Kit can't contact us by phone," Numpty began carefully. "There's an embargo on communication between those on the PCC and those outside it."

"And how do you know that?" Eve asked.

"Intuition," Numpty declared. "I just know. You'll have to accept it."

"What's a PCC?" asked Uncle Rambler, notebook in hand.

"A Parallel Coincident Construct," Numpty replied. "It's the proper name for what Andrew calls anomalous constructs. Or rather it's the name the people on the PCC use. I suppose Andrew has as much right as they to decide on its name. After all, he discovered how to set one up on his own when we observed the creation of the universe and the birth of life. In any case, he understands the phenomenon rather better than those on the PCC."

"Why do you say that?" asked Rambler, stopping his note-taking for a moment.

"Because he's been taken to the PCC to work on the paradox device and to help them build their own."

"You mean Andrew is helping the people who are holding Adam, the people we think are possibly trying to destroy us?" said an incredulous Prune Leach.

"I didn't say that. I said that's why he's been taken there, not that that's what he's doing."

"Wait a minute," Eve interjected. "Where are you getting all this from? Intuition? Intuition just might tell you that Kit can't contact us directly, especially as he promised he would and he hasn't. But how do you know so much detail?"

"I told you," Numpty minded to Luke. "Now what do I say?"

"Well, prove you have extraordinary intuition," minded Luke.

"Great! How do I do that?"

"Tell them that in a minute I will get up, go up to Eve, Prune, Rambler and the Storyteller in that order, and offer my right paw to each of them in turn."

"You'll what?"

"You heard. Eve, Prune, Rambler and the Storyteller in that order. Go on."

Numpty cleared his throat. "I have developed an acute intuitional sense. For example, in a minute Luke will get up and offer his right paw to each of you in turn – first to Eve, then to Prune, then to Rambler and, finally, to the Storyteller."

The others looked puzzled, but Luke got up and followed his own instructions precisely.

Prune was unconvinced. "That's a clever trick but what does it prove?"

"Well, it certainly proves that young Numpty can foretell the future," interjected Rambler, determined to defend his nephew.

"Either that or the dog understands English," Prune half-conceded.

Numpty decided to carry on. He would tell them everything Luke had told him. It was up to them whether they believed him.

"Adam is being put through some kind of brainwashing by the Praesidium. The Praesidium is the organisation that operates from the Westminster PCC, and claims to be in control of all human affairs. They call the brainwashing a training programme, but as far as Kit can tell they're trying to turn Adam into a completely heartless monster. Kit is being held prisoner, and is being forced to witness Adam's progress as he undergoes 'training'."

"And Andrew?" Prune asked. He was, of course, concerned about the welfare of his partner, but he was even more eager to ask Andrew how to operate the paradox device. Prune was convinced that without the paradox device they would lose their fight with Minofel and whoever, or whatever, was behind him.

"Andrew is building a new paradox device, but I'm pretty sure the Praesidium will never get their hands on it."

"Can I communicate with him?" asked Prune.

"It won't be easy," said Numpty, "but I think it could be possible."

"Hold on," said Eve. "Did you just say Kit is being held prisoner? Are you serious? We have to do something. We have to rescue him."

Even as she said it, she realised how weak and vulnerable they were. With Adam in the hands of David Minofel and the Praesidium, Kit had been the driving force in the group. He had known of the dangers they faced, and had been prepared to risk all. He had gone willingly to Geneva, but evidently was now in the clutches of this Westminster PCC. Their enemies had Adam and Kit. And they had Andrew Rimzil, probably the most brilliant engineering innovator the world had ever produced. Apart from Prune Leach, most of the talent among the questors was already at the mercy of the enemy.

"We need help," said Prune, voicing what Eve had been thinking.

There was silence. What could they do?

"There's always Prometheus," offered the Storyteller.

The Storyteller's contribution was met with astonished silence.

"Come on," said Eve, eventually. "That was a different world and an age ago."

"Beautifully put," said Rambler, scribbling in his notebook.

"You're right, Eve," said the Storyteller, "and as you know I'm loath to interfere. But Prometheus has been a good friend to man. He risked and suffered much for man. He betrayed his own kind, the Titans, and the gods of Olympus, because he saw something in us worth preserving, worth nurturing. He gave us hospitality and encouragement when we visited him. He will help us if he can. Don't be dismissive just because when we met Prometheus, it was far away and long ago. Very little of what matters to each of us is in the here and now. Almost all that matters to anyone is in the past or the future. The present is so ephemeral."

Eve shook her head. "This is nonsense. We are not taking off in a camper van again. We're not going back to the Caucasus of ancient times. Our problem is twelve miles from here, just down the road. We certainly need help, but we need it here, and we need it now."

The Storyteller appeared to have accepted what Eve said. He left the room, pausing only to invite Luke to join him. Once out of earshot of the others, the Storyteller addressed Luke.

"Your telepathic powers have developed well – better, far better than you know. You can communicate through space. Space and time are one. *Ergo* ...?"

It took a moment for Luke, whose knowledge of Latin was still rudimentary, to understand.

12. Excursion 2 – Lotte Axelrod

Lotte Axelrod, Head of Depravity, had adopted human form that morning with unwonted enthusiasm. It would be stretching it too far to say that she had emerged from her pool of yellow essence in the Crucible chamber like Aphrodite from the waves in the sea off Paphos, but as the twinkling, glutinous liquid coalesced into human form, she imagined herself as she had been before her work had left its mark on her. She had never been a beauty, but in her youth, she hadn't been entirely repellent.

Setting aside such pointless recollections, Lotte prepared herself for the challenge that lay ahead. She had ensured she was fully charged with energy from the Crucible of Eternal Light, absorbing yellow until she was close to overload.

oooOooo

Adam found himself in a lorry park off the M20. Beside him was an exceedingly unpleasant-looking elderly woman in a bright yellow dress that did nothing for her sallow complexion. Her hair was dark, as were the rings under her eyes, and her body was thin, desiccated, wizened.

"Watch what happens," ordered Lotte Axelrod.

A fat white man drove into the park in a battered blue van. He looked around furtively. There was no one else in sight. He walked over to a container that was standing on its own where a lorry had dropped it off. He went round to the back and undid the padlock. He pulled down the lever and opened the door. Light poured into the container, revealing more than a dozen children cowering behind the empty freight boxes.

"Out!" shouted the fat, white man.

One of the children, who understood some English, translated the order to the others. All but one of the children stumbled forward and climbed down from the container to the ground. They were thin, dirty, terrified and blinded by the light.

"And you," the man shouted to a child that had not moved. "I said out!"

The man stepped into the container and marched over to the child.

"Bugger!" he said when he realised the child was dead. He turned round and shouted at the frightened, confused children, "Get in the back of the van. Now."

The children obeyed.

The man poured a can of petrol over the body of the dead child, then around the rest of the container and over the empty freight boxes. He stepped out of the container and threw a lit match under one of the boxes. With the container and its contents ablaze, he hurried over to the van and, after checking all the children, less the dead one, were present, drove off.

As the fat white man drove away, he used his mobile phone to contact his employer.

"It's Tubbs here," he said when his call was answered. "I've got the packages, but one was damaged in transit, so we're one short."

"Did you clear up?" asked the voice at the other end of the call.

"'Course. The damaged package was burnt to ashes. I should be able to drop the rest off in about two hours – depends on the traffic."

oooOooo

Back in the lorry park, Lotte Axelrod gave Adam what she thought was a winning smile.

"I'm here to give you an insight into another aspect of human nature. In my opinion, it's the most powerful, the most direct, and the most wholesome of all human drives."

Adam looked at Lotte. She was old and dried-out, and her skin had a yellow hue. Certainly she was ugly, but that was not the cause or the justification for the feelings of disgust and nausea he felt when he looked at the woman's face, especially the grimace, that he took to be her version of a smile smeared across its bottom half.

"I'm sorry," he muttered as he averted his gaze.

For a moment Lotte was disconcerted, but she quickly regained her composure. She wanted to explain that adopting human form had always been a problem for her, but she couldn't. After all, the reason Monitaurs adopted human form was to deceive humans into thinking they were interacting with fellow humans. She could scarcely explain that she looked a good deal better as nature intended: a sparkling, yellow, glutinous, pulsating mass.

"There's no need to apologise," Lotte said. "It is perfectly normal to find the old, the sick and the ugly distasteful. Only the hypocrite pretends otherwise."

"No, no," was all Adam could manage.

"Yes, yes," said Lotte. "But no matter. I expect you would like to see where our van-load of trafficked children are heading, both literally and metaphorically. Literally, they are heading for a London suburb, which is where we must now go."

oooOooo

Adam found himself in a large semi-detached house in a London suburb. There were three large bedrooms upstairs; two of them had floors covered with mattresses.

"The children will stay here for a couple days – no more," Lotte explained. "They will be cleaned up and fed, then they will be assessed. The customers for these children will have expressed preferences based on age, sex, colour, et cetera. The man Tubbs phoned, known to his clients and their victims as Daddy, is very careful to match the children as closely as possible to the client's specification. He has a very select clientele – senior politicians, civil servants, wealthy businessmen, all with a predilection for children. Daddy takes some pride in his work and is paid well for his trouble. The children will be distributed around London and the Home Counties within forty-eight hours. Brothers and sisters will be separated and will never see each other again. Some of the children may be assessed as too traumatised to be of any use. They could be a danger to the paedophile community. They might attract public attention. So if there are any such, they will be disposed of – with the greatest reluctance, I should add, because Daddy doesn't get paid anything for dead children."

"Why are you showing me this?" asked Adam. "And what will happen to us if we are caught here?"

Lotte laughed. "Don't worry. No one can see us. We are simply observers. As for why you are here, it is part of your training programme. I'm told the Praesidium has high hopes of you. All senior Praesidium staff need to demonstrate that they have a full grasp of human nature."

Adam bridled. "I don't think forcing me to witness a paedophile operation is going to tell me very much about human nature. Paedophiles are deviants. They're not the norm."

Lotte shrugged. "Paedophiles are people too," she said. "Whereas you fancy women, and gay men fancy other men, paedophiles are attracted to children. It's not their fault. It's as natural for them to lust after children as it is for you to lust after women."

"I don't lust after women," said Adam, feeling uneasy about the direction in which the conversation was going.

"I'm sorry," said Lotte, "I assumed because you are married that you're heterosexual."

"Of course I'm heterosexual. I just don't lust after women," said Adam.

"I'm sorry again," said Lotte. "Penile dysfunction. I had no idea. There is an effective treatment in most cases."

"Are you making fun of me? asked Adam

"Certainly not," said Lotte. "I'm just making the point that men have a very strong drive to insert their tumescent penises into the various orifices of other humans – and, in some cases, animals – they find attractive. Paedophiles find children attractive."

The doorbell rang. Tubbs had arrived.

Daddy's assistant, known as Mother, opened the door. "Bring them in," she said. "Daddy is in the kitchen. He will settle up with you."

Tubbs was in a hurry. As soon as Mother had taken charge of the children, he went straight to the kitchen. "Have you got my money?" Tubbs demanded.

"Yes, I have your money, but I have made a deduction for the dead child."

"Sorry, mate, but you can't do that. My boss won't go for it. The contract was for me to pick up the kids from the container and bring them here. It's not my fault if one of them snuffed it."

"I would have thought it obvious that I'm not going to pay for something I can't sell. I have deducted pro rata."

"You can deduct in any way you like, mate, so long as you give me the agreed price," said Tubbs.

"Take it or leave it," said Daddy. Daddy resented being called "mate".

"I'll take it," said Tubbs, "but my boss won't." Tubbs took the envelope and left.

"Are we done here?" Adam asked Lotte.

"More or less," Lotte replied. "I just want you to appreciate the scale of this type of activity. It's much more widespread than most people think. It has been said that if the Crown Prosecution Service prosecuted all the paedophiles in the country, it would need a rolling programme of prison building, and even then there might not be enough land available on which to build the prisons. And don't imagine it's just men. It's estimated that some 64,000 women are involved in child sexual abuse in England and Wales. The total number of sex offenders in the United Kingdom is probably not far off half a million. Imagine that, and then imagine what that figure is globally."

"You sound almost proud," said Adam.

"You still don't understand," said Lotte. "It is true that this type of activity falls within my remit, but we are not the drivers of any aspect of human activity. We simply believe that human nature is what it is, and that it should be allowed to express itself. It's true we oppose those who try to pretend that human nature is not as it is. We fight those who shackle man with guilt by fabricating codes of behaviour that are alien to human nature, and which demand standards of conduct that men cannot meet. Above all, it's true that we want you, Adam, to understand the world you live in. We want you to see the truth. Isn't that what you have always wanted? Never forget," Lotte added with emphasis, "the Praesidium is on your side."

Adam said nothing.

"It's time for us to move on," said Lotte.

oooOooo

"Where are we now?" asked Adam.

"We're in a town in the north of England. It's 2011."

Adam looked up and down the street. It was full of terraced houses. On the steps of one, several girls in their early teens were sitting chatting to each other and to a middle-aged Asian man. All the girls were drinking alcohol; two of them were smoking spliffs.

"You might think it odd that these children are here," said Lotte. "They are younger than they look."

"I'd have thought they should be in school," Adam suggested. "Aren't the school, social services or the police on the case?"

Lotte laughed. "You'd be surprised. No one cares. This is a multicultural town. Customs vary."

"Come on," said Adam. "Customs may vary, but we don't tolerate paedophilia."

Lotte became serious. "If you are going to play an important part in guiding man along the path of life, you must use all the weapons at your disposal. I can't claim all the credit, but I've certainly played my part in developing a number of key concepts that have allowed men to be the best they can be, by which I mean, the truest to their nature. One of the most effective and popular concepts is that of multiculturalism, and its associated philosophical position, moral relativism.

"You would have thought the concept of a multicultural society would have fallen at the first hurdle," Lotte continued, musing to herself as much as to inform Adam. "After all, to anyone with an operational brain, it's a contradiction in terms. Most people would define a society as a group of people with shared values and customs. You don't have a society if people have different values and customs. But despite this inherent flaw in the concept, we managed, by exploiting feelings of guilt and the natural propensity of human beings to ignore difficult problems, to get the idea off the ground. We planted and nurtured the concept until some members of ethnic minorities could behave in the most depraved manner and the authorities simply let them get on with it." Lotte paused, and then said, "I do hope I'm not loading you with too much information."

Adam's brow was furrowed. Lotte had certainly given him a lot to think about. It was true that human beings tended to ignore difficult problems. That was something he had learned from David Minofel. But he had also learned that the man who can face and solve difficult problems has power. Of course, when solving problems you sometimes had to make difficult choices. Sometimes you had to select the lesser evil to achieve a greater good. But none of that mattered. The main thing – the only thing – was to get it done, to solve the problem.

"So you're telling me the authorities knew these underage girls were taking drugs and having sex with these older men and they did nothing?"

"Absolutely," said Lotte. "No one wanted to rock the multicultural boat. Asian men looked at the girls and despised them. They locked away their own daughters until they could offload them into forced marriages. But white girls, with their short skirts and their permissive attitudes – they were fair game, to be corrupted, debauched, used. And it wasn't just these girls. Some 1,400 underage white girls were handed round among syndicates of Asian men in this and other nearby towns for all types of sexual abuse, including gang rape. All this was permitted, or at the very least not prevented, by the authorities – in the interests of racial harmony, and in the name of maintaining the fiction of a multicultural society."

"So, what are you saying?" asked Adam, now completely confused. "Are you saying multicultural societies are bad things?"

"Oh dear!" said Lotte. "You have much to learn. Of course I'm not saying multicultural societies are bad. Anything that encourages man to express his true nature is a good thing. And the failure of the authorities to stop it, because they were weak, misguided and foolish, was also a good thing. Why? Because the vast majority of men and women of all races are weak, misguided and foolish. Here, they were simply doing what seemed natural to them. But you, Adam, are not among that vast majority. Your training programme is to ensure you are strong, focused and wise, not weak, misguided and foolish. Then, like the others, you will be what you truly are, but unlike them, you will know the truth and have real power."

oooOooo

"That little girl over there," said Lotte, indicating a small, bemused black child holding on to a man's hand, "is Ayania. She is Somali, although she was actually born in Lambeth. Her name means 'beautiful flower'. Today is her fourth birthday. She has come from England to Mogadishu with her father on holiday. He is the one holding her hand. As yet, she doesn't know very much about Somalia, its history, or its customs. But she will learn."

Adam looked around. The temperature was around thirty degrees centigrade. The air was hot but dry.

"Looks like quite a big city," said Adam. He had visited the Middle East on business as an IT adviser, but he had never been to Somalia.

"It is," said Lotte. "It has a population of more than two million. This is an ancient city."

"Why are we here?" Adam asked, keen to avoid an informative but irrelevant history lesson.

"The population is Sunni Muslim. In Somalia, they have a custom that is going to affect young Ayania. It is not an Islamic custom because it predates Islam, but it has survived in, or been adopted by, a number of Muslim societies. The custom is Female Genital Mutilation, or FGM. Ayania's father has brought her here because FGM is illegal in England.

"I'll be honest with you. The Praesidium has mixed feelings on FGM. The practice is all about the repression of women, the attempt of a patriarchal society to take control of a woman's sexuality. It involves a particularly barbaric, cruel and intrusive form of surgery. While we fully understand the natural desire of men to assert proprietorial rights over their womenfolk and, of course, we are not at all against barbaric and cruel behaviour, we are uneasy about the possible consequence of inhibiting female promiscuity in adult life."

"And I am here why?" Adam enquired. If the Praesidium itself was ambivalent, what conclusions was he, as a trainee, to draw?

"You have seen what man can do to man. Now we want you to see what man can do to woman. We want you to see how men can take the natural bond between human beings, the loving bond between a man and a woman, and because of other natural drives – the desire for power, for ownership, for exclusive access to an object of his sexual desire – take a razor to a little girl and cut out her sex for fear she will be difficult to control when she becomes a woman."

Adam struggled to grasp the twisted logic Lotte was describing. "And her father is prepared to let this happen?" asked Adam.

"He insists upon it. That's why he has brought her here."

"Where is Ayania's mother?"

"She is at home in England. She pleaded with her husband not to take Ayania. So Ayania's father beat his wife for daring to take a stand against him. He was angry and disappointed. In his view, she should have known better. After all, she had been subjected to FGM herself as a small child. Surely he now had every right to expect her to be an obedient wife and a responsible mother."

oooOooo

In the observation booth, Kit asked if he could be taken back to his cell.

"You've found Lotte Axelrod's training programme a bit rich?" asked Simon hopefully.

"I found it, and I find you, disgusting. I will concede that if you persist in exposing Adam to all the vilest aspects of humanity, you will desensitise him to such an extent that, to all intents and purposes, he will cease to be a human being. But given that you say your purpose is to make him fully human, not to destroy his humanity, your programme will have signally failed."

"You really are a stupid and naïve man," snapped Simon. He was becoming increasingly irritated by the blind man's complacency. It had crossed Simon's mind that Kit was protected by his blindness, that he didn't feel the full impact of Adam's training programme because he couldn't actually see the perpetrators or the victims. After all, it was called an observation booth, and was designed for the sighted. "You talk about Adam as though he is a fine, upstanding citizen. How well do you know him?"

"Well enough to know that he is, like all of us, a fallible human being. Well enough to know that he has fears and weaknesses. But I also know he has courage and strength. He's like the rest of us – sometimes good, sometimes bad – but he maintains a certain integrity, a desire to find the truth."

Simon Goodfellow laughed. "He's finding the truth all right. Every excursion he takes is bringing him closer to the truth. As for Adam as a man, I could tell you of the things he's done that might put a dent in your benign assessment of his character. I could tell you, but I won't – not yet. It's always good to have something to look forward to."

13. Communication established

While Adam was with Lotte Axelrod, there had been progress in Harrow.

Luke's telepathic powers were becoming increasingly sophisticated. He could now hold two-way conversations with Andrew Rimzil, as well as with Kit, Numpty and the Storyteller. He could even observe what was going on in the minds of others. Although unable to communicate with the latter group, he was able to slip the odd thought into their subconscious.

His conversations with Andrew Rimzil had revealed that Andrew was now in the Westminster PCC, working hard on a new paradox device. His nominated host was Manfred Bloch, the Praesidium's Technical Director. John Noble had told Manfred to provide Rimzil with whatever technical equipment or assistance he wanted. He had allocated Rimzil a large, well-equipped laboratory on the ground floor of the main building. The work on the device was going well – amazingly well – but Andrew's relationship with Manfred was not an entirely happy one.

"We need to persuade him to make a paradox device. We need to understand the technology and we need to know how to use it," John Noble had said.

There was no problem in persuading Andrew to make the device. He'd already done most of the work in Geneva, and Minofel had made sure all of Andrew's work had been carefully packaged and transported to the PCC in London. No, from Manfred's point of view, it was Andrew himself who was the problem. The Praesidium's Technical Director was used to giving orders, and was accustomed to respect from all those who worked in his division. Manfred was a large, powerful man with a short temper. His staff feared him, and Manfred liked it that way. Indeed, they feared him so much, no one had ever even hinted at his wife's enthusiasm for extra-marital sexual adventures. But this strange man, Rimzil, with his peculiar accent and his almost military bearing, neither feared nor respected him. He didn't request equipment or materials; he demanded them. When Manfred had complained to John Noble about the man's demeanour, the Chairman had simply told him to put up with it.

There was another problem with Rimzil: he gave nothing away. It was obvious that the man was not merely building a second paradox device, he was also developing it, exploring its properties and its potential. He'd even caused a momentary blip in the Praesidium's power supply, as though the device had somehow connected with the Crucible and accessed the Eternal Light.

When Manfred had questioned him, he had been treated like a none-too-bright lab assistant. "Just running a few tests," Andrew Rimzil had said, before dismissing him.

Luke had also conversed with Kit. Minofel's plan to undermine the blind man was having an effect, although he was putting a brave face on it. Kit's biggest problem was not being able to talk to Adam. The Praesidium was building a case, and without anyone to dispute it, Adam seemed to be accepting it. But the case was based on a concept of man very different from the one in Kit's head – and very different from the man Adam had been. And just as Minofel had predicted, as Adam moved closer to the Praesidium, Kit felt his own strength diminish.

Luke passed on all the information he'd gathered from Andrew and Kit to Numpty, who relayed it, word for word, to the other questors. Luke knew that if they were to form a plan to save Adam and bring both Kit and Andrew home, it would be best for them to know as much as possible about the enemy.

Perhaps the most exciting development in Harrow had been a tentative experiment that Luke had undertaken following the advice of the Storyteller. He had told Numpty what the Storyteller said, that "space and time are one, *ergo* ..." Numpty knew well enough what *ergo* meant from his struggles with *cogito ergo sum* – it meant there was an obvious conclusion to be drawn. And so Numpty suggested to Luke that he should explore whether his telepathic powers could operate through time as well as space. If they could, then he might be able to contact someone – anyone – in Prometheus' cave.

The first couple of attempts were complete failures. Luke was unable to find, much less grasp, a timeline. He said he felt as though he was trying to swim through air. There was nothing there, nothing to take hold of. Numpty suggested he should think of space as a flat piece of land, and time as the hidden depths beneath that land. There's little doubt that in deploying this rather clumsy metaphor,

Numpty was influenced by his continuing obsession with the concept of an osmotic gouger.

"If you can stop wandering across the land and dig down, you could find the past in layers underneath. If you dig in the right place, you may be able to open a channel with the past so that the past can rise up osmotically out of the ground into the clear, fresh air of now."

"That would be more like a tunnel than a channel," Luke had minded. "Or a channel tunnel, even."

"I was thinking more of a tree," Numpty explained, "with its trunk and branches in the present and its past in its roots, or with its roots in the past."

"Whatever," Luke had responded, unimpressed by Numpty's metaphorical peregrinations. Nevertheless he tried what Numpty suggested. He marshalled all his memories of their visit to the Caucasus and focused them as sharply as possible, looking down deep into his mind. And something entirely unexpected happened.

"Hello," said a tentative female voice. "Is there anybody there?"

Luke recognised the voice immediately. "Chione. How are you?"

Chione had been one of Prometheus' delightful nymphs. It was Chione who had taken a shine to Gwoat when the questors had stayed with the Titan.

"I'm fine," said Chione, "but you sound a bit faint. Where are you?"

"Don't worry about that. Just give our best regards to Prometheus."

"You did it," said Numpty. "Bit odd that it was Chione you reached. I'd have thought you would've have made contact with Prometheus."

"Obviously I need some practice," minded Luke.

"Sorry," said Numpty. "I wasn't criticising. It's absolutely amazing what you've just done. Chione heard your thought as a voice. What's even more amazing is that I heard Chione too. You must have put her on speaker. Uncle Rambler will devote an entire notebook to you. I mean, contacting a land not only far away but long ago is extraordinary. That it should be done by a dog – well, wow! That's all I can say – wow!"

"Treat yourself," minded Luke, reading Numpty's mind, "Go on. Say it. Bow wow!"

14. Excursion 3 – Oliver Nates

"Hello, I'm Oliver Nates," said a man in a grey suit. The man had a long, straight nose on top of which rested some very academic-looking glasses.

"Hello," Adam returned.

Oliver cleared his throat. "I need to say a few words about my role in the Praesidium before we begin. I'm in charge of obfuscation and negativity. Yes, I know it sounds a bit dull, but you're wrong. You've already spent some time with Edgar and Lotte, and I'm sure you found their excursions very exciting. I can't promise beheadings, murder, rape, or the burning of people alive, but if you think hard about your excursion with me, you'll realise that, in the long run, what I do contributes more to the Praesidium's goals than the efforts of Edgar and Lotte combined."

"Are you feeling all right?" Adam asked. The man looked grey, even ashen. "You don't look at all well."

"I'm fine," said Oliver. "Did you hear what I said?"

"Yes, absolutely. It will be quite a relief not to have to witness burnings, et cetera. I have no idea how what you do contributes to the Praesidium's goals, but I'm ready to be enlightened."

Oliver pushed his glasses up his nose, for they had slipped a little, and began. "There is a misconception promulgated by those who wish to harm mankind. It is that man is aspirational. He is not. He is essentially conservative, apathetic and lazy."

"Right," said Adam. "Don't you think that's a bit of a sweeping generalisation?"

"All generalisations are sweeping. Sweepingness is in the very nature of generalisations," observed Oliver tartly. "But if, when you deploy that tautological cliché, you are implying that I am wrong, then you are wrong, profoundly wrong. Given a choice, man will settle for what he has. Otherwise, in the typical hierarchical society there would be insurrections the whole time. No, in the main, man is more than content with being content."

"I see," said Adam, still not entirely convinced.

"There are exceptions," Oliver conceded. "You are an exception. You are genuinely aspirational. You want to discover the truth. But that's the last thing most people want to discover. They fear the truth. Hence the appeal of stories – fairy tales, myths and religions. They want to be happy, not informed."

"Don't tell me the Praesidium is opposed to education," said a surprised Adam.

"Not at all," Oliver responded. "Every society needs an educated population. It needs clerks and administrators. It needs technicians. It needs skilled and unskilled workers. It needs all the professions. What it doesn't need is people who can think. Happily, thinking is the last thing most people want to do. People who think are never content. They're never satisfied. They want more. They want to know more. They want to understand more. They want to be more. More, more, more! Well, they can't have what they want – and, more to the point, we can't have them having what they want. Thinking is the preserve of the Praesidium and those it recruits."

"Sorry, but I don't understand," said Adam. "You say you want the people to be educated, but you don't want them to think. Isn't that a bit of a contradiction?"

"Excellent! First class!" said Oliver Nates, both pleased and relieved. "You and I are going to get on very well."

oooOooo

Adam found himself in a large school playground close to the centre of London. Oliver stood at his side. No one seemed to think that the presence of two grown men in a playground full of children was odd, if not alarming, but that was because no one could see them.

"I'd really like someone to explain how you do this," said Adam. "Lotte pulled the same trick in her excursion. Are we here or not?"

"You're here well enough to see what is going on," said Oliver. "Tell me what you see."

"We're in the large playground of an inner London school, with hundreds, if not thousands, of children who are speaking lots of different languages."

"Good," said Oliver. "Now, let's consider the contradiction of creating an educated population who cannot think. Do you have any suggestions on how to resolve the contradiction?"

"Not really," said Adam. "I've always thought the main purpose of education was to enable and encourage people to think."

"Let me help you," said Oliver. "I think we agreed that we

needed people to be sufficiently educated to run things. What we didn't consider was how many educated people were needed. More importantly, we didn't give a thought to what you do with the educated people you don't need. The Praesidium's solution, for which I can justifiably take most of the credit, was brilliant. It was to extend education as widely as possible while, at the same time, eroding and degrading the standard of education."

Oliver paused, clearly expecting Adam to gasp with astonishment, or to express undiluted admiration in some other way.

"I'm not sure I see how that helped," said Adam at last.

Oliver's eyes widened a little in surprise. He pushed his glasses up his nose towards the frown that had developed on his forehead.

"Let me explain. The state decided to educate more people for longer, a decision supported – indeed, initiated – by the Praesidium. Why? To mop up surplus labour as the requirement for manual labour declined. You follow so far? Good. But it was obvious that, if we expanded education, there wouldn't be enough white-collar jobs for all the educated candidates.

"Governments and industry came up with a number of means to mop up surplus labour. They created largely spurious new functions, like public relations for governmental tax-gathering departments, or safety officers enforcing elaborate risk-minimisation procedures in offices where the most serious possible accident would be a nasty paper cut. They insisted on the unnecessary expansion of existing functions, like expanding small, efficient personnel departments into massive, overweening human resources organisations. They recruited staff to fulfil numerous coordinating functions to improve communications between the burgeoning, and mostly purposeless, new departments. But there was still a problem.

"That's why reducing the standard of education was a stroke of genius. By putting poorly educated graduates, often only semi-literate and largely innumerate, into demanding administrative roles, organisations inevitably became unwieldy, sclerotic and slow. Unable to perform efficiently, rather than dismissing existing staff and seeking out properly educated replacements, government departments, and even commercial companies, took on more staff in a forlorn attempt to compensate for the inadequacies of their existing employees. Result! More people employed and, therefore, content. Education degraded. Threats to the status quo diminished.

Aspiration discouraged. Best of all, the risk of Emergents greatly reduced."

"Sorry," Adam interrupted. "What's an Emergent?"

Oliver's grey face became suffused with a red flush, which actually improved his appearance considerably. "Whoops!" he said. "Shouldn't have said that last bit. Please delete 'risk of whatever'. Silly slip of the tongue."

Adam wondered whether Oliver was talking to him or to some unseen observer. In fact, it was to both.

"Were you blushing?" asked Adam.

Before Oliver could answer either of Adam's questions the school bell rang. With some reluctance, the children divided into groups and made their way to their classrooms.

"We need to observe a class," said Oliver, eager to put some distance between himself and his verbal indiscretion.

The class Oliver chose was on history – on the evils of colonialism, and the major, and generally iniquitous, role Britain had played in it. There was one teacher, a white woman, who clearly felt the shame of the country's colonial past personally and acutely. There was one assistant teacher and two translators. The pace of teaching was slow. Each module of information was first expressed in English by the teacher. Then there was a pause while the translators, who had varying degrees of expertise and knowledge of English, translated what the teacher had said. Progress was painful and snail-like, but it didn't matter because there were at least a dozen children who didn't understand English or either of the translators' languages. In any case, few of the children were paying attention to the lesson. A fight had broken out at the back of the class between an Indian child and a Pakistani child. The scuffle was of considerably more interest to the children than the teacher's halting exposition of the evils Britain had done over the centuries to their respective home countries.

"Multinational, multicultural and mixed-ability teaching – you can't beat it," said Oliver proudly.

"Seems a bit chaotic," Adam hazarded.

"Chaotic!" Oliver exclaimed. "Chaotic? It's not chaotic at all. It's perfectly focused on our objectives. By not laying the foundations of a good education, by denying the importance of literacy and numeracy, and by ensuring the children are fed with ideas that encourage tribalism and hostility to the host country, overlaid with a veneer of tolerance and political correctness, we are able to produce an adult population that carries prejudices against both other ethnic groups and the country they live in. But they're unable to express their prejudices because of the demands of political correctness. They're unable to analyse them because of a defective education, and they're unable to debate them because of both."

"But how does this fit in with the Praesidium's objective to enable man to fulfil himself?" Adam asked.

"I'm truly surprised that, at this stage in your programme, you can ask such a question," Oliver replied. "This type of education is precisely designed and then carefully calibrated to meet man's requirements. Man is a tribal animal. He thrives on group thinking and prejudice. He is hostile to reason because of reason's insistence on consistency. He is opposed to elitism because it implies his inferiority, he distrusts those who are clever because he fears they think him stupid, and he despises the stupid because that makes him feel clever. There are those who deny this, but they are ignorant of human nature. They appeal to the brotherhood of man when, in fact, my brother and I see others as our enemy, just as they and their brothers see us. They call for social cohesion, despite the fact that everywhere, at every time, like seeks like, whether in terms of ethnicity, social class, religion or sexual orientation – and each group that forms, embraces those within and excludes those outside. They regard education as a panacea, whereas in practice it destroys the bonds that hold the tribe together and leaves man alone on a windswept mountain top, friendless, hopeless and confused."

Adam observed the class for a few minutes. "So the Praesidium has caused all this?" he asked, eager to be sure he understood the Praesidium's philosophy and role.

Oliver winced. "'Caused' is not the right word. 'Facilitated' or 'enabled' would be better. We always work with man, not against him. Yes, we gave a nudge here and a prod there, but once the ball was rolling, no more nudging or prodding was needed. In education, once you've put one generation through the system, it's self-perpetuating. The pupils become teachers. They bring with them the standards by which they were taught. Rather like a copy of an original, you lose a little definition each time you copy a copy. In any case, a general decline in educational standards is built into any system of education that continually expands its pupil pool. As you work your way down the ability levels of those you educate, you have to lower the standards in line with the average ability of the pool. Those taught at the lower standard then become teachers and bring that lower standard with them. They have no idea the standard is lower. To them it is the norm. It's perfect."

"I still don't see how this enables people to fulfil themselves," said Adam. He was having a real problem with what seemed to him to be a determined effort to undermine education. "If the Praesidium truly wants to help man to be fully himself, then surely a good education is essential."

"Yes, of course," Oliver sighed. "That's what you've been told by everyone all through your life. And it is true, there is a form of education that truly empowers – the education you are currently undergoing, a full and proper understanding of human nature. But such education is certainly not for the masses. Let's move on, so I can illustrate my point."

oooOooo

"I think you probably gathered from your excursion with Edgar Exton that man thrives on conflict," said Oliver as he and Adam handed in their tickets and took their seats in the audience of a television discussion programme. "Fighting and killing others makes man feel alive, which is why my division developed the concept of tolerance."

The programme had not begun. The producer had yet to prime the audience on how the discussion would proceed, so Adam had the opportunity to question Oliver.

"Sorry, but what you just said makes no sense at all. Man thrives on conflict, so you promoted tolerance. Surely tolerance resolves conflict."

"I'm going to be honest with you, Adam," said Oliver Nates, a subtle combination of irritation and sadness in his voice. "The Praesidium is convinced you are destined for high office, but I have to say that wherever they decide to place you, it is most unlikely to be in the Obfuscation and Negativity Division. Let's just listen to the discussion."

The subject of the debate was whether religion did more harm than good. On the panel were representatives of the three great monotheistic religions, together with a humanist, a moral philosopher, an historian, a liberal politician and a regular panellist from the atheist militant tendency.

As is usual in such discussions, the chairperson, an attractive young lady with a rather short skirt and exemplary legs, gave no one sufficient time to deliver anything more than a soundbite. Individual participants presented incoherent propositions without any embarrassment, and obviously contradictory views without feeling any need to resolve the inconsistencies. Many comments were prefaced by "With all due respect..." or "I hear what you say...", both of which meant, "I haven't been listening to what you said, but whatever it was you are wrong". Occasionally, one of the panellists would battle through the programme's conventions to make a telling point, but no sooner had the point been made than the chairperson would invite someone else to comment on some other issue entirely. It was as though she wasn't listening to the content of the debate at all, but was following a predetermined schedule to ensure that everyone, regardless of the quality of their contributions, had their fair share of airtime. The three religious spokespeople showed extraordinary deference to each other, despite the fact that two of them were, spiritually in one case and literally in the other, hell-bent on world domination. The discussion had no sense of direction, and no conclusions were drawn.

When the programme was over and Oliver and Adam had left the building, Oliver said proudly, "That was one of ours."

Adam said nothing.

"Don't you see?" Oliver prompted.

"I saw a typical discussion programme."

"That's right. That's what my division has done to the quality of debate. Each point made was given equal value, whether it was a profound insight or total bollocks. No one, except possibly the moral philosopher, said what he or she really believed. Each of the three religious spokespeople despised and feared the others, but pretended otherwise. The militant atheist believed that all three of the theists were mentally challenged, which he implied but feared to say explicitly. The historian was convinced he was the only panellist who could speak with any real authority."

"So they were all tolerant of each other. That's good, isn't?" Adam was finding his excursion with Oliver the most difficult of all to understand.

"Of course it's good. That's why we promote tolerance. But you will have noticed that none of the underlying conflicts in the group – and therefore among the constituencies each of them represents – was addressed, much less resolved. Even you must see that unresolved conflicts will fester and grow. Tolerance and its sibling, political correctness, have closed down any serious critique of ideas. Everyone's view must be respected, whether it is truly insightful or obviously drivel. By combining sub-standard education masquerading as first-class, with uncritical acceptance of aimless and incoherent public discourse on all major issues, we have created the perfect conditions for social conflict – and social conflict is what the people need."

"I thought they just wanted to be content?" said Adam.

"They won't be content without social conflict," said Oliver, clearly irritated. "People form groups, like goes with like. They are loyal to their group. From that feeling of belonging they derive contentment. But belonging to a group is meaningful only if everyone else is outside the group. Those inside the group are naturally hostile to those outside it, hence the inevitability of social conflict. It's quite simple really."

Adam decided not to argue.

"There's one more point I should make before we conclude this excursion," said Oliver. "It's a concept we've adopted and promoted. This one you must take away with you and ponder. If you've understood nothing else, you need to get your mind round this one – relativism.

"Relativism is the key to tolerance. It is also the key to incoherent thinking. Take societies, for instance. If you can persuade people it is wrong to make value judgements about societies simply because there are no absolute or objective standards of value, you have to show tolerance to all societies. Even the primitive head-hunting tribe that has a tradition of cannibalism should be protected, respected and studied because, as relativists, what right do we have to judge their society inferior? It's a small step from that position to tolerating voodoo in an enclave of a modern society on the grounds that it's an ethnic tradition of some in the West Indian immigrant community."

"So you think that's wrong?" asked Adam.

"Are you pretending to be dense?" Oliver responded, close to exasperation. "Of course we don't think it's wrong. It's right that every man should be able to express his true nature in his own way. Who are we to say that the witch doctor in Brixton, who inadvertently kills a child while attempting to exorcise an evil spirit, is wrong?"

oooOooo

"Not going quite as well as you'd hoped?" suggested Kit. "It seems Adam isn't quite as damaged as you'd thought."

"I'll admit I'm disappointed with Oliver Nates," Simon Goodfellow conceded. "He usually puts in a better performance, but then, this is only the first of his excursions. I'm sure he will improve."

"What was that about an Emergent?" Kit asked. He had noticed Oliver Nates's embarrassment.

Goodfellow laughed. "That's not something for you to worry about," was all he said.

oooOooo

As soon as Kit had been returned to his cell, Simon summoned Gustave Houry, the Head of the Internal Discipline department. Houry, who was of Franco-German origin, was a quietly sadistic man with a deceptively kind face, marred only by a twisted smile. Houry deployed his smile a good deal for he had at last found fulfilment, and a kindred spirit, in the service of Goodfellow.

"I want the blind man given a thorough beating. And while your men are carrying out the beating, I want you to make a record of everything he says and anything he does."

The Head of Internal Discipline smiled, nodded and left.

Simon was worried. In the last training session, Adam had undoubtedly shown some cognitive limitations. Admittedly, Oliver Nates was not the most persuasive of the Monitaurs, but apart from the slip when he mentioned "Emergents" he had done a passable job. Yet Adam had shown some resistance. Simon wasn't worried about Adam. He had gone too far to turn back. But Adam's hints of recalcitrance had given the blind man some reason to hope, and hope was the last thing Simon wanted Kit to have.

There was something else. David Minofel had informed the Praesidium of the incident with Kit and Jedwell, Minofel's factotum, when, according to Jedwell, Kit had exercised some kind of mind control over him. Jedwell had been unable to lift a salt cellar or some such nonsense. So far, throughout his time in charge of the blind man, Simon had seen no sign of any unusual powers. Indeed, he had seen no evidence at all that the man was an Emergent. But he was showing remarkable resilience. It was possible the blind man had chosen to conceal his true nature, had decided to keep his powder dry.

What better way to nip any stirrings of hope in the bud and provoke the man into showing himself than the administration of a thorough beating. It was time Kit realised how this would end, both for Adam and himself. As Simon often said, "Pain is an undeniable reality. Pain is its own truth. Fear eats the soul and pain shrinks the heart."

15. Chinks

When Adam returned to his apartment Miss Tomic was waiting for him.

"Let's go up on to the roof," she said, handing him a cup of coffee.

Adam was surprised. Miss Tomic had kept very much to herself since their arrival at the Westminster PCC. While he'd been on his excursions, she had spent some time with David Minofel, but for the most part she had been alone, reading books from the well-furnished library in the apartment and watching world news on the 110-inch television screen. She hadn't seemed eager to socialise with Adam, and, given the odd circumstances in which they found themselves, he had thought this probably for the best.

"If you say so," Adam replied.

Once on the roof, Miss Tomic made for an open space in the middle of the lawn.

"Do you have something against pergolas?" Adam asked, referring to the only place on the roof that provided any seating.

"Not at all," Miss Tomic responded quietly. "Only when they are equipped with microphones."

Adam's features showed surprise, but he said nothing.

It was a beautiful day in Westminster, both in the real world and in the PCC. The sun was shining through a perfectly blue sky and there was a light, cool breeze, which took the sting out of the sun's midday rays.

"You've almost finished your first round of excursions," Miss Tomic began.

"That's right," Adam agreed. "I have one more to go. It's with someone called Charlie Cornick, I believe. You said 'first round'. I didn't realise there were going to be more rounds."

"Well, it all depends," Miss Tomic explained. "If they think you are ready, they will end the excursions immediately."

"Ready for what exactly?" Adam asked. He had been wondering what his "training programme" was training him for. In particular, he had wondered how any opportunities they offered him would fit with life in Harrow with his wife and their second chance at parenthood.

"That's why I asked you to come up here." Miss Tomic's

green eyes seemed to express both compassion and fear. "Do you understand what they are doing to you?"

"Now you come to ask," Adam responded at once, "not entirely. I'm guessing that if I pass all their tests, they'll make me a job offer I can't refuse. But I don't really understand why I'm being sent on these excursions – unless it's just to familiarise me with the organisation's operations."

"They are training you to take a senior position in one of the operational divisions, with the intention of appointing you, in the medium term, as operational head."

"Since signing up with Slievins, I seem to have been fast-tracked at every opportunity," Adam laughed. "I was parachuted into ZeD as marketing director, even though I had no marketing experience, and now, if you're right, I'm heading for the top here as well. Clearly, I'm on a roll. Any idea what my remuneration package might be?"

"If I were you, I should focus on the price you will pay, rather than the money you will earn." Miss Tomic was speaking so softly her voice was almost a whisper.

"And what price will I pay?"

"They are desensitising you," said Miss Tomic bluntly. "They are systematically extracting from your mind any capacity for empathy. They are draining your heart of all compassion. They are excising from your being any moral sense you still have."

"Steady on," said Adam, shocked by both what Miss Tomic had said and the obvious passion with which she had expressed it. "That's a bit harsh. We all know – at least we at Slievins know – that the primary requirement is to get *it* – whatever *it* is – done. David Minofel taught me that, and I'm pretty sure that's what he taught you too. You may have to jostle a few moral qualms out of the way to reach your goal, but reach it you must. After all, you were the one who slept with Geoffrey Reed and Giovanni Spinetti, clearly without caring much for either. You, like me, were an essential part of the scheme to break ZeD. You and I both betrayed the man we worked for. The only difference is I'm pretty sure you knew about the scheme long before I did. So I really don't think you're in the strongest position to lecture me on moral rectitude."

"You have a wife, with a child on the way," Miss Tomic said. She seemed to be pleading with him.

"I'm well aware of that," Adam interrupted. "I've done nothing to harm Eve, and I will love and protect my child. Let's face it, you're really not the best person to lecture anyone on the sanctity of marriage. After all, you destroyed your fiancé by committing adultery with Dr Reed."

"Listen to me. They will break your marriage and take your soul," said Miss Tomic flatly. "At least I have warned you." With that, she turned away and left the roof garden.

oooOooo

Despite Miss Tomic's precautions, there were two witnesses to her secret conversation with Adam. David Minofel heard everything Miss Tomic said via the drone that hovered high in the PCC sky.

Andrew Rimzil also heard and saw everything using the small scanner he had attached to his new and improved paradox device. He was now able to observe what was going on throughout the PCC. He'd been particularly interested by what he had found in the chamber containing the Crucible of Eternal Light – interested and, once he'd understood what it was, shocked.

Both Minofel and Andrew Rimzil took some action as a result of what they had learned from the conversation between Adam and Miss Tomic.

David Minofel summoned Jedwell to his side, explained the problem presented by Miss Tomic, and told him to teach her a lesson she wouldn't forget.

Andrew immediately contacted the questors through Luke and sent a simple message: "If you are going to do anything to save Adam, you need to do it quickly."

16. Action

"We've spent long enough debating what we should do," said Numpty when he had finished delivering Andrew's message. "We need to agree a practical plan to get Adam, Kit and Andrew back."

"We have to find a way into this PCC thing," said Prune. "If we can get in, we have at least a chance."

"That's not a plan," said Numpty.

"Wait," Eve interrupted before an argument could start. She addressed Numpty. "You can communicate with Andrew and Kit. Is there any way we can involve them in devising a plan? After all, they know what is going on in the PCC. We don't. Without their input, we're flying as blind as a deaf bat." Eve's trip with the Storyteller through the vast blackness of intergalactic space had ruffled her metaphorical imagination.

"I'm going to have to tell them," minded Numpty to Luke. "I told you. I should have done it before." Without waiting for Luke to object, Numpty said; "Listen, I'm sorry I didn't tell you, but it's not me who communicates with Kit and Andrew. It's Luke."

"Luke!" exclaimed Eve and Prune together.

"Don't be daft," said Prune. "He's a dog."

"You see," Luke minded to Numpty. "You humans! You share ninety-eight per cent of your DNA with chimpanzees, but you think you're one hundred per cent superior. You can't run as fast as a dog, your jaws are weaker than a dog's, you aren't as loyal as a dog, but you're totally convinced that you're not just special and different, you're in an altogether higher league. You actually believe that you will go to heaven, wherever that is, and that we dogs won't. I'm sorry, but on your own scale of moral values, which I assume is your basis for determining access to heaven, dogs knock humans into a cocked hat." Like Eve, Luke's gift for metaphor had been extended – although, in his case, not necessarily enhanced – by the initiation of the Fourth Beginning.

"You're not helping," Numpty minded to Luke. "What do I do?"

"Tell them the truth," snapped Luke mentally. "And while you're at it, you can really blow their minds. I can't reach Adam. There's some kind of block I can't penetrate. But I can set up a conference call between us here and Kit and Andrew there. I can act as a hub so that you will be able to talk to each other."

"How on earth can you do that?" minded Numpty.

"Does it matter? I just can. It doesn't matter how."

Numpty took a deep breath and told the others what Luke had said.

With varying degrees of emphasis, Eve, Prune and Rambler expressed incredulity, intermingled with some concern for Numpty's sanity, until they heard Andrew Rimzil's voice.

"Could you stop talking and listen?" said Andrew. "I'm shielding our conversation, but communication between the PCC and the real world is strictly regulated. I can't be sure they won't notice some irregularity on their scanning devices."

There was a stunned silence for a few seconds. Then Prune asked, "Are you all right? Why haven't you contacted us?"

"I haven't contacted you because ..." Andrew began, then stopped. "I don't have time to explain now. Ask Luke. I'll give him all the details. For now, let's focus on what's important. Both Kit and Adam are in danger, although for different reasons. We have to do something to save them."

"But what can we do?" Eve had known Kit was at risk, but she was alarmed to hear Adam was in danger as well. "All three of you are prisoners in the PCC thing."

"I'm not a prisoner," said Andrew. "I can leave here whenever I want. My new paradox device means I can transport myself anywhere instantaneously. And Prune, before you interrupt, I'll bring you up to speed as soon as we're back together."

"How about now?" suggested Prune.

"There's a problem. I can use the device to transport me, but obviously I can't take the device with me because it's doing the transporting, and it can't transport itself. It's a bit of a paradox. The device can transport anything, except itself."

"You could leave it behind," suggested Prune.

"Oh no I couldn't," said Andrew. "You don't realise what it can do. If the people here get hold of it, it's game over."

"Fascinating," said Rambler. "When you say it can transport anything, is there a size limit?"

"Well, I guess mountains would be a tall order," Andrew replied with some impatience. "Now listen, all of you. Luke told me you'd been considering calling on Prometheus for help, so I contacted him. I hope you don't mind, but I know how urgently Kit and Adam need help. I asked Prometheus what he could do. We discounted him coming here himself to help. After all, he's a Titan. He'd be a bit conspicuous in Westminster, in either the PCC or the real version."

"So, is there anything he can do?" asked Eve. "He's always been on our side. Surely he could at least give us some advice?"

"He can do better than that," said Andrew, "and that's why I'm contacting you. He's willing to send his daughter, Aletheia, to help. As soon as we've finished talking, I'm going to transport her from Prometheus' cave to your door. Aletheia is dearer to Prometheus than anyone else, in his world or ours. I'd ask you to look after her, but Prometheus tells me not to worry. According to him, she's perfectly capable of looking after herself. I've been completely honest with him about the dangers we face here and the kind of people we're up against."

There was a faint clicking sound from Andrew's end of the conversation. "That's it. I think Security may have registered an irregularity," he said. "We'll talk later." And he was gone.

There was a stunned silence. They all had so many more questions to ask. No one noticed that Luke was lying flat on his back with his legs in the air.

Rambler spoke first. "How did we do that? It was as though he was here with us in the room."

Numpty tried to explain. "Although the Fourth Beginning was aborted, it did bring about some changes that persisted. It opened my mind. I find it much easier to understand so much more than before. It left Adam fifteen years older than he should be. The ageing he suffered during his ordeal in hell at Cadnam wasn't reversed. And Luke – well, Luke ..."

Suddenly, they all noticed Luke.

"Oh God, what's the matter with him?" shrieked Eve.

It was probably psychological, but Luke found it easier to act as a relay station if he lay on his back with his legs in the air, as though his legs were transmitters or receiving antennae. Of course, the actual processing of sounds and their onward transmission took place in Luke's brain, but when he was so engaged he found it helped to adopt a supine position, with legs reaching skywards.

"Would you like me to tickle your tummy?" enquired Numpty,

who was familiar with Luke's relay station posture and thought his tummy-tickling suggestion was the best way to put Eve's mind at rest.

"Certainly not," minded Luke indignantly, righting himself. "We have plans to make and things to do."

He was about to continue his canine call to action when there was a knock on the door.

17. Excursion 4 – Charlie Cornick

"At last," said Charlie Cornick, grabbing Adam's hand in both of his and then embracing him in a warm, manly hug. "I'm Charlie Cornick. Call me Charlie. I'm here to open your eyes."

Adam looked at his new excursion guide, taking in Charlie's florid complexion, his large, fat body and his cheerful, ebullient persona.

"They've kept the best to last, my friend, believe me. You and I are going to have a helluva good time."

There was something rather endearing about Charlie. He was full of life and, at the same time, larger than life. It was clear the Monitaur in charge of corruption knew how to enjoy himself.

"Adam, I'm going to be straight with you. I promote corruption in all its forms, of which there are many. Yes, you are shocked. You think it disgraceful that a major division of the Praesidium should dedicate itself to encouraging corruption. But you must hear me out. We are going on an excursion you will never forget. Before we set out, I want you to take on board a couple of truths. First, corruption is what makes the world go round. The grease on palms is the oil that enables human civilisation to chug along smoothly. You haven't realised it yet but everywhere, in every society at every level, corruption is the lubricant of human affairs. Secondly, we are not corrupting man, we are simply allowing his inclination to be corrupt to fulfil itself without guilt. This last point is crucial, not just in the work of my division but in all the work of the Praesidium.

"In a way, Adam, the ultimate goal of the Praesidium is to free man of guilt. We just want humanity to accept what it is and get on with life, without the dreadful burden of guilt that comes from aiming, but always failing, to be better than we are. Many of the powerful organisations in your world are against us. Governments enact laws that are designed to prevent man from being himself. Religions set entirely unrealistic moral standards which man is doomed to fail to meet. Why do they do this? Is it, as they all pretend, for the benefit of mankind, to create a better society, to make the world a better place? Is it really to make man better than he truly is? No, absolutely not. It is simply to maintain power over him. The guilt that ensues from perpetual failure is the chain that keeps man in wretched servitude.

Sinners of the world unite. You have nothing to lose but your guilt. Whoa! I'm getting ahead of myself. I love my work and I tend to get a little carried away. I just wanted to set the scene for our excursion."

oooOooo

"Let's begin with everyone's favourite," said an ebullient Charlie.

He and Adam were in a large meeting hall where it was obvious that a major shareholders' meeting was taking place. It was March 2007. On the stage were several representatives of the Royal Bank of Scotland.

In the centre of the group was Sir Fred Goodwin, the bank's chief executive. He was being questioned about possible exposure to the disastrous sub-prime market in the United States.

He replied emphatically, "We don't get involved in sub-prime lending."

A month later, the RBS annual report for the previous year was published. In it, Sir Fred's assertion about non-involvement in sub-prime lending was confirmed. *"Sound control of risk is fundamental to the Group's business ... Central to this is our long-standing aversion to sub-prime lending, wherever we do business."*

There was a flicker and Adam looked questioningly at Charlie.

"We've just moved forward a little. It's now 7th June. Sir Fred Goodwin is addressing city analysts again."

"We don't do sub-prime, so we have not, perhaps, been exposed to some of the more boisterous elements of the market that others have."

The meeting faded away, and Adam found himself sitting in the reception area of the £350 million RBS headquarters built on Goodwin's orders at Gogarburn, outside Edinburgh.

"I want to tell you a bit about Sir Fred," said Charlie. "I'm sure you're familiar with the outline of the story, but I'd like to put a bit of flesh on the bone – not because his story is exceptional but because, in one way at least, it's typical.

"Fred was a grammar school boy, attending Paisley Grammar School, then going on to Edinburgh University, where he studied law. He then joined the accountants Touche Ross and qualified as an accountant in 1983. He became a partner in 1988. His work at Touche Ross brought him into contact with the banking sector, especially the National Australia Bank. In 1998, he joined the

Royal Bank of Scotland as deputy CEO. While in that role he was the driving force behind the RBS takeover of NatWest. He became CEO of RBS in 2001. By then he'd earned the nickname 'Fred the Shred' for ruthlessly cutting jobs while effecting bank mergers. In the merger of RBS and NatWest, he made eighteen thousand people redundant.

"In short, Adam, he was our kind of guy. Sharp, focused, efficient! Indeed, I understand that Slievins considered taking him on in his early years, but then decided to leave him in banking, mainly because he lacked your vision and your desire to find the truth. He thought he was exceptional. In fact, he was merely ordinary in the extreme."

"But things went dreadfully wrong," said Adam.

"And how!" said Charlie, gleefully. "In August 2008, RBS revealed a pre-tax loss of £691 million. Fred insisted he was still the best man for the job, despite the fact that he misled shareholders and analysts over and over again about the bank's involvement in the sub-prime market. Bit like Groucho Marx when he asked, 'Who are you going to believe – me or your own eyes?' Then, in February 2009, RBS posted a loss of £24 billion for the preceding year, the largest loss in British corporate history. The British government had to step in to save the bank and its depositors. Now we come to the really interesting part."

Adam waited.

"It's what Fred did next that is most interesting and informative for our purposes. Did he willingly fall on his sword? Did he slink away in shame? Did he, as the man who had brought a bank to ruin and a country to its knees, cry out *mea culpa* and throw himself on the mercy of the population he had helped to impoverish? Did he, hell! No, siree! He had to be ousted from his job. When he 'retired', he took with him a pension of £703,000 a year from the bank he had bankrupted. Actually, that's not quite right. He took a pension of £703,000 a year from the taxpayers who provided the money to save RBS. There was a bit of an outcry when it dawned on the public what was going on, so Fred graciously agreed to a reduction in his pension. He agreed it should be slashed to a mere £342,500 a year. But the reduction was not quite what it seemed. He kept a lump sum of £2.8 million which he'd already taken out of the pension fund, and – you'll love this – he kept a bonus of £2.6 million for his sterling efforts in the last year of his employment with RBS."

Adam shrugged.

"So, as we sit here in this £350 million tribute to Fred's arrogance and extravagance, what conclusions should we draw?" Charlie enquired.

"Well, as you say, he was arrogant and extravagant," Adam hazarded. After the difficulties he'd experienced with Oliver in judging the right response, he felt the need to be cautious.

"Yes, of course, but he also exhibited a number of other very human characteristics. That's why I like to start my training programme with him. He was avaricious, he was callous, he was incompetent, he was deluded and – perhaps most telling of all – he was unrepentant. Yes, he had these qualities in an extreme form, but they are – and this is the main point – essential components of human nature. If you aspire to govern the affairs of men, and you wouldn't be here if you didn't, you have to understand and respect human nature. You have to work with the grain of human nature, not against it. Sir Fred is an excellent example of what a man can be when unchained from the nonsense of religious and moral constraints."

"But there aren't many men like Fred Goodwin," Adam suggested.

"You'd be surprised. Why do you think Fred was able to negotiate the absurd terms of his severance? It was because all those at the top of the financial sector are as avaricious as Fred. And, since they all determine each other's remuneration, they understandably tend to be as generous as possible when setting salary and bonus levels. They're not all as successful as Fred in extracting money from their shareholders and the public, but they would all like to be."

"So Sir Fred is a model in your eyes?" Adam suggested tentatively.

"He's no longer a knight. They stripped him of his knighthood. Funny, really! They missed the point. Fred Goodwin was not about honours. Of course, he took them as appropriate recognition of his outstanding abilities, but that wasn't what drove him. If they had really wanted to hurt him, they should have stripped him of his money. He may resent the loss of his honour, but he is more than compensated by the £28,000 he receives every month as a pension from the taxes of the very people who hate him. What's important is not that Fred's a model, although of course he is, but far more important, he's an indicator. He shows what a man with drive and ambition can achieve if he sets aside all the spurious moral precepts that shackle men and make them so much less than they can be."

"But in the end wasn't Goodwin an outstanding and egregious failure?" said Adam, still tentative in drawing this conclusion.

"It's not about success or failure," said Charlie. "It's about being what you are. Anyway, we must leave Fred Goodwin now. We have much more to see and ponder."

oooOooo

"Where are we?" Adam asked.

"It's a Texas ranch. It belongs to the man who was, at the time, the most powerful dyslexic in the world. It's April 2002. The United States is still reeling from the 9/11 terrorist attacks. President George Bush and his neo-con buddies have plans that include regime change in Iraq. The British Prime Minister, Tony Blair, who has developed a taste for sending young men to war, is spending time with George. We don't need to eavesdrop on their private conversation, although it would be a privilege to see Tony hiding his contempt for his intellectual inferior behind an impenetrable cloak of sycophancy. No, it's sufficient for us to know that Tony Blair has committed the United Kingdom to joining the United States in an invasion of Iraq. Of course, he's blathered on about 'ideally going through the United Nations', but he's assured George Bush that when America invades Iraq, the UK will be at its side."

"What has this to do with corruption?" Adam was feeling bolder. Charlie seemed happy to answer questions without implying, like Oliver Nates, that they could only have been asked by an idiot.

"Patience," Charlie replied. "Corruption takes many forms. Following his meeting with George on his ranch, Tony Blair is determined to take the UK to war, but being a lawyer, he is desperate to find a legal basis for such a serious political decision. He also wants to have the backing of the House of Commons. So he stakes everything on finding weapons of mass destruction (WMDs) in Saddam Hussein's arsenal. Saddam has an evil track record. If it can be proved that he has secretly stockpiled WMDs, it will probably be possible to persuade the UN to endorse the war. Trouble is, after years of sanctions, Iraq is in pretty poor shape, and Saddam doesn't have any WMDs. The weapons inspectors have not been able to find any. As a result, the attorney general, Lord Goldsmith, the highest legal authority in the land, expresses doubts about the legality of invading Iraq. So, exploiting the difficulty of proving a negative,

Tony demands a dossier to prove Saddam has something that he doesn't have. His loyal hack, Alistair Campbell, does his master's bidding. He checks the dossier, tightens it up where necessary, eliminates the odd namby-pamby qualification and – hey presto! – Tony feels able to tell the House of Commons, one hand on his heart, and the other behind his back with fingers crossed, that Saddam has '*existing and active military plans to use chemical and biological weapons*' which '*could be activated in 45 minutes*'.

"It's difficult to be precise about the ensuing number of deaths, but leaked US military statistics put the number of dead people at well over 100,000, of whom the majority were civilians. Some estimates put the figure closer to one million."

"This is history," said Adam, dismissively. "We all know the story."

"Yes, but it's what happened next that's important," Charlie continued, unperturbed. "Blair never really recovers from the Iraq war. It's particularly unpopular with his own party's supporters. He quits office. Then what does he do? It's classic. Having initiated military action in Kosovo, Sierra Leone and Afghanistan – not forgetting the war in Iraq – he takes on a job as Middle East peace envoy. What do you say to that?"

"Well, I guess it was inappropriate, especially as it was generally agreed that he had a very shaky grasp of Middle Eastern culture, religion and politics."

"Yes, of course it was inappropriate – no, it was not merely inappropriate, it was absurd, but that's not the point. The point, dear Adam, is this – if you're a full-on human being, as undoubtedly Blair and Goodwin are, you can perform the most extraordinary feats. Goodwin broke a bank and shook a nation. Blair, in concert with Bush, shoved a country a few centuries back into the past, and laid the foundations for chaos across the Middle East. Yes, some would say that their goals were not completely fulfilled, but in terms of revealing what man is all about, they are stand-out characters. Don't you see? When lesser men would have fled, they remained unmoved and unrepentant. They retained all the many benefits they had acquired during their careers and then, despite their final cataclysmic failures, they brazenly faced down the criticism of those whom they had most damaged. Also note, they became extremely wealthy, not by accident of birth, but to a large extent as a result of their unequivocal commitment to the pursuit of power and money."

"All that's true, but most people see them as bad," Adam pointed out. "Many would like to see Blair in prison and Goodwin begging for a crust in the Gorbals."

Charlie laughed. "The Praesidium would never let that happen. Men like Goodwin and Blair are role models for mankind. They're not hamstrung by guilt. They're not plagued by moral uncertainty. Even when things go wrong, they carry on. They don't buckle. It's part of my job to make sure such men reach their full potential."

"I see," said Adam. "But you pick exceptions. I accept that power tends to corrupt, but most people don't have power."

"I started with a couple of exceptional examples. I have hundreds of other 'exceptions', but I picked those two just to lay down the ground rules. We are now going on excursions into other levels of society where we will find that the aspects of human nature which Goodwin and Blair exemplify so forcefully are present in everyone, albeit perhaps in paler form."

18. Aletheia

It was Numpty who answered the knock on the door. Before him stood a tall, fair-haired girl with blue-green eyes, fine features, a surprised expression on her face, and a rather fine sword and dagger at her side.

"I am Aletheia. Is this the dwelling of the woman Eve?" she asked, looking quizzically at the young man who stood before her. She spoke quietly, but with an air of confidence.

Numpty, too, wore a surprised look. The girl was naked except for a belt around her waist, from which hung the fine sword and dagger.

"There's a young lady at the door asking for Eve," Numpty managed.

"Well, bring her in," said Eve.

"She has no clothes on," Numpty added.

Eve went to the door. She took a coat from a peg in the hallway and put it round Aletheia's shoulders. Aletheia placed her sword in the umbrella stand. She kept the dagger on her belt.

"Come in, come in," said Eve, taking Aletheia by the arm. "Would you like a cup of tea?"

Eve wanted to put her visitor at ease. In any case, if this was Aletheia, then she had just travelled a few thousand miles, and several thousand years, to be with the questors. A cup of tea seemed somehow apt.

The others gathered round and greeted their new guest.

The Storyteller smiled when he took Aletheia's hand and spoke to her as though they had met before. "It's good to see you," he said. "We follow different paths, but we are heading for the same destination."

Eve wondered what he meant, but Aletheia seemed to understand. By way of reply, she smiled and nodded.

Prune was not much of a lady's man and was slightly embarrassed by the arrival of a naked girl. Although Aletheia was now covered up, Prune kept his eyes to the ground when he greeted her. When he took her hand he simply muttered, "Welcome."

Rambler, on the other hand, had much to say. "It is truly a privilege and honour to meet you," he gushed. "How was your journey?"

"I will be better able to answer that when I know how I was transported here. A moment ago, Prometheus was briefing me on your situation. He had just finished explaining the terrible dangers you and your friends are facing, when there was a disturbance of light and air at the mouth of Prometheus' cave where he and I were standing. Then, in the blink of an eye, I'm here."

"Without any clothes," murmured Prune, still a little disconcerted by the arrival of a naked goddess.

"Apparently that's something to do with the teleporting system in the paradox device," said Numpty. "Andrew told me that while he is still testing the system it's best if the only thing teleported is the person – no possessions and no clothes."

"Clothes are a matter of no importance to the goddess of truth," said Aletheia, dismissively. "I just hope I have not caused too much embarrassment.

"Not at all," said Rambler quickly. "As soon as I heard we were to be honoured by a visit from Aletheia, I half-expected you to appear unrobed."

Eve frowned. Rambler was behaving oddly.

Prune was blunter. "What are you drivelling on about? Give the girl a chance to collect herself without inflicting your nonsense on her."

"It's not nonsense," said Rambler, appealing to Aletheia.

Aletheia smiled. "It's true enough that I am often depicted naked in pictures and statues by artists. They think it helps to convey my character, and in any case both men and women in my time – and no doubt yours – find the naked female form appealing. Clearly you have studied our customs. By the way, what is this thing called tea?" Aletheia asked.

"It's something we drink, especially when we are tired or need comfort," said Eve.

"It's an aromatic beverage produced by pouring boiling water over the cured leaves of a subtropical evergreen shrub, *Camellia sinensis*, native to Asia," Rambler chipped in. "It was first drunk more than five thousand years ago in China, and is considered a healthy drink. Not, I fear, in quite the same league as nectar, but perfectly acceptable to human palates. Indeed, it is second only to water as man's favoured drink."

"Enough," Eve interrupted. "Let's drink some tea and get to know our guest."

"Excuse me," said Numpty, "but if you had to be transported here without any possessions, how did you bring the sword and dagger?" The image of Aletheia's naked figure, with her weapons at her side had burned itself into Numpty's consciousness.

"I made it a condition of my participation in your venture that I should bring my trusty blades, and your comrade, Andrew Rimzil, relented. I was perfectly happy to forgo my clothing, but without my sword I would be truly naked."

Although Eve had intended that Aletheia should talk about herself and relax in her new and unfamiliar surroundings, the conversation swiftly turned to the questors' predicament. Eve explained that, as far as they could tell, Adam was somehow being corrupted by Slievins, a sinister organisation that had first taken him on as an employee, and then taken him over as a person. There was bitterness in her voice when she told Aletheia that although she was pregnant with their child, Adam had effectively cut her out of his life.

In an attempt to satisfy Aletheia's curiosity about how she had arrived in Harrow from long ago and far away, Prune did his best to explain the paradox device and the work in which he and Andrew Rimzil were engaged. Aletheia listened attentively. When Prune had finished, she thanked him and surmised that his and Andrew's expertise would be a valuable asset in the battle that lay ahead.

Eve then talked of Kit, the blind man who had accompanied them on all their adventures and who, on learning of Adam's plight, had once again put himself in harm's way.

"He sounds like a very special man," said Aletheia, "I look forward to meeting him."

When the briefing was over, Eve asked Aletheia to tell them about herself.

"I was not born of woman, nor came I from the seed of man. Prometheus was my creator. He fashioned me from clay, then sculpted me in a form as true as the great Titan could achieve. He baked my clay-moulded form in his potter's kiln, and then infused my form with life. Prometheus was proud of, and deeply moved by, what he had created.

"When Zeus, king of the gods, saw what Prometheus had made, he grew jealous. He said that any girl as fine as me should be a goddess and live among the gods. I should explain that this was before Prometheus had made Zeus angry by favouring man above the gods. Zeus asked Prometheus if he could adopt me as his own child. In return, he promised Prometheus that he would make me, like all the gods, immortal. Prometheus, who loved me dearly – and still does – agreed, but fearing Zeus's lascivious nature he took a simple precaution.

"In fact, Zeus had lied. He desired to have me as his lover, not his daughter, but he knew Prometheus would object. Even then, there was tension between Prometheus and Zeus, and a lack of trust on Prometheus' side.

"As soon as I had been made immortal, Zeus showed his true intentions. He tried everything to seduce me. He did his swan thing, his golden cloud. He even took the form of a dove as he did with that girl from Phthia. But I refused, partly because I feared the vengeance of Hera if I succumbed, but more because Prometheus had inclined me to favour Lesbos over Olympus – or, to put it more clearly, Sappho over Zeus.

"That was Prometheus' precaution and it worked. In the end, Zeus gave up and sent me home. He wanted to strip me of my immortality, but when Prometheus threatened to tell all the other gods and all men that the king of the gods had been rejected by a piece of Prometheus' handiwork, he relented.

"Since then, I have travelled much and had many adventures. In the end, though, I have always returned to the Caucasus, to my home in the cave of my creator, Prometheus. To the great Titan I have been, and still am, a daughter.

"I am here now to fulfil the wish of Prometheus that I assist you. The man Andrew Rimzil has told Prometheus all he knows, and Prometheus has briefed me. Prometheus has explained to me that this is a fight for the heart, mind and soul of man."

When Aletheia had finished, Rambler was the first to speak. "So that is why some texts, including Pindar in his Olympian Ode, say you were the daughter of Zeus."

Aletheia smiled. "For all his power Zeus was insecure. He couldn't bear to lose face. So he persisted in claiming paternity, despite his attempts to take me to his bed when I was in his company. But no matter – in the end, truth will out."

"Perhaps of even more interest would be any hint as to how you might help us," suggested Prune, who had little interest in Greek mythology and even less knowledge of it. He did not intend to be rude, but like the other questors, he was only too aware of the urgent need to take action.

"That's simple enough. As soon as Andrew Rimzil has apprised us of Adam's condition, and of Adam and Kit's precise locations, we will ask him to use his paradox device to teleport us to the Westminster PCC, to the heart of the Praesidium. There we will rescue Adam and Kit. If any oppose us, we will destroy them."

The questors looked at Aletheia, then at each other. Clearly, Aletheia had been well prepared for the mission. It was Prune Leach who voiced the question that was troubling them all.

"And how exactly are we going to do that?"

Aletheia smiled. "With the truth, of course, with the truth."

19. Gloating

Simon Goodfellow was pleased with the work Charlie Cornick was doing. In Simon's opinion, Cornick was the most accomplished of the Monitaurs. Of course, he had an advantage over the others in that his brief centred on a human characteristic that was ubiquitous. Even so, he had a very attractive, laid-back mastery of his subject. There would be no *faux pas* and no slips of the tongue with Charlie. Adam was in safe hands.

With this in mind, Simon decided to visit the blind man in his cell. He had not seen him since he had issued instructions that Kit should be beaten. Following the beating, Kit had not been well enough to attend the observation sessions.

Goodfellow had asked Gustave Houry, Head of Internal Discipline, who supervised the punishment, what the blind man had said and whether he had shown any signs of being an Emergent. The answer to both questions had been negative. Kit had said and done nothing – other than bear his beating with extraordinary fortitude.

"Good to see you once again," said Simon as he entered Kit's cell. "Healing well, I hope?"

Kit, who was still in intense pain, ignored the question.

"You've become remarkably taciturn," Simon goaded. "Nothing to say to your beaters, and now nothing to say to me! Never mind. I'm happy to do the talking. I just wanted to bring you up to speed with the progress Adam is making. We've moved on to corruption with Charlie Cornick. Charlie is really good at what he does. Adam's learning a lot."

Still Kit said nothing.

"I guess your back is giving you gyp. All those lacerations take time to heal, and it must make sleeping difficult. Still, I'm confident you'll soon be well enough to join me in the observation booth once again. I feel it's really important you appreciate how well Adam is doing."

Simon noticed tears in the blind man's eyes. He wondered whether the cause was pain, frustration, anger or despair. There was no way of telling. Simon decided to goad him one more time.

"It's really important for you to take an interest in Adam's progress. You see, when he has completed his training, I plan to place your fate in his hands. It's obvious how this is going to end for you, but I think it somehow right that Adam should be the one who takes the decision and does the deed, don't you? It will answer all your questions, and his, at the same time."

Simon left. As he checked that the door of Kit's cell was locked, he said to himself, "If that man is an Emergent, then I'm a Netherlander." Then he laughed.

oooOooo

With Simon gone, Kit tried to move himself into a more comfortable position. He desperately needed sleep, but the pain kept waking him.

"You need proper medical treatment," said the voice of Andrew Rimzil.

"Where are you?" Kit asked. Although he couldn't see, he knew he was alone in the room.

"I'm in my quarters, here in the PCC. I've been working on the paradox device. There are things it can do now that it couldn't before – or, if it could, I didn't know how to do them. It doesn't matter. One of the things I can now do is teleport you out of here back to Harrow in the twinkling of an LED."

"You mustn't do that," said Kit quickly. "I have to stay here to the end. It's not just Adam they're testing, it's me too. If I leave, they win. My fate and Adam's are bound together."

"If you stay Simon Goodfellow will kill you," Andrew predicted. "He wanted to kill you from the start. It's only because David Minofel stipulated you should be witness to all of Adam's training that you are still alive. Simon thinks he knows better than Minofel. In fact, he thinks he knows better than everyone."

Kit groaned. The pain in his back was almost unbearable. The cuts were not healing well. Every time he moved it felt as though the wounds in his back were being scrubbed with a wire brush.

"Won't you help yourself?" Andrew asked. "You knocked Nick Peters off Mount Strobilos."

Andrew had always thought Kit had more power than he admitted. There were small things he had done which were out of the ordinary to say the least. He had somehow managed to feed them all when they were leaving the Garden of Eden, although they had previously been unable to find food. Then there was the disappearing broken glass in the Elm Tree pub. And, most recently, the incident with the salt cellar and Jedwell in Geneva, which was the subject of much gossip among the PCC technical staff.

"The time for tricks is over," said Kit. "This is the endgame."

"Not much of a game – either for you or for Adam."

Kit said nothing. Andrew conceded defeat. He promised he wouldn't move Kit without his consent, which evidently Kit was not going to give.

oooOooo

That afternoon Simon was looking forward to enjoying the favours of Kathrin. Apart from the physical pleasure engendered by their encounters, there was Kathrin's promise that today she would be able to confirm that Simon had a majority of board members ready to back his coup. John Noble might not relinquish the chairmanship willingly or graciously. He would almost certainly appeal to the Praesidium's High Council, but if Simon had a majority and Noble were to meet with a tragic, fatal accident before any appeal could be heard, the High Council would be certain to endorse Simon's appointment.

20. Alarm bells

While Simon and Kathrin were disporting themselves in Simon's apartment in the accommodation block, David Minofel burst into John Noble's office and told Cynthia, Noble's secretary, that he must see her boss immediately.

John Noble had just finished reviewing Kathrin's most recent report on Simon Goodfellow's machinations; she had done an excellent job. He agreed to meet Minofel.

"Are you sure you have everything under control?" Minofel demanded.

"Rather better than you have control of your temper," Noble responded. "What's the problem?"

"I thought your man Bloch was taking care of Andrew Rimzil?"

"Well, so he is," Noble replied.

"When I said 'taking care' I meant extracting information from him about the paradox device, and taking advantage of his genius to improve the Praesidium's far-from-perfect Technical Division."

John Noble remained calm. "As I understand from Bloch, Rimzil is making remarkable progress in building a paradox device for us. Our people are keeping a close eye on him at all times. What is the problem?"

"Well now, let me see," said Minofel, in his most irritating manner. "You say he's making remarkable progress. Well, you're right there. He's built an upgraded version of the device he used with the questors. It seems his first enhancement was to incorporate a shielding function to prevent your people from knowing what he is doing. So much for keeping an eye on him! And let me tell you, the new device is not intended for the Praesidium. Rimzil has simply taken advantage of the facilities we have provided to develop the device for his own use and to help the questors."

"So, what has he been doing?" John Noble asked uneasily.

"He's been contacting Eve and her friends in Harrow. They've been hatching a plot to rescue their friends from the clutches of the Praesidium and to create havoc here in the process."

"And how do you know this?"

"I'll tell you how, and the reason I'm here. They have a new ally, and we have a new enemy – an enemy whom even I regard as serious opposition. My man Jedwell has been observing the activities of Eve and her friends. Some days ago, Jedwell mentioned that they had discussed the possibility of contacting Prometheus."

"Prometheus?" John Noble queried. He knew of the mythological Titan, but assumed this was a codename for another, more contemporary individual.

"Prometheus," said David Minofel. "Prometheus, son of Iapetus and Clymene, one of the Oceanids. The Prometheus who tricked Zeus out of the edible portions of sacrificial animals, who stole fire from the gods for man, and who in ancient times was considered man's greatest benefactor. That Prometheus!"

"But that's just mythology," objected John Noble. He was now rubbing his neatly trimmed moustache with untypical vigour. "He didn't exist, and even if he did, he doesn't exist now."

David Minofel laughed. "You have a lot to learn. Given that you have regular meetings with the Monitaurs, entities which in their natural form appear to humans as sparkling, glutinous, formless masses, I'm surprised you baulk at accepting the existence of a Titan."

"But even if he did exist, that was thousands of years ago. Not now." Noble was reluctant to accept what Minofel was telling him.

"You put too much reliance on your limited grasp of time," Minofel replied. "Rimzil has already demonstrated with his paradox device that time is a rather flaky concept. Anyway, whether you have a problem with what I'm telling you or not, you really need to take on board the fact that Prometheus' finest creation, the goddess Aletheia, is in Harrow. She is here and she is now. Believe me, she is a powerful ally and a formidable foe. And she has been sent by Prometheus to help the questors."

It was a long time since John Noble had felt that he was losing his grip on things. He had managed his branch of the Praesidium for many years. There had been ups and downs, but on balance he had run things well. He had kept the Monitaurs focused, and they had responded well to his leadership. Goodfellow's latest report on Kit Turner suggested that the blind man was most unlikely to be an Emergent – one less thing to worry about – and with Kathrin's help, he was taking in his stride the challenge that Goodfellow was mounting to his position. But all this nonsense about a Titan and a goddess introduced an anomaly into John Noble's domain – and he hated anomalies.

"Who is this Aletheia?" he asked.

"You're asking the wrong question," said Minofel. "You should be asking what she can do. I will tell you this. She is strong. She will not give up. If she decides to eliminate you, she may not succeed, but you will never be able to destroy her. And she will keep coming back until she has what she wants."

"You sound as though you fear her yourself," said John Noble, strangely pleased that the practitioner seemed to be showing some vulnerability but concerned at the same time that even his powerful ally feared their new enemy.

"Slievins fears no one," said Minofel quietly. "But I respect her, and I will do all in my power to help you to fight her. And for this assignment there will be no fee."

"No fee?" said John Noble incredulously. Practitioners never accepted a task without first negotiating a fee.

"No fee," Minofel confirmed.

Of all the disturbing news Minofel had delivered, John Noble considered the words "no fee" to be the most frightening.

oooOooo

Simon lay beside Kathrin. He admired her finely proportioned curvaceous body, her full breasts, her perfect buttocks. She had taken him through her full repertoire of sensual delights. For his part, he was pleased with her performance, but he had to admit that he was beginning to feel the familiar stirrings of his sadistic appetite. He pondered the possibility of enhancing his pleasure by inflicting at least a little pain on his partner. A flicker of fear in Kathrin's clear blue eyes would more than compensate him for any ensuing diminution in the pleasure he took from caressing her previously unblemished skin. Yes, next time he would take the platinum chain to her. After all, what did it matter if it damaged their relationship? Her work was done. He had his majority on the board.

"So, when will you make your move?" Kathrin asked softly.

"At the next full board meeting, my dear," he replied.

"That would be next Friday," said Kathrin.

"Friday it is," said Simon.

21. Remission

Jedwell was waiting in the accommodation block, out of sight of the door to Adam's apartment. At 9 a.m. he saw Adam depart for a training excursion with Charlie Cornick.

When his master had told him to apply himself to solving the problem of Miss Tomic, Jedwell had known exactly what he meant. Happily, it was not a death sentence – he was to teach her a lesson, and you need to be alive to remember a lesson – but it was an instruction to ensure that the beautiful Miss Tomic did not deviate from Minofel's instructions ever again.

Let's be clear: Jedwell had no problem with inflicting pain or physical damage. If it was part of the brief, generally speaking, moral qualms didn't enter into it. He felt less comfortable if the victim was someone he knew, even more so if it was someone he had known and admired for years. Nevertheless, a job was a job, and Jedwell Boon always took satisfaction from a job well done.

Jedwell had known Gorgeous Tomic from childhood. She had suddenly appeared as part of the Minofel household when she was seven years old. Jedwell had asked his master where she had come from and Minofel had spun some yarn about a bungling imp, a fearful mother, and a curse. Jedwell knew well enough not to pry any further when David Minofel was evasive, so he'd asked no further questions.

Miss Tomic had turned from a pretty child into an extraordinarily beautiful woman. Throughout those years Jedwell had watched over her. He had seen himself as a protective uncle, complementing and to some extent compensating for Minofel, who was a rather inadequate and often absent father.

For her part, Miss Tomic had seen Jedwell as a trustworthy, reliable friend and an always-loyal servant to his master.

There was no denying that over the years Jedwell had become fond of Miss Tomic. Indeed, if Jedwell Boon had been inclined to indulge in the intimate relations favoured by most people, his fondness would almost certainly have expressed itself in stronger terms. Of course, Jedwell would never have expected such feelings – either fondness or love – to conflict with his duty to his master, and yet on this occasion that was precisely what was happening.

He pressed the buzzer of Adam's apartment. Miss Tomic answered the door. She smiled at Jedwell, her green eyes sparkling, pleased to see a friend. Since arriving in the Westminster PCC, she'd spent too much time alone, reading or watching world news on the television.

"Come in," she said. "It's good to see you." Miss Tomic was immaculately dressed in a white blouse and a black skirt that ended at the knee.

They walked through to Miss Tomic's wing of Adam's apartment. Miss Tomic offered Jedwell a coffee, which he accepted. It was obvious Jedwell was ill at ease.

"Is something the matter?" Miss Tomic asked, as she sat down in an armchair opposite Jedwell and crossed her long, shapely legs.

"Mr Minofel is angry with you," Jedwell blurted out. "You spoke to Adam. On the roof. You tried to interfere in his training."

Miss Tomic had a look of resignation. She had taken precautions when talking to Adam. Even so, she feared that however careful she'd been, Minofel would know what she had done. "I see," she said.

"And he's sent me here to teach you a lesson."

Miss Tomic had never asked for, or been told, any details of Jedwell's work, but she was highly intelligent and knew this powerful man was his master's enforcer.

"To teach me a lesson? That's sounds ominous," she said. Then she added, "Do you have any idea of what they are doing to Adam?"

Jedwell was shocked. "It's no business of mine," he replied.

Miss Tomic resigned herself to her punishment. "In that case there's no more to be said."

An embarrassed silence followed, filled only by Miss Tomic's fear and Jedwell's confusion.

Eventually Jedwell spoke. "Mr Minofel has left it to me to decide the precise nature of the lesson. The purpose of the lesson is to ensure you don't ever go against his wishes again. Specifically, he doesn't want you talking to Adam. If you promise to obey Mr Minofel and never to speak to Adam again, we will leave it at that, which I would very much like to do."

"And do you think that will satisfy David?" Miss Tomic asked.

"Let us hope so. Do you promise?"

"Your leniency in this matter is as effective in imposing David

Minofel's will as any punishment you can possibly imagine," Miss Tomic replied.

"Then I guess I have done my job," said Jedwell. A broad grin spread across his face.

"A job well done," Miss Tomic agreed.

When Jedwell had left, Miss Tomic spent the rest of the morning wondering why she had felt compelled to speak to Adam, why, after years of doing Minofel's bidding, something inside her had told her to stop and think. She struggled to understand. Then she realised she was asking the wrong question. She should have asked why she had done Minofel's bidding for so long. True, she was well cared for; true, she could have whatever she wanted in the way of clothes and other possessions. But why had she obeyed Minofel without question? He had exercised absolute authority over her, even determining her sexual partners. She was a beautiful, well-educated, intelligent, articulate woman. Why had she entirely subordinated her will to that of her mentor? And then suddenly she knew the answer: fear. Somewhere deep inside her was the conviction that if she disobeyed Minofel, all manner of misfortunes would befall her.

After talking to Adam she knew things would never be the same. She also knew that if she had the chance, she would talk to Adam again. She had told Jedwell that his reprimand would be as effective as the most brutal of punishments and she had not lied. No matter what he did to her, she would, if she were able, persist in trying to save Adam.

22. Excursion 5 – Charlie Cornick

"On our last excursion," beamed Charlie Cornick, "we came close to a truth that eludes many observers of human nature all their lives – the degree of corruption is directly related to the opportunities to be corrupt. That's why there is the saying 'Power corrupts and absolute power corrupts absolutely'. But for all the wisdom encapsulated in that old saw, it is misleading. It suggests that corruption thrives only if the person has power. But that's not the key – the key is opportunity combined with the absence of risk."

Charlie was wearing a very expensive bright blue suit, which accentuated the colour of his eyes. He was a big man, a figure that stood out in a crowd. Adam was concerned that such an imposing figure would intimidate the little old lady standing at the door of her bungalow. But he soon realised his concerns were misplaced. The little old lady could see neither Charlie nor Adam.

"Garden's done," said a thin, middle-aged wiry individual who came round from the back of the house to the front door. He was wearing a gilet emblazoned with the company logo.

"So, how much do I owe you?" asked the little old lady.

"That'd be two hundred and fifty pounds without the VAT," he said. "With the VAT, it's three hundred pounds."

"Three hundred pounds is rather a lot," said the little old lady. She waited.

"Well, I can understand that. Money must be short for you. Tell you what," said the man conspiratorially, "if you pay cash, we might be able to forget about the VAT."

"That's very kind of you," said the little old lady. She had the cash ready in her purse.

"If there's anything else you want done around the house or garden, give me a call," said the man, giving her a card. "That's my mobile. Call me direct. It's best to call me direct."

He packed his van with various pieces of gardening equipment and was gone. The little old lady waved the man goodbye, went inside her bungalow and closed the door.

"What do you make of that?" asked Charlie.

Adam shrugged. "She saved a bit of money by paying cash," he suggested.

"Quite so," Charlie agreed. "Obvious thing to do. Most people wouldn't think twice. Why put the man to the trouble of filling out an invoice when as a result you have to pay twenty per cent more?"

Adam nodded.

"Of course, it means she's avoided tax, which is a criminal offence," Cornick added. "And he's conspired with her to enable her to commit the crime. At the same time, he's defrauding his company because he's not going to put the two hundred and fifty pounds through the company. So, while he's being paid by his company to do this type of work, he is slipping the odd job through as a cash transaction, effectively being paid twice. And, of course, he's not paying tax on the cash."

"That is dishonest," Adam conceded.

"And so is the little old lady," Charlie beamed, "with her purse full of cash at the ready."

oooOooo

Adam found himself in a large, detached house in suburbia. He saw another old lady, this time sitting in an orthopaedic wheelchair. The house and its furnishings suggested she was a lady of means. A fat woman, who could have benefited from a good bath herself, was bustling around, preparing to wash the old lady.

"You're lucky I could fit you in, dearie," said the fat woman. "I can't spend too long. I've got one to do for the Council at twelve thirty."

The fat woman trundled the old lady into the ground floor bathroom. She ran some warm water into the basin and, using a flannel, began to carry out a cursory wash. "I think it's dreadful, the Council deciding not to wash you any more. It's not as though you're getting any better. It's just the cuts, and they reckon you can afford to pay anyway. Still, I weren't goin' to see you left high and dry."

"I'm very grateful," said the old lady. "It's so difficult to find anyone."

When the fat woman had finished, she said, "Sorry it's been a bit of a rush. The Council runs us ragged. We said twenty-five pounds, didn't we?"

"Hand me my purse," said the old lady. "It's on the mantelpiece." The old lady paid the fat woman.

"Same time next week," said the fat woman as she showed herself out.

"Well?" said Charlie.

"Yes, I get the picture. The fat woman is doing a bit of moonlighting during her regular job, earning extra cash when she's supposed to be doing Council work."

"Right," said Charlie gleefully. "And that's why she's had to rush this lady, and it's why she's late for her next appointment, which she will also have to rush. Double pay for half the service! Don't you just love people?"

"Doesn't anyone complain?" asked Adam.

"Some do," said Charlie thoughtfully, "but that presents more opportunities for the general encouragement of corruption, this time in Council and social services. Because of the cuts, social services have reduced frontline staff and demanded that those who remain work a little harder. The alternative of making themselves and their office co-workers redundant was, not surprisingly, unappealing. As a result, the level of service provided to the disabled has taken a bit of a knock. Hence, the increase in complaints. But from the manager's point of view, complaints are just a pain in the bum. So they ignore them. After all, what can the complainant do? They're disabled and vulnerable. They're afraid that if they complain about the poor quality of service, the service will be further reduced or withdrawn altogether. And if, when you complain, nothing happens or things get worse, you learn pretty quickly not to complain. The Council and social services people are quite happy. After all, they couldn't do anything to improve the service anyway, and it's not as though the people they're looking after mean anything to them personally, so why worry?"

"They could resign in protest. If what you say is true, they don't have the resources to perform their duties. So if they stay, they are taking money, their salaries, their pensions and their other benefits under false pretences."

"But they don't resign, do they?" said Charlie. "And no one really expects them to. The whole purpose of this exercise is to show you human nature as it is."

oooOooo

Adam took in the scene. He and Charlie were in a large car park at the front of a DIY store. To their right and left were rows of disabled parking spaces. A middle-aged woman in a Mercedes drew up and took one of the disabled spaces close to the store entrance.

"She doesn't look disabled," Adam observed.

"She's not," said Charlie. "She's the daughter of the old lady we saw being washed by the fat woman. The disabled sticker is for her mother, but the daughter uses it all over town, whether or not her mother's in the car."

In one corner of the car park was a man with a bucket and sponge, vigorously cleaning one of the parked cars.

"Do you see that fellow?" said Charlie.

"Yes, I see him," said Adam. "He seems to be doing a good job."

"He's doing an excellent job – especially when you consider that he's on disability benefit."

oooOooo

"These are all pretty minor transgressions, compared to the political and financial examples," Adam commented.

"Transgressions!" exclaimed Charlie. "Transgressions! What kind of talk is that? I'm not showing you transgressions. I'm showing you human beings simply being themselves, doing what comes naturally. I thought I'd made it clear. We're not in the business of making moral judgements. We're here to help man be true to himself."

"Sorry," said Adam. "I wasn't really making a moral judgment. I just thought that in comparison with the likes of Goodwin and Blair, these instances were pretty petty."

Charlie immediately accepted Adam's apology.

"'Course," he said. "I understand. But don't underestimate how widespread and how gratifyingly endemic, such practices are. In 2014, the UK's black economy was worth about £160 billion, more than enough to wipe out the UK's total current account deficit. The shadow economy – cash transactions to avoid tax – alone was worth about £64 billion. That little old lady at the door of her bungalow was part of a £64,000,000,000 tax scam. Each pound she paid her gardener was one of the one in every eight pounds paid in cash to avoid tax. Across Europe, the black economy was reckoned to be about two trillion euros, that's €2,000,000,000,000, much of it the result of a cash-based, tax scam conspiracy between the middle-class and the working-class."

23. Swordplay

"You shouldn't really do that," said Eve to Aletheia, "at least not in the garden."

Aletheia was practising her swordplay. She was dressed in a white exercise tunic, which showed to advantage her finely toned, lightly tanned body.

"Sorry." Aletheia dropped the sword to her side. "I shouldn't do what?"

"The thing with the sword," said Eve. "If the neighbours see you, they may wonder what's going on."

"Surely sword practice is common enough," Aletheia replied. "I practise every day in Prometheus' cave. I have travelled widely in my time – through Mycenae and Lukka, across the Hittite empire into Assyria, and on to Babylon, Nippur, Uruk, Eridu, Lagash and Elam. Nowhere has anyone objected to my swordplay."

"This is a different world," Rambler intervened. "We have modern weapons and different customs. In this country, you are not allowed to carry an offensive weapon. It is against the law."

"How can a weapon be offensive?" Aletheia asked. "The weapon-wielder can be offensive, in which case he needs to be taught a lesson, but a sword is just a sword. It is neither courteous nor offensive."

"You cannot carry any weapon that can be used to attack someone," Rambler elucidated.

"But every weapon can be used to attack someone. Is that not the definition of the word 'weapon'?"

Rambler was beginning to regret his intervention. It reminded him of his lengthy and often frustrating debates with his nephew.

Eve stepped in. "If you wish to practise with your sword, we can clear the sitting room."

"Of course not," said Aletheia. "Soon we shall be going to the Westminster PCC. I'm sure I will find time and space to exercise my sword arm when we are there."

"Do you think you could teach me to use a sword?" asked Numpty, who had followed Rambler to join Eve and Aletheia in the garden.

Aletheia laughed. "I could teach you the basics, but it would take a year. To master the sword takes a lifetime."

Numpty was disappointed.

"Perhaps we will have time to make a start," said Aletheia, hoping to console the eager young man, "when we reach our destination."

Numpty, who was even more attracted to Aletheia than to swordplay, was content.

"When are we going to mount our rescue mission?" Aletheia asked Eve.

"We are waiting to hear from Andrew. It seems there are tensions at the top of the Praesidium. Andrew believes there will be a coup attempt."

"This is both good news and bad," said Aletheia. "It's good news in that our enemies may well be preoccupied with their own internal conflicts and so not too alert to what we are doing. On the other hand, it complicates our planning. We may find ourselves in the middle of a power struggle, uncertain of the outcome. For myself, the sooner we begin, the better. I am looking forward to engaging the enemy."

For the first time in months, Eve felt a glimmer of hope.

24. Excursion 6 – Charlie Cornick

Adam found himself sitting alongside the corpulent body of Charlie Cornick in a rotorless, helicopter-shaped machine, hovering high above Westminster.

"Look down," instructed Charlie. "I've shown you the nature of man when he has great power. And I have shown you that same nature when he has little," said an ever-cheerful Charlie. "Different circumstances, different opportunities, but same nature. Now let's fill the gap."

"What gap?" asked Adam.

"All the people in between – not the rich, not the poor, but those in the middle. There are whole industries where my division leads the way. Take advertising – a discipline honed to perfection in order to persuade people they are getting value for money when buying products that have to be outrageously overpriced, partly in order to pay for the obscene cost of advertising. Take public relations – the art of presenting greedy, profit-obsessed corporations as consumer-loving, entirely benign organisations akin to charities, which, I should add, are quite often as greedy as the corporations that wish to steal their clothes."

"That's a bit strong," Adam objected. "You seem rather fond of unfavourable generalisations." He looked down at the busy streets of central London, where human beings the size of small dots hurried busily through the streets, all set on fulfilling their own goals.

"Well, this is one generalisation that has universal application," said Charlie. "It's inherent in any system humans devise. Whether it is working under capitalism, socialism or a mixed economy, human nature ensures that, as I think Jonathan Swift said, all humans reveal themselves as either fools or knaves. That might sound unfair to some, but it isn't – because all humans are knaves some of the time and fools at other times. The banker who defrauds his customer by selling him insurance he doesn't need will then spend his ill-gotten gains on a grossly overpriced product that delivers far less than it promises and never fully satisfies. The man who unwisely buys a second-hand car that turns out to be a potential death trap will happily sell it on to a stranger without warning him of the risk. Marketing people routinely price products in such a way as to confuse and deceive their customers. Companies use clever packaging to disguise reductions in product size while at the same time maintaining or increasing prices. Banks disguise identical interest rates on savings accounts with meticulous care to create an entirely false impression of competition, and then quietly reduce the interest they pay on existing deposits, confident that many of the depositors won't notice or take any action. Health foods are sold, in which the only active ingredient is hope. Lawyers, accountants and architects routinely inflate their fees by exaggerating the hours they spend on clients' business, so much so that cumulatively the hours billed by some individuals exceed the number of hours in their eventual lifespan. Top managers agree among themselves their rewards in salaries, bonuses and share options – rewards that bear no relationship whatsoever to the work they do or the results they achieve. The white-collar worker avails himself of any opportunity to show creativity in compiling his expenses, while the blue-collar worker takes pride in minimising the work he does for the money he is paid. Both use spurious claims of sickness to further cheat their employer and the public by forcing price increases to cover the cost of their absenteeism. Even shop assistants spend more time socialising with each other than they do attending to customers."

"Stop!" cried Adam. "You've made your point."

"Have I?" said Charlie. "I do hope so. In every case, the extent of man's cupidity is directly proportional to the opportunity he has to indulge it. The whole purpose of your training programme is to show you the true nature of human beings. Man is essentially a selfish creature. This is not a criticism. To describe any of the behaviour I have mentioned above as bad, much less evil, would be ignorant and, dare I say it, unfair. Selfishness is inherent in his condition. All his experience of existence is acquired through his own distinct, separate body. He could not be other than self-centred. There are, of course, occasional aberrations. He is exhorted to be selfless, especially by religions. But this is like asking the wind to be still or water to be dry. Asking man to be selfless is an act of evil. Asking man to be good is perverted. It goes against nature. It cannot be."

"I understand," said Adam. He felt slightly sick.

"If you truly understand," said Charlie Cornick, with a gentle smile, "your training is complete."

oooOooo

"I'm sorry you missed the earlier sessions, but I'm so glad you could be here for the finale," said Simon Goodfellow. Kit had been dragged from his bed and propped up in a wooden chair in the observation booth. "Assuming the other Monitaurs agree, Adam is ready for the next stage."

"Which is?" croaked Kit. On Simon's orders, Kit's rations had been cut, so he was weak from hunger. As intended, the lack of nutrients was impeding the healing process. Some of the cuts on Kit's back were now infected.

Simon laughed. "That is for me to know and for you to wonder about. But I will say this – there are going to be changes here, and whatever they are, Adam will have a chance to show what he is really made of. As for you – however things turn out, your prospects, you will not be surprised to learn, remain depressingly poor."

25. Prepping Adam

Following the conclusion of his final session with Charlie Cornick, Adam retired to his capacious apartment, poured himself a double whisky and settled back into an armchair. He had been troubled by the embargo on any contact with the outside world. He had wanted to talk to Eve, to apologise for the abrupt way he'd ended their previous telephone conversation. But as the days passed, his need to talk to her had diminished. Of course, he wished to explain what he had been doing, to set her mind at rest, to support her through the remainder of her pregnancy, but he no longer felt any sense of urgency about it. He would talk to Eve when he had concluded his business with the Praesidium.

"A penny for your thoughts," said David Minofel.

Adam was startled.

"You left the door open, a sign you feel confident and secure," said David with a laugh.

"More a sign of presenile dementia," said Adam, who was sure he had shut the door.

"We'll come back to that," said Minofel. He didn't give Adam time to query his remark. "Are you ready for what is going to happen now?"

"I don't know," said Adam. "I hope so, but since I don't know what's going to happen I can't be certain."

"There will be a board meeting today. Some of these meetings are rather tedious, but this one will be an exception. Whatever else happens, you will be offered a place on the board. If you accept, you will have power beyond your wildest dreams. Do not ask about remuneration. You will have access to so much wealth that it will be a matter of total indifference. Whatever you want you will be able to have. As a matter of interest, you may well be surprised by how little you want when you know you can have it all. But there are conditions."

"Which are?" asked Adam.

"You must dedicate your life to the Praesidium and to furthering its interest and goals."

Adam frowned. "That's a bit open-ended. I'd prefer a more specific account of my duties and responsibilities."

"Do you have reservations about the Praesidium?" Minofel asked, his voice quiet but combative.

"No, no," Adam replied at once, "but I need to know what I will be doing."

"Why?" said Minofel. "Obviously you will be contributing to the Praesidium's programme of enabling man to fulfil himself. Is that not sufficient?"

"Can I be frank with you?" Adam asked.

"If not with me, then with whom?" Minofel replied.

"I completely accept the Praesidium's account of human nature. Let's face it, after my excursions with Lotte, Edgar, Oliver and Charlie what else could I do? And I'm not quibbling – really I'm not – but it does seem to me …"

Minofel was losing patience. "Get to the point," he snapped.

"It does seem to me that to some extent at least the Praesidium is not just enabling man to fulfil his nature, it is actually encouraging him to indulge the worst aspects of his nature."

There was a stony silence. Then David Minofel, practitioner in the service of the Praesidium, spoke.

"The worst aspects of his nature? Who are you to rank the 'aspects of human nature'? I think you should ponder your own actions since you and I met. You began by becoming an accessory to murder. Then you accepted a job with ZeD out of avarice, abandoning your pregnant wife shortly after she had experienced the trauma of a burglary and attempted rape. You must agree that you found it relatively easy to condone the summary execution of the offenders, unlike your wife who at least had the misguided decency to express moral qualms. At ZeD one of your first managerial actions was to act as facilitator in a bribe to ensure the launch of a drug that had killed a patient in a clinical trial, a trial you conspired to suppress. You followed that with blackmail of the good doctor Reed. And then there was the murder, yes murder, of Giovanni Spinetti. Would it not be fair to say that somewhere along the line you forfeited the right to blather on about morality?"

Adam was stunned. He wanted to defend himself, to explain the reasons for his actions, to argue that at every stage he had put the greater good ahead of the lesser evil, but there was no point, given that he would be offering an explanation to the very person who had been his mentor throughout the events described.

"Don't misunderstand me," Minofel continued. "I'm not criticising you. We've gone beyond applying commonplace morality to our actions. You are, after all, a Slievins man. The sole purpose of your time with me, at ZeD and here with the Praesidium, has been to reveal that moral concerns ensnare and emasculate ordinary people. It elevates weakness to a virtue. Man fails to fulfil his nature because he is persuaded there is something wrong with his nature. The lion that decides not to kill not only starves but also ceases to be a lion. All you have done needed to be done to fulfil our objectives. The Praesidium will ask no more of you than that."

Adam was subdued.

"Cheer up," said Minofel in his hearty voice. "I have a reward for you – something a little out of the ordinary. It's a personal, unconditional gift from me, no strings attached. When you were in hell at Cadnam you were tested. You survived the test, but it took fifteen years of your life. I am going to restore those fifteen years to you as a reward for all the progress you have made."

Adam didn't know what to say. It was a generous gift, a priceless gift, but surely beyond Minofel's means to deliver it?

"What is taken away can be restored," Minofel answered Adam's unasked question.

"Thank you," said Adam.

oooOooo

Adam set out for the Praesidium board meeting, which he would attend as an invited guest.

David Minofel smiled. Goodfellow had reported that the blind man was broken and close to death. David had instructed that Kit must be kept alive, so Goodfellow had increased Kit's rations just sufficiently to sustain him. All was as it should be. Kit had to remain alive so that one of Adam's first actions, as a Praesidium board member, would be to play a pivotal role in the blind man's termination.

As for Miss Tomic, well, she had brought disaster on herself. Jedwell had failed to discipline her, but she must not escape punishment. She would lose fifteen years of her life. After all, the world called out for balance, and if Adam was to gain fifteen years, someone had to lose them. What is restored to one must be taken away from another. After all, as Roland Samiat, Slievins CEO, was wont to say, "life is the quintessential zero-sum game".

26. The coup

On the Friday morning of the day on which the Praesidium board was to meet, Simon Goodfellow invited Kathrin to join him in his apartment for a pre-coup celebratory drink. She was not keen to attend, but she complied. So far everything had gone according to plan. It would be a great shame, and possibly dangerous, to do anything that might raise Simon's suspicion at this final stage.

"By this evening I will be Chairman of the Praesidium board," Simon declared as he poured champagne into two crystal glasses. "Tomorrow, a new day will dawn for the Praesidium – and you will be rewarded." In a finely tailored grey suit Simon felt he was appropriately dressed to assume high office. He looked authoritative but restrained. His was not an ambitious grab for power; it was a rational decision. The time had come for a younger, more energetic man to guide the Praesidium into a new age.

"Here's to Nastafilu Verdicel," said Simon, invoking the name of the Praesidium's founder. "And to us," he added.

Kathrin drank. She tried to put out of her head the revulsion she now felt for Goodfellow. At first, in her self-appointed role as John Noble's spy, she had felt curiosity about the character of the Deputy Chairman, as well as some excitement at embarking on a sexual relationship with someone whose reputation for exploring the more arcane and exotic corridors of sensual gratification was legendary in the PCC. But as she had got to know him, curiosity and excitement had gradually been replaced by disgust and contempt. How such a man could think he was fit to replace John Noble as Chairman was beyond her. He had no new agenda, despite his vague assertions about a new day and a new dawn; he simply wanted power. And for Simon Goodfellow, the attraction of power derived entirely from the freedom to abuse it.

"Drink up," said Simon. "I need to be preparing myself for the board meeting. I want to put the finishing touches to my speech."

Kathrin tried to get up. To her surprise her legs ignored her. She tried to speak. No words came.

"I'm going to leave you now," said Simon. "I don't want you to worry. You will be paralysed until I administer the antidote, but you will be fully conscious, with a fully functioning autonomic nervous system. You'll just be unable to move or speak. I will feel more at ease knowing you are safe here in the comfort of my sitting room. I do not expect trouble, but there's no telling what Noble might do when he finds out you have betrayed him. When I return I will be Chairman. I will inject the antidote and we can celebrate – and I mean celebrate. So far, my dear, I have allowed you to teach me your take on the art of love. When I return, it will be my turn to teach you mine. It will be an exquisite celebration for both of us."

oooOooo

All ten members of the board were present, seated around the boardroom table. In addition to the Chairman, the Deputy Chairman and the Technical Director, there were the directors of Accounting, Human Resources, House Services, Internal Discipline, Planning, Research, and Security. The Monitaurs (Edgar, Charlie, Lotte and Oliver) were not present. They, along with Noble, Goodfellow and Bloch, were members of the Executive Committee, but not being human, were not on the board of directors. Adam had been told to wait with Cynthia in John Noble's office until summoned to join the meeting.

The routine board meeting business was despatched with unusual speed, as though everyone knew that more important matters lay ahead.

"Is there any other business?" John Noble asked, when they had concluded the discussion of the final item on the agenda.

The tension in the room was palpable.

"I have something," said Simon Goodfellow.

"I hope it is a matter of some importance," said John Noble, with a smile. "I was hoping we could break the record for completing a board meeting in the shortest time."

"I think you will agree it is a matter of some importance," said Goodfellow. "I propose a vote of no confidence in the Chairman."

There were various gasps of surprise and an exchange of looks around the table.

"On what grounds?" enquired Manfred Bloch. Bloch was secretly delighted that Goodfellow had made the first move. Whether Goodfellow succeeded or failed, everyone would know that it had been the Deputy Chairman who had initiated the move. There's always something rather distasteful about disloyalty.

"First, on the grounds of financial mismanagement," Goodfellow replied. He had notes with him but, having rehearsed the speech many times, had no need of them. "Secondly, for poor management skills in general, and especially in relation to the hiring and control of the practitioner. Thirdly, because of a lack of vision and drive."

"And you can substantiate each of these alleged failings?" asked the Director of House Services.

Simon smiled. He had House Services down as a supporter of John Noble, so some resistance from this quarter was only to be expected. "Of course," he replied. "No one calls for a vote of no confidence lightly, and I should add at once that it is only with great regret and reluctance that I am tabling this no confidence motion now. But given the circumstances, and the risks to the Praesidium, I feel I have no alternative."

"Then present your case," said John Noble.

"The costs of retaining the practitioner were high from the beginning, but the additional fees for dealing with the possible Emergent, agreed by the Chairman without prior consultation with anyone, were prohibitive. The Head of the Technical Division will confirm that his budget has been savaged to meet the demands of Minofel and Slievins.

"As for the quality of management, it has been slack to the point of negligence. From the start I expressed scepticism that the blind man was an Emergent. I can now confidently report that he is not. I have put him through some pretty stringent testing, both physical and mental."

"That's a tad euphemistic," John Noble observed. "You stabbed him, and then had him beaten and starved."

"Precisely," Simon agreed. "I followed Minofel's programme of forcing him to observe Adam's induction training, but I complemented it with some enhancements of my own."

"Enhancements more to your taste," said Noble. "More to your own very personal taste."

"As a result," Simon continued, "the man is broken and awaits his fate with commendable resignation. We, on the other hand, will find it rather less easy to resign ourselves to paying Minofel's astronomical fees for disposing of a non-existent Emergent."

Silas Drahan, the Director of Internal Security, a man Goodfellow knew to be on his side, spoke. "It is undeniable that the Chairman's arrangement with the practitioner means that we have spent a very considerable proportion of the Praesidium's annual budget needlessly."

There were murmurs of agreement.

"But none of these are my main reasons for tabling this motion," Goodfellow continued. "The key reason is that under John Noble's chairmanship the Praesidium has lost its way. We sit here listening to the reports of the Monitaurs, praising them when appropriate, cajoling them if they seem to be slacking. Is that all we are supposed to do? Are we not utterly complacent? What would our founder Nastafilu Verdicel think of us? Where is the drive in us that was so powerful in him?"

"And what is it that you think we should be doing?" asked John Noble.

"I despair," said Simon, as though the Chairman had condemned himself out of his own mouth. "Don't you see? The man has no idea. Think. For decades now we have had no major wars, no global wars. We have allowed the Monitaurs to fob us off with local skirmishes in which the major players have used proxies to settle their rivalries. Yes, hundreds of thousands have died in battle, and millions in famine. But the population of the world grows inexorably. The conditions for a global war are perfect. The major powers have the means to kill tens of millions in a matter of minutes."

"And that is what you want?" enquired Manfred Bloch. He was not particularly interested in the answer to his own question, but he felt the need to assert his presence. Above all he needed time to think. The Technical Director was in a quandary. Goodfellow would not have made a move unless he thought he had a majority on his side. Was the Deputy Chairman assuming that Manfred would support the motion? Or since Goodfellow had given Manfred no warning of the coup, was the Deputy Chairman assuming he would vote against? This must mean that Goodfellow thought he could win without Manfred's support. More importantly, which way should he vote? He wanted Noble ousted. It suited him that it was Goodfellow, not he, who had initiated the ousting. But there was a danger that if Goodfellow succeeded in winning the vote, he would move immediately to claim the chairmanship. Since he was Deputy

Chairman, he would have a good chance of succeeding. And if he, the Technical Director, voted against the motion and Goodfellow still won, his own position would be under threat. Even Simon would not have numbered magnanimity among his qualities. On the other hand, if he voted against the motion and Goodfellow lost, John Noble would no doubt appreciate his loyalty, but it would then make it difficult for Manfred to make his own move to take the chairmanship.

"We want man to be true to himself," Simon responded. "It is unnatural for man to have the power to destroy his enemies and not use it. We listen to the Monitaurs reports on conflicts around the world. We applaud them and their work. But what is the best they can do? Revive a medieval religion, locked in a sixth-century time warp, and set it against the modern world? What is the most we can hope for? A series of barbaric atrocities, perhaps one or two significant outrages? And then the modern world will put them down. A mere skirmish. Not a real battle, much less a global war. Where is our ambition? When the history of the Praesidium is written, where will our names appear? And if they appear at all, what will they say about us?"

"Enough!" John Noble interrupted. "You have said enough. Now we will vote."

Simon was taken aback at the Chairman's interruption. He had scarcely started his comprehensive trashing of the Chairman's character and record. What's more, where was the Chairman's response? Surely he would wish to offer a rebuttal. After all, the Chairman had implicated his deputy in at least some of the negotiations with the practitioner, so he could at least attempt to spread the blame. And he could try to take credit for some success, since the threat from the initiators of the Fourth Beginning seemed to have been eliminated. Simon had prepared answers to any defence the Chairman chose to offer, but he offered none.

"Those in favour of the motion?" said John Noble, his voice quiet but firm.

According to Kathrin, Simon could count on six votes for sure, seven if Bloch sided with him. Even without Bloch, he would win by six to three.

Two hands went up. Only the directors of Internal Discipline and Security were voting for the motion. That couldn't be right. Adding his own vote, there were only three board members in favour of the motion. Kathrin had assured him Accountancy, Research, and Planning would also back him. He stared at the three directors. They looked back unabashed, as though he had no right to expect their support.

"Those against?"

Six hands went up – the five directors whom Kathrin had assured the Chairman he could rely on, and Manfred Bloch, who saw no point in supporting a motion that would be defeated anyway.

"I think that settles the matter," said John Noble. "Except that, in the circumstances, I think it would be appropriate for the Deputy Chairman to consider his position. It will not be necessary to take a vote on that motion. That is my decision."

Simon nodded his head, gathered his papers and, without a word, left the boardroom.

"There is one other matter before we conclude this meeting," said the Chairman. "I have been informed that Adam Smith's induction programme has been completed. All four Monitaurs have certified his preparedness, albeit with one or two minor caveats. I therefore propose to call him into this board meeting to congratulate him on his outstanding progress and to offer him a place on the board."

There were grunts and murmurs of approval, and a general feeling of relief at Simon Goodfellow's abrupt and self-inflicted fall from grace. Truth to tell, Simon Goodfellow had been disliked by most members of the board. Even those who had supported his bid for power held some reservations. If asked to express their feelings towards him in a word, most of his colleagues would have chosen either fear or contempt – if permitted two words, they would have chosen both. His fondness for cruelty, especially towards women, was frowned upon – not that there was anything wrong with cruelty in itself, but there was a convention within the Praesidium that employees within the Westminster PCC should enjoy protection from it. The disappearance of several young women while working for the organisation was rumoured to be the result of Goodfellow's overenthusiastic exploration of the bleaker corners of sexual depravity.

On entering the boardroom, Adam was greeted by a round of applause.

"Please take the empty seat," said John Noble, indicating the chair vacated by Goodfellow.

"We are delighted to welcome you here," the Chairman began, "and to congratulate you on the extraordinary progress you have made. I am assured by the practitioner and the Monitaurs that you have been an excellent student. You have understood why the Praesidium exists, the purpose of all we do, and our essential goal of enabling man to fulfil himself to the fullest extent. With this in mind I would like to offer you a place on the Praesidium board. Furthermore, in view of the events that occurred in the course of this meeting I have a vacancy in a key position within our organisation. I will discuss this possibility with you outside this meeting."

There was renewed applause and a general hubbub of congratulations from members of the board. Only Manfred Bloch showed some lack of enthusiasm. He felt that if the post of Deputy Chairman was vacant, surely he should at least have the right of first refusal.

oooOooo

Simon Goodfellow was not a man to take disappointment well. What's more, it was obvious he had been tricked and betrayed. Noble had been so confident of the outcome that he hadn't even offered a defence. He had allowed his deputy to commit himself, then cut him down. Unsurprisingly, the Chairman had made it clear that Simon's position as deputy was now untenable.

Simon's morning had begun with the certainty that he would be Chairman of the Praesidium by the evening. Now, he had forfeited his post as deputy, and it seemed likely that he would lose his place on the board as well. The fate of former board members who had been forced to resign was invariably miserable, assuming they lived long enough to endure the misery.

So Simon decided something had to be done.

oooOooo

"Quite a day," said a voice.

Simon was halfway across the bridge that connected the main Praesidium building to the accommodation block.

"I think we should talk." It was David Minofel.

Simon needed time to think, to plan his next move. The last thing he wanted was to pass the time of day with the practitioner. "Not now," he said.

"If we don't have a chat, my friend," said Minofel, "you may well have even less time than you think." He took Goodfellow by the elbow and propelled him to one of the empty benches off the walkway. "This is a good place to talk," he confided. "The security system on the bridge is well overdue for an upgrade – something you should look into as a matter of urgency when you take over the chairmanship."

The quiet hum of the moving walkways, with their cargo of chatting Praesidium personnel, made it difficult for the microphones to pick up the conversations that took place on the benches.

Minofel now had Goodfellow's total attention.

"So, things didn't go as well as you had hoped," Minofel continued.

"How do you know what happened at the board meeting?" Simon asked.

"A better question would be what are you planning to do about it?" said Minofel.

"Even assuming I intend to do anything, I'm unlikely to share my plans with someone whose loyalty almost certainly lies with the man, my enemy, who is paying his fees."

"You really should stop obsessing about my fees. I get paid no matter who the Chairman is. I know that and you know that. I'm more interested in making sure the Praesidium survives and succeeds. The Praesidium is, after all, Slievins' most valued client."

"I haven't decided on any course of action yet," said Goodfellow cautiously.

"Oh dear, that's a little disappointing," said Minofel. "I really rather like your ideas on global war – you know, the vision thing, raising the Praesidium's sights ..."

"Why?" asked Simon. "What's it got to do with you, or with Slievins?"

Minofel gave a "tsk" of disapproval. "You're so defensive. I'm here to help. Tell you what, I'll set out a plan of action, and you tell me what you think of it. Is that all right?"

Goodfellow felt deeply uneasy. This could be a trap. If Noble could prove his deputy had been conspiring to overthrow the legitimate Chairman of the Praesidium, he would lose more than his place on the board. "That's up to you," he said.

"Let's assume John Noble is eliminated. As Deputy Chairman,

you become acting Chairman, right? Of course your appointment will have to be ratified by the High Council, but you will have weeks to consolidate your position."

"It's unlikely to be ratified if I've killed the Chairman," said Simon dismissively.

"True, but only if it's known that you killed him," said Minofel. "Let's say he disappears without a trace. What then?"

"The inexplicable disappearance of the Praesidium Chairman would demand the most thorough investigation by the security services of the High Council."

"But what if it wasn't unexplained?" asked Minofel. "What if it was the work of an Emergent? It would be perfectly possible for an Emergent to effect a disappearance. After all, many Emergents have been associated with so-called miracles. Alternatively, an Emergent could simply kill a man by willing him to die. That might be a better way. Yes, if there's a body, there can be no doubt about the death. And if the only person who could have carried out the murder were to be an Emergent, albeit a weak, unarmed and injured one, so much the better."

"But we don't have an Emergent," Simon objected. "I've spent the last few weeks conclusively proving the blind man is not an Emergent, and we don't have any other candidates." Goodfellow had the distinct impression that Minofel was planning on the hoof, and the last thing he wanted was to be implicated in a half-baked, ill-thought-out act of treason.

"You're being very negative," Minofel chided. "Let's say you're wrong. Let's say he fooled you."

"He wouldn't be the only one," Simon conceded bitterly.

"Ah yes! Kathrin," Minofel smiled. "She really has made a fool of you. Don't be offended. Any man might be misled by such an accomplished seductress."

"Since you know so much, perhaps you can tell me why she misled me?"

Goodfellow was genuinely puzzled. The fear he inspired in his lovers was usually strong enough to ensure their loyalty, even after any attraction or fondness had turned to revulsion.

"For someone who prides himself on keeping well informed, and who has the directors of Security and Internal Discipline under his thumb, you seem to have been extraordinarily myopic. She and John

Noble have had a very deep, decade-long relationship."

"But Kathrin is Bloch's wife!" Goodfellow seemed genuinely shocked.

Minofel laughed. "Clearly there are aspects of Kathrin's life that you failed to uncover in your pillow talk."

"You mean she's been sleeping with Noble, as well as with me – and, I suppose, with Bloch."

"You seem upset," Minofel was still laughing. "But relax. She hasn't slept with Noble. She just has a strong relationship with him, a good deal stronger than the one she has with her husband, or with you. But we seem to be drifting off the point. This morning you hoped to be Chairman. If you act promptly you can fulfil that ambition by tomorrow at the latest. Persuade Noble to come to your apartment when the board meeting ends. Warn him to tell no one, and to come alone."

"But why would he come?" asked Goodfellow.

"For someone who bases his claim to the Chairman's post on his superior planning ability you are being particularly dense," said Minofel sharply. "I do hope I won't have to spoon-feed you for much longer. Given Noble's affection for, and attachment to, Kathrin, and given that Kathrin is defenceless in your apartment, it's not that difficult to see how to persuade Noble to do what you want."

"But even if I kill him, how do I dispose of the body?" Goodfellow asked. He was beginning to warm to Minofel's scheme.

"As soon as it's done, I will send my man, Jedwell. He is an expert in the removal and disposal of bodies, and is absolutely discreet."

"Why are you doing all this for me?" asked Goodfellow. He knew that practitioners always had a price, a price you had to pay.

"Several reasons," said Minofel lightly. "As I said, I rather like your idea of stirring things up, of aiming higher. Slievins is a very aspirational company, and we like to encourage ambition wherever we go. Secondly, in my estimation you are the man to get the most out of the Monitaurs. Noble has been too laid-back in his management style. As a result, I sense some degree of complacency wafting around in the Crucible of Eternal Light. Thirdly, you will owe me, and someday I will call in the debt. Now, before you ask further questions, I suggest you get on with the plan. You need to act quickly and efficiently. Don't allow your sadistic tendencies to tempt you to complicate any part of it. Just persuade Noble to come to your apartment and then kill him. Jedwell will pass by later and clean up. Try not to make too much of a mess. And while you're at it, you'd better tell your people to start feeding the blind man properly and to sort out his infected lacerations. If he's the Chairman's killer, we need him to be in reasonable shape. He will need to look credible at the trial and, ideally, able to stand at his execution."

With that, David Minofel got up from the bench and set off towards the Praesidium's main building. Simon Goodfellow stepped on to the walkway and set off in the opposite direction towards his apartment.

27. Teleportation

In the laboratory the Praesidium had allocated to him, Andrew Rimzil leaned back in his chair, his hands behind his head, his long legs outstretched. He was satisfied. Using the paradox device, he had created a precise replica of the laboratory and had superimposed it on the original – a Parallel Coincident Construct within a Parallel Coincident Construct; a bubble within a bubble. There were now two laboratories: the original, which Security was watching all the time, and the replica, which was as real as the original but, cloaked by the paradox device, invisible to Security.

Andrew could either switch between the two laboratories or be in both at the same time. When Andrew was in both, to an observer there were two of him, although the observer would only be able to see one of him at a time. By cloaking the replica, Security could see only the Andrew in the original laboratory. But for Andrew, there were definitely two of him, two bodies and two brains that could do entirely different things simultaneously, with both under his control. It was a strange but exhilarating experience. For a less exalted intelligence, this double existence might have threatened the individual's sanity; for Andrew Rimzil, it was a tantalising glimpse of what the paradox device could do and what the human mind was capable of. "Who says men can't multitask?" he had minded to Luke when updating the dog on progress.

Luke had passed the news on to the other questors. Only Prune Leach fully grasped what Andrew had done; even he was mystified by the science. Through Luke, he'd asked Andrew if he could do one thing in one laboratory and the opposite in the other. The rather tactless example Prune offered was dying in one place, and continuing to live in the other. Andrew had replied that he thought it was perfectly possible but hadn't tested the hypothesis, for fairly obvious reasons. He'd added that he was still feeling his way and that mastering the paradox device was more an art than a science, a proposition that left Prune rather more bemused than enlightened.

This construction of a cloaked replica laboratory meant that Andrew was now completely free to do whatever he wanted in the new laboratory. All that Security and Internal Discipline could see was "their" Andrew running checks on various developmental prototypes in the "real" laboratory. Meanwhile, in the parallel replica laboratory, of which the Praesidium was entirely unaware, he had made significant progress, having developed, refined and installed a number of very substantial enhancements to the paradox device.

There was one aspect of the paradox device that puzzled Andrew. From the very start, the device had called on Andrew's mind to be somehow conscious of it in the performance of its functions. It had been just a feeling at the beginning, but the more he explored the device, the more it seemed that it had a need to involve Andrew's mind in its processes. It sounded ridiculous, but Andrew felt he had a developing relationship with the device.

"I'm ready," Andrew minded to Luke. "I can bring you all over to this replica laboratory. I've improved the teleportation function. You can bring whatever you need with you. I tested the enhancement when I allowed Aletheia to bring her sword and dagger with her – she refused to travel without them – and there was no problem. We can decide how to proceed when you're here. It's urgent. There's been some trouble at a board meeting. The Deputy Chairman's been thrown out and he's not happy. Adam's been offered a place on the board, which he's likely to accept. He may even end up as Deputy Chairman. And Kit's in a bad way. I've kept offering to teleport him out, but he refuses. They've kept him alive, but he's in pretty bad shape. We need to act now."

"Are you sure they won't know we've boarded the PCC?" Eve asked.

Luke passed on Eve's question and relayed Andrew's reply, via Numpty, to Eve: "Don't worry about it. You'll be as safe here as you are in Harrow – perhaps even safer. The Praesidium knows about Harrow. As far as the Praesidium is concerned, this laboratory doesn't exist. They're perfectly happy watching me in the original. I find it rather amusing. They are in a virtual world over Westminster, and I'm in a virtual world in their virtual world. Anyway, I suggest we all stay in the replica laboratory until we've agreed a plan. We may be here for a few days. It's going to be a bit crowded, but I've put a curtain across one of the alcoves to give Eve a little privacy. There are washroom facilities attached to the lab, all within the safety zone. Outside this laboratory, it's a different story. Once you step outside, you will be observable.

"By the way," he added, "I don't know if Aletheia explained this, but the paradox device teleports you instantaneously. One moment, you'll be in Harrow, the next you'll be here. You're not travelling through time and space, you're circumventing it."

"Right," minded Luke, making a mental note to ask Rambler, when time permitted, what "circumventing" meant.

oooOooo

The questors quickly made preparations for their teleportation. Uncle Rambler checked that he had sufficient notebooks to record every detail of what promised to be, as he said, "yet another unique experience".

"Is it possible to have more than one unique experience?" Numpty enquired, assuming a wide-eyed, naïve expression.

Uncle Rambler began to explain that you could have any number of unique experiences – unique in the sense that the experience had not been experienced before. Then he realised his nephew was joshing him.

Aletheia had given Numpty one lesson in swordsmanship, and as a reward for his modest progress she'd lent him her dagger and sheath. Numpty had put the sheath on his belt and carried the knife with him at all times, except when he left the house. The six-inch blade far exceeded the length of blade which could legally be carried in public.

Prune took a selection of tools from the camper van and wrapped them up in a canvas tool roll. He suspected that none of them would be of much use – Andrew's replica laboratory, being a perfect copy, must be as well-equipped as the original – but Prune never liked to travel anywhere without some of his own tools. "They're like old friends who've never let me down," he explained.

Eve, by now visibly pregnant, took her favourite cushion and a dog bed for Luke. She was well aware they were going into a strange and dangerous world, but she reasoned that if Andrew Rimzil's laboratory was safe, she and Luke might as well be comfortable while they were there.

Aletheia, now fully clothed, took the sword, the only thing other than the dagger that she had brought with her from Prometheus' cave.

"What are you taking?" Eve asked the Storyteller.

"A hunger for the truth and a thirst for meaning, as ever," said the Storyteller, with a smile.

oooOooo

When the questors confirmed they were ready, Andrew switched on the paradox device. To avoid draining too much power from the PCC's resources when the paradox device was activated, he had added an energy storage element. When he pressed the button to effect teleportation, there was scarcely a flicker in the power supply in the main Praesidium building.

Andrew's replica lab, which he alone had entered since its construction, was now full of people.

"I was right," he said to himself. "It's going to feel a bit crowded."

They all greeted each other, much relieved that, courtesy of the paradox device, they had survived the instantaneous journey. Luke settled down quickly into the dog bed Eve had brought. He had never been keen on these expeditions and felt the need for the comfort of something warm and familiar.

"It's good to be together," said Numpty. "Adam's not here, and Kit has yet to be rescued, but we're all in the same place. If we're lucky, we will all soon truly be together once again."

"That's the spirit, my boy," said Rambler.

"We need a plan, as well as luck," said Andrew. "And that's what we must agree this evening."

"And we will need courage," added Aletheia. "Prometheus told me that if we take on the powers ranged against us, we will all be risking our lives. Even I will be risking my life. The evil that we face could sweep away my immortality as easily as Zeus bestowed it on me."

"Let's hope we can save Kit and recover Adam, if that's what he wants, without violence," said Eve. "We're scarcely equipped for battle."

"It is always best to resolve conflict by negotiation," Aletheia responded, quoting Prometheus. "But in my travels, I have found that sometimes a point is best made with the tip of a sword."

"Yes," said Numpty, patting his dagger.

"You say 'the evil that we face'. What is this evil?" Eve queried.

"Prometheus told me that man is capable of achieving far more than the gods, but he is hampered by weaknesses rooted deep inside him. Those we must fight have dug deep into the nature of man and have told him that those weaknesses are his true nature and should be nurtured."

"We face an osmotic gouger," suggested Numpty triumphantly. "Someone who digs down deep into the dark recesses of the soil and draws up nutrients to produce a plant." His enthusiasm for the concept of an osmotic gouger had got the better of him.

"Perhaps. But this plant is the flower of evil," said Aletheia, rebuking Numpty. "And it is a flower that our enemy wishes man to wear in his buttonhole."

"Les fleurs du mal," mused Rambler. "The flowers of evil."

"Like William Blake's sick rose," suggested Numpty, who had recently developed a taste for the poet's work. "Perhaps we're up against the invisible worm – except Blake's worm flew. Those that the osmotic gouger encounters tend to be earth-bound."

"What I meant," Eve interrupted, addressing Aletheia, "is do you know what we are up against? Is it an international organisation, a secret government body, or something else?"

"I asked Prometheus precisely that question," Aletheia replied. "He said we shall be fighting with man, for man, against man."

Now Andrew interrupted. "I can tell you what we are fighting. We're fighting an organisation called the Praesidium, a secret organisation that has been guiding human affairs throughout human history. It has a particular view of man that it is determined to impose and/or maintain. It has control of a power source, the Eternal Light, which, apparently, gives them limitless amounts of energy, enough to create and maintain such things as this Parallel Coincident Construct, this PCC. They are aided by entities they call Monitaurs who intervene in human affairs, in order, so they claim, to help man fulfil his true nature. The Monitaurs are not human, although they can assume human form. I'm pretty sure the Praesidium is what stopped the Fourth Beginning. We tapped into a potential in man, a potential the Praesidium is determined will never be realised."

"Entities?" asked Eve and Rambler in unison, and then both added in unison, "Monitaurs?"

"Don't ask me," said Andrew. "I've only seen them on my scanner as humans, but that is not their natural form. The answer lies in the chamber containing the Crucible of Eternal Light. They withdraw to the chamber to do whatever it is they do and where,

I reckon, they revert to whatever they really are. I realise this all sounds like bollocks, but sadly it isn't. You'll just have to take my word for it. Frankly, I'm more interested in the Eternal Light. As a seeker of knowledge, I'm naturally curious about what seems to be an inexhaustible source of energy, but even more importantly I'm also pretty much convinced that if we took control of the Light, the Praesidium would be finished."

"That sounds like something we can work on together," said Prune. He had scarcely spoken since arriving in the laboratory, preferring to examine the paradox device on the main bench. He was eager to catch up with Andrew Rimzil's modifications and enhancements.

"How does Slievins fit into all of this?" asked Rambler, who had been quietly scribbling down everything Aletheia and Andrew had said into his notebook. "Is it part of the Praesidium?"

"It works with the Praesidium but it's not part of it," Andrew answered. "Slievins is a bit of a mystery. David Minofel is a partner in Slievins and is known to the Praesidium as a practitioner. Practitioners help the Praesidium when they have difficulties. I can't be sure but I have a feeling they're even more dangerous than the Praesidium."

28. The breath of death

While Andrew Rimzil was briefing the questors on the Praesidium and Slievins, Simon Goodfellow was busy implementing the plan that David Minofel had outlined. He had just spoken to John Noble on his mobile, adopting a casual tone, as though his recent reversal at the board meeting had just been a trivial embarrassment. "Kathrin is in my apartment and would like you to pick her up," he had said, then added, "Come alone and don't mention where you're going. We don't want Bloch to know his wife has been with one lover, and is being picked up by another. He might throw one of his temper tantrums."

Noble had said he would be over within the hour. He had discounted everything the deposed, and no doubt resentful, Deputy Chairman said, except the underlying message that someone he loved dearly was in Goodfellow's power and that no good would come of it.

Simon waited for him. Kathrin, fully conscious but still paralysed, was in a state of literally inexpressible terror. She realised that, by now, Goodfellow would know he had been betrayed and that she had played an essential role in the betrayal. She also knew that Goodfellow was a man who took pleasure in gratuitously inflicting pain. What extremes of pain he would inflict if he had cause were almost beyond her imagining.

"Well, my dear, this is a fine pickle you've created," said Simon, patting her knee. "Of course, you know what happened at the board meeting, and I have to be honest, I'm not best pleased with the outcome. You have let me down and I feel truly disappointed. Anyway, not to worry. I'm sure we can sort things out. It's all just a misunderstanding. I've asked John to come over. We can talk things through and put all this behind us."

While chatting to Kathrin, Simon filled a syringe with liquid from a small green phial. "No, my dear, it's not the antidote," said Simon, smiling. "I think it best you stay as you are for a little longer. No, this is for John Noble, your mentor, the man, so I'm told, who means more to you than your husband, more even than me."

There was a buzz at the door.

"Enter," said Simon to John Noble, ushering him into his sitting room. "Good of you to come. I'm not one to worry unnecessarily, but there seems to be something wrong with Kathrin. She's fallen into some kind of waking trance."

"Where is she?" There was panic in John Noble's voice. "What have you done to her?"

"Done? What have I done to her?" Simon was shocked. "Why should I have done anything to her? I can't think of any reason why you should think I would harm her. Can you?"

By now, John Noble was kneeling in front of Kathrin. He could see at once she was paralysed. He could also see the fear in her eyes. "We must get medical help at once. I brought a guard with me. He's at the end of the corridor," he said.

As the Praesidium Chairman started to get up, Simon jabbed the needle of the syringe into his neck. He sank back to the floor. Administered by injection, the drug took effect immediately. John Noble was now in the same state as Kathrin.

"I told you to come alone," said Simon. "I'm really disappointed. It's as though you didn't trust me. Now I wonder what instructions you gave your guard. Oh, of course, you can't answer. Well, I'll just have to guess. I expect you told him to break in if you weren't out of here in fifteen minutes. Am I right? Well, whatever you told him, I'd better try to get rid of him."

Simon was uneasy. Noble had brought a guard with him. The first priority must be to send him away, and that might be difficult. The guard might insist that the order should come directly from Noble. If he did, Simon realised he would have to deal with the guard himself. Although no slouch in martial arts, he was no match for a trained personal guard charged with the protection of the Praesidium's Chairman.

Simon opened the door of his apartment, stepped out and looked up and down the corridor. He could see no one. He closed the door behind him and walked to one end of the corridor and then the other. There was no guard. Simon was puzzled. Could Noble have been bluffing? That explanation was unlikely. When Noble had mentioned the guard, he'd been desperate to help Kathrin. He would hardly have invented a fictitious guard.

Simon returned to his apartment. Kathrin and Noble were exactly as he had left them: Kathrin in the chair, Noble with his head resting on Kathrin's knees. Both were now clearly terrified.

"What a picture you look," said Simon. "The most desirable adulteress on the entire PCC cradling the head of her paternalistic, platonic lover in her lap!"

Simon went into the kitchen and returned with a large plastic bag. "By the way, I can't find your guard anywhere," he confided. "I guess he thought you would be here for a while and so took a break. Whatever. I can't worry about him now. I have to take a chance. After all, I'm playing for high stakes – indeed, the highest. I realise you won't be happy with what is about to happen, but I want to emphasise that I'm doing this for the good of the Praesidium. While I was Deputy Chairman, there was at least one senior member of the board with both a backbone and a vision. By requiring me to resign you have brought this on yourself. I have no choice but to act, and act decisively."

With some care, Simon Goodfellow gently lifted the Chairman's head from Kathrin's knee just long enough to put the bag in place. "I have no idea whether this is going to cause you any pain, given that you are paralysed, but I must emphasise that, perhaps unusually, I would take no pleasure from it even if it did."

Every struggling breath sucked the bag into John Noble's mouth. Simon could see John Noble's eyes through the plastic. He could also see the strange mark in the plastic above the Chairman's mouth created by his neatly trimmed moustache. The eyes were staring at him, expressing a mixture of terror and incredulity.

"Oh dear!" said Simon, now turning his attention to Kathrin, whose eyes were fixed on the head of the man she loved as he struggled to hang on to life. "I can see that you are in some distress, and to be honest, in your case I am rather enjoying it. After all, you tricked me, and you betrayed me. Really, how could you?"

Noble was struggling for breath. He could still take in some air through his nose. Simon adjusted the bottom of the bag, fitting it tightly into the Chairman's collar so that no air could enter. He then began to stroke Kathrin's blonde hair. "On the way back from the board meeting, I must admit I struggled to think of an appropriate punishment for your perfidy," he said. "I considered the usual options – application of pain, disfigurement, mutilation. Of course, these options are still on the table, but I realised the best and most appropriate punishment would be this – for you to watch the man you love, the man who thought that with your help he had outwitted me, breathe his last."

The sucking of the bag ceased. "There we are," said Simon. "Dead as a dodo and not a mark on him – and no mess. Minofel was most insistent about that. Let me move his head off your knees. I'm sure if you weren't paralysed you'd be most uncomfortable. I'm not going to give you the antidote just yet. I think it best to dispose of the body first. You women can be so emotional, and I really don't want you to cause a scene."

The door buzzer sounded. Simon felt a rush of adrenalin. If this was Noble's bodyguard, he must be ready to strike immediately. From his kitchen, he took a knife with a blade short enough to be concealed but long enough to kill. He opened the front door.

"My master tells me there is a package for disposal," said Jedwell.

"Perfect," said Simon, much relieved. "The package is in the sitting room."

"I found a guard waiting in the corridor when I arrived," said Jedwell casually. "I removed him."

Jedwell followed Goodfellow into the apartment. He took in the scene in a glance. "What is the matter with the woman?" he asked. There was a look of desperate pleading in Kathrin's blue eyes.

"Nothing," Simon replied, somewhat taken aback that one of Minofel's minions should dare to ask him a question. "What business is it of yours?" he snapped.

"None," Jedwell replied, apparently unoffended.

"What are you going to do with the body?" Simon asked.

Jedwell gave Simon a big, open smile. "None of your business," he replied.

29. First move

The following morning, the questors put the first part of their plan into action. It was risky, but they all agreed the risk was worth taking. It was decided that Eve should find Adam and talk to him. Andrew knew where Adam was staying. Indeed, everyone knew where Adam was staying because he had been allocated the best guest apartment in the entire PCC accommodation complex.

"How do I leave this virtual laboratory and enter the real PCC?" Eve asked.

Andrew laughed. "The PCC itself is a virtual world, but I know what you mean. It's easy. Just walk through the laboratory door and you will find yourself in a corridor leading to the main reception hall. Outside the reception hall you will see the walkway that takes you to the accommodation block. When you come back here, you will see that the laboratory door has two handles, one on the left, which only we can see and which exists only for us. The other handle is on the right. Open the door using the left handle and you will be back in here with all of us. Open the door using the handle on the right and you will find yourself in the 'real' laboratory, the only laboratory the Praesidium people can see. If you went in there, you'd probably find me working on the paradox device. Don't ask me how I can be in here and in there at the same time – it's a paradox."

Eve made her way from Andrew's laboratory, along the corridor and out into the main Praesidium building, then through the vast reception hall and on to the bridge walkway that led to the accommodation block. Most people were heading in the opposite direction, towards the main building, but there were enough service staff going towards the accommodation block for her presence and progress to go unremarked.

Within fifteen minutes, she was taking the elevator to Adam's penthouse apartment. When Adam answered the door it was impossible to tell who was the more surprised.

Adam was astonished that Eve had found a way to reach the PCC. Indeed, she shouldn't have known of its existence. She should have thought he was living in an apartment in Westminster, not in a substantial virtual construct hovering over it. He was also surprised how radiant she looked. Pregnancy agreed with her; she had blossomed. And, of course, she benefited from the effort she'd devoted to her appearance that morning, given that she had not seen her husband for weeks and not heard from him for almost as long.

As for Eve, it was Adam's appearance that struck her. He looked ten, perhaps fifteen, years younger. He looked as he had before going through the ordeal at Cadnam.

"Come in," said Adam after they had stared in silence at each other for thirty seconds.

Eve looked around as they walked through the vast, thickly carpeted entrance hall into the spacious, superbly equipped kitchen. From the kitchen window she could just about see the Houses of Parliament and the crowds of people thronging Parliament Square far below.

"Coffee?" asked Adam.

"Thanks," said Eve. "Just a dash of milk. No sugar."

Adam frowned. He knew how his wife liked her coffee, and she knew he knew. Was she sniping at him? He said nothing.

"This is quite an apartment," Eve observed, taking the offered cup of coffee. "You must feel like a pea in a drum."

Adam considered telling Eve he was sharing the apartment with Miss Tomic but thought better of it. She might well misunderstand the arrangement.

"Why are you here?" said Adam eventually. "Of course, it's wonderful to see you, but you shouldn't be here. I told you I'd soon be back home."

"Do you have any idea what is happening to you?" Eve asked. There was no point in small talk. Neither of them had time for it.

"Yes, I have a very clear idea of what I'm doing. I'm pursuing my career, and with the help of Slievins it seems to be going rather well. According to David, my reputation is flying high. As soon as I've finished my induction here I'll either become a senior member of the Praesidium board, operating from here, or I'll be back in play on the London scene. No door will be closed to me. I'm the man who risked all to expose corruption at ZeD. I'm a hero. And you're the wife of a hero. We could be popping in and out of Number 10 like that couple on a Swiss weather clock."

"Do you know what the Praesidium is for?" Eve asked, beginning to realise the scale of the task she faced.

"What it's for?" queried Adam. "I may not know 'what it's for,' but I know what it does. It helps man to be himself. It frees man from the shackles of false aspirations. It resolves all those neurotic tensions that come from pretending to be what you're not. And for the truly exceptional, it removes all limits to ambition."

"And you're one of the truly exceptional?"

"I guess so. Do you remember what David Minofel said when we first met him? He said that I'd been chosen. I don't know why, but it's obvious that Slievins must have seen something in me, something I didn't know was there. Whatever it was they saw it's been unlocked. I learned a lot at ZeD, but that was just preparation for my induction here. I now understand human nature, how to guide it, how to work with it, and how to allow it the freedom to fulfil itself."

"And how to exploit it, I guess," said Eve. "How to use human nature for your own ends. Otherwise, you wouldn't have been promoted. You wouldn't be paid obscene amounts of money. You wouldn't have been raised above everyone else."

"You really have no idea what you're talking about," said Adam. "People need mentors, they need counsellors, and yes, they need leaders. All we do here at the Praesidium is lead them along the path they wish to follow, the path best suited to their nature. As a result, we have power. But it is a power that men willingly cede to us. It cannot be bad if we use that power to help man to fulfil himself."

"Do you know what your friends have done to Kit?" Eve asked, changing the subject.

"What do you mean? Kit's not here. I had a brief meeting with him in Geneva weeks ago. That was the last time I saw him."

"He came here to persuade you to come home," said Eve. "He came here to tell you the truth about the Praesidium, Slievins and David Minofel."

"Well, obviously he didn't make it because I haven't seen or heard from him since Geneva."

"He made it all right," said Eve. "Jedwell Boon picked him up from our home and brought him here. Since his arrival, in the care of a man called Simon Goodfellow, he has been brutalised, beaten and starved. He has also, when well enough, been compelled to witness what you call your induction – what he calls your corruption."

"You're making this up," said Adam. "You have to be. And what do you mean 'my corruption'? Slievins – in particular, David

Minofel – has put a great deal of effort into expanding my skill set. Yes, they've shown me how to focus, and yes, they've encouraged me to think clearly about how best to achieve precisely defined goals – is that what you mean by corruption?"

"Adam, you're not a stupid man," Eve sighed. "You must realise what they've been doing to you. I don't know what you've been taught, and I don't know what you've done, but I do know they have damaged you. I'm really afraid you are damaged beyond repair."

"Eve, you're being a bit theatrical," said Adam. "Let's try to talk sensibly. I admit I've been an absentee husband, and I'm sorry for that. I realise I should have been there to support you through the trauma of the burglary, and I'm sorry for that too. As soon as I've finished here I will make it up to you. I'll do my very best to be a good husband and, very soon, a good father."

"When you've finished here – or, rather, when they've finished with you here – I'm terrified you'll be good for nothing."

"Eve, you're being silly. I'm your husband, the father of the child you are carrying. I'm faithful to you and I will take care of you."

"If that is so," said Eve, getting up to leave, "why, after weeks apart, did you not greet me with a kiss? Not even a kiss on the cheek."

When she was gone, Adam ran through their conversation. She was obviously upset, and from her point of view she had every right to be so. But everything he had done had been for them – for her and their child. She would see that when she calmed down. Only two things continued to worry him: first, the suggestion that unbeknownst to him Kit was being held by the Praesidium; second, Eve's final remark.

As Eve made her way back to the Praesidium's main building she too pondered their conversation. Adam's bizarre image of them being like the couple on a Swiss weather clock seemed to sum it up. They might be a couple but they were not together; they were at opposite ends of the spectrum. When he was in, she was out, and vice versa.

30. Murder most foul

All hell broke loose in the Praesidium building when the Chairman's body was found in Kit's cell.

According to Simon Goodfellow, who was still Deputy Chairman and now, following the death of John Noble, acting Chairman, there were no marks on the body. There was no sign of a struggle. It seemed that a strong man, in the prime of life, with no record of any illness, had visited the cell of a suspected Emergent and died.

No one knew why John Noble had decided to visit the blind man. As soon as word spread that the blind man was a suspected Emergent, the rumour grew that Kit had somehow summoned the Chairman to his cell. When John Noble had heroically refused to do the Emergent's bidding, he had been terminated by the power of the Emergent's will.

Simon convened a meeting of the board. He invited the Monitaurs to attend, knowing they would support him if any board member objected to his assumption of the chairmanship. No one did. They were all stunned, and many were saddened by John Noble's death. Having lost their leader, no one had the stomach for a fight with the man who had, until the previous day, been indisputably second-in-command.

Only Manfred Bloch seriously considered challenging Simon Goodfellow, but he was more concerned about the absence of his wife. It was not unusual for Kathrin to disappear for a day or two to spend time with her theatrical friends, but she usually told him where she could be found. On this occasion, there had been no word.

"The Emergent must be put on trial as soon as possible," said Simon.

Despite his worries about Kathrin, Manfred Bloch felt compelled to question Goodfellow's proposal. "I thought you were convinced the blind man was not an Emergent? Even if he is, if he has the power to kill at will, not an accomplishment normally associated with Emergents, why should we risk a trial? Surely we should have him put down immediately?"

"Absolutely not," Goodfellow replied. "John Noble's death must be investigated thoroughly. I've no doubt there are those who will ask themselves who stands to benefit from the Chairman's death. I can assure everyone here that I am as saddened and sickened by John's death as any, but I can't deny that I am the one who benefits. I challenged him and failed. It is absurd and outrageous, but I'm sure there will be someone who will point the finger of suspicion in my direction. It is therefore imperative that we take no shortcuts. There must be an investigation that will satisfy even the most scrupulous member of the High Council. It will be a trial that follows Praesidium procedures to the letter. And then, when the guilty party has been condemned, there will be a fitting punishment."

"Are you confident it is safe to put an Emergent on trial in the very heart of the Praesidium?" Manfred Bloch persisted. If anything did go wrong, he would be remembered as the one who questioned Goodfellow's decision. If nothing went wrong, he had lost nothing. Goodfellow didn't like him, but he wouldn't dare to dismiss the Praesidium's Technical Director.

"We will take every precaution," Simon replied. "There will be two guards with the blind man at all times. If he shows any sign of manifesting Emergent capabilities, they will have orders to execute him immediately. We will have cameras on him, with twenty-four-hour monitoring. And I am having our medical people provide an intense magnetic resonance imaging head coil for the accused so that we will be forewarned of any signs of abnormal brain activity. Finally, I have asked the Monitaurs to be especially sensitive to any Emergent resonances. The guards and the Monitaurs, together with the Praesidium's other security resources, will be able to ensure that we conduct the trial and the execution in complete safety."

The meeting ended. There was no more to be said. The trial would proceed.

As Manfred Bloch left the boardroom, he muttered, "That's a first."

He was overheard by the Director of House Services, who enquired, "A first what?"

"Didn't you notice? It's the first time Goodfellow has ever referred in our hearing to our former Chairman by his first name. Obviously, our new Chairman finds it easier to relate to John Noble in death than in life."

31. An act of kindness

Jedwell had been busy. In the last twenty-four hours, he had disposed of the bodyguard stationed outside Simon's apartment and, later, he had collected John Noble's body from the apartment and placed it, as his master had instructed, in Kit's cell. Jedwell had opened the cell door with the key Minofel supplied. Kit had been asleep and heard nothing. Jedwell was a heavy, powerful man, but he could move silently, even when carrying a dead body.

After these exertions, Jedwell should have enjoyed an untrammelled rest, but he slept poorly that night. The image of the woman in Goodfellow's apartment preyed on his mind. In the world of his master, people had to be despatched from time to time. There were always good reasons. Those who died generally presented obstacles to the fulfilment of a plan. And obstacles to plans had to be overcome. But a professional took some pride in eliminating such obstacles in an efficient manner, away from prying, observant eyes. Why had Simon Goodfellow killed John Noble in front of the woman? It was a stupid thing to do. A witness to a killing created a new, separate problem for the executioner.

But there was more to it than that. The woman had known the victim. Of course, she had been terrified for her own safety. Anyone who found themselves in Goodfellow's clutches had reason to fear. But the fear visible on the woman's face had been mixed with grief and despair. She was grieving for the dead man. It looked as though Goodfellow had somehow paralysed the pair of them, then murdered one in front of the other, in part at least for reasons unconnected with the efficient fulfilment of a plan.

What Jedwell did not know was that Simon Goodfellow's conduct had tapped into a blocked memory of his own father, Ogody, a brute of a man who had taken pleasure in hurting other people. Jedwell had suffered at his father's hands throughout his childhood, but it was his mother who had borne the brunt of Ogody's savagery. When Jedwell was fifteen, his father had killed his wife. He had beaten Jedwell's mother once too often; the final blow cracked a rib and drove the broken bone into her heart.

When Jedwell returned from school that day, he had found his father dismembering his mother's body, intending to dispose of the corpse discretely by dumping the body parts in various waste disposal sites around town. Jedwell was an unusually strong fifteen-year-old, but under normal circumstances he would have been no match for his father. These were not normal circumstances. The murder of his mother, on top of the years of abuse, unleashed a tsunami in Jedwell's psyche. He struck his father – one blow in the middle of his forehead. It was a blow of unbelievable force. It cracked Ogody's skull. Blood filled his father's eyes and poured from his nose. This hulking brute of a man died, standing, with the carving knife still in his hand.

If these events had been dealt with in the normal way, Jedwell might well have spent the next few years in detention. He might have been accused of killing both his parents and sent to a mental institution. But David Minofel, who had been observing Jedwell as a possible recruit for a junior post at Slievins, intervened. He extracted Jedwell from the situation. Minofel's people cleared up the mess. The entire family disappeared. It was assumed that Ogody's criminal past had caught up with him and the family had been abducted and eliminated, or that Ogody had fled with his wife and son to a safe haven abroad.

Jedwell was taken under David Minofel's wing. He had no recollection of the events of that dreadful day, and Minofel made sure the memory was locked away deep in Jedwell's unconscious. Minofel was Jedwell's protector, both from the memories and from the consequences of his actions. Jedwell owed Minofel everything and would repay his master with unqualified obedience.

Of course, Jedwell hadn't realised that Simon Goodfellow's conduct had stirred up suppressed memories of his father – the scene of Kathrin, paralysed and entirely at the mercy of a sadistic and brutal man, had triggered a faint recollection of his kind and gentle mother.

Jedwell got up early. He began the day with his usual routine. He showered, then shaved his face and head. When he had dried himself, he applied some baby oil to the top of his head and massaged it into the skin in a clockwise circular motion. When he'd achieved a satisfactory shine, he dressed, drank a cup of coffee and set out for Simon Goodfellow's apartment. He was unsure how he would proceed.

All Jedwell's missions were driven by David Minofel's precise instructions. Occasionally, if circumstance demanded, he would deviate a little, as he had done to protect the young girl on the tube journey to Harrow, but in the main he followed instructions. Funnily enough, on this morning, although he was uncertain how to proceed, the uncertainty and the responsibility he was taking for any decision gave him an odd feeling of liberation.

Just as he arrived at the accommodation block, he saw Simon Goodfellow leaving to chair the emergency board meeting. Jedwell waited until Goodfellow had gone, then made his way to Goodfellow's apartment. He decided not to press the buzzer. Instead, he used one of Minofel's master keys to open the door.

Jedwell made his way to the sitting room. The woman was nowhere to be seen. Quietly, he moved on to the bedroom. He was keen not to disturb the servants in the annex. There, on the master bed was Kathrin, no longer paralysed but strapped to the bed, naked, face down and gagged. Kathrin turned her head to see who had entered the room. The look of abject fear faded, replaced by a flicker of hope. At least he wasn't Goodfellow. Jedwell removed the gag.

"Please help me," Kathrin whimpered. Her plea lacked confidence, for she recognised Jedwell as the man who had removed John Noble's body.

Jedwell placed a sheet over her body, then cut her free. "When you have dressed, I will take you out of here," he said.

"Where will you take me?" Kathrin asked. It would be some time before she could trust anyone, least of all an accomplice of Goodfellow.

"Wherever you want to go," said Jedwell.

While Kathrin dressed, she tried to think of the best thing to do. She wanted to be safe. Above all, she wanted to be away from Goodfellow. She knew he hadn't finished with her. He had killed the man she loved and he had defiled her, but that was not enough to expiate her sin of fooling and betraying the newly appointed Praesidium Chairman. And in his new position he would enjoy almost absolute power.

"I would like you to take me to my home," she said.

Manfred Bloch lacked almost all the attributes that would attract a licentious woman. He was not a great companion, he had a limited, rather dogged sense of humour, and his performance between the sheets could be criticised in a myriad of ways, but he did have two compensating advantages: he loved his wife, and he had the strength and courage to protect her. Of course, Goodfellow might decide to tell her husband about her general promiscuity, or even about his own affair with her, but he would have to be careful. Kathrin knew her husband; his rage would most likely be directed not against her but against her lovers. And Chairman or not, woe betide Simon Goodfellow if he found himself on the wrong side of Manfred Bloch's temper.

She might not be safe with Manfred, but she could think of nowhere safer.

32. Best laid plans

When Eve returned to the Praesidium's main building, she made her way through the reception hall and along the corridor back to the laboratory. Reaching the laboratory, she opened the door using the handle on the left.

"How was it?" asked Andrew.

Eve shrugged. "He really doesn't seem to know what's going on. And I'm not sure he wants to know. Even if he is aware, I'm not sure it will make any difference."

"Not a wholly positive conversation then," observed Rambler. "Perhaps we should concentrate all our energies on Kit. We know he needs our help. And, more importantly, *he* knows he needs our help, unlike Adam."

An animated debate about priorities ensued. Eve was concerned that the questors might settle for saving Kit and abandoning Adam if he showed no wish to be extracted from the clutches of Slievins. Rambler argued that if Aletheia was right, rescuing Kit would put them in mortal danger, so there really was little sense in adding to the risks by spending time trying to persuade a reluctant Adam to change course. Aletheia supported Eve, saying that as she understood it the mission was to save both Adam and Kit, and there was no reason to change the mission objectives before the action had begun. Rambler commented that Aletheia's attitude had hints of male machismo, which Aletheia took to be a reference to her sexuality. Aletheia, irritated, explained that whether straight or lesbian, women could be at least as dangerous as men. Having no wish to engage in an argument with a goddess, and feeling his remark had been misinterpreted in any case, he hastened to apologise. He conceded that women of all sorts in power had shown at least as much enthusiasm for war as men, citing from recent times Sirimavo Bandaranaike, Golda Meir, Indira Ghandi and Margaret Thatcher, all of whom had enthusiastically engaged their countries in wars. In passing, he observed that three of those belligerent female leaders had been educated at Oxford University, not usually thought of as a hotbed of violence, at least not of the militaristic variety.

While this discussion was wandering off track, Andrew Rimzil and Prune Leach were totally absorbed in speculation about the potential of the paradox device. Andrew had brought Prune up to speed on the enhancements he had incorporated into the device, and the results of his research and experimentation. Prune could scarcely contain his excitement. Andrew, on the other hand, seemed almost intimidated by his own invention, and found Prune's more exotic suggestions of possible applications deeply disquieting.

Suddenly, Luke barked. Andrew immediately broke off his conversation with Prune and turned to the monitor covering the reception hall of the Praesidium's main building.

"What's going on?" enquired Prune, looking over Andrew's shoulder.

"I'm not sure," Andrew replied. He tapped on one of the wireless keyboards linked to the paradox device. "I've asked for a scan of all conversations in the building to see what's trending," he explained.

In less than three seconds Andrew had an answer. His face grew pale.

"It seems that John Noble, the Praesidium Chairman, is dead. And that's not all – Kit has been charged with his murder. He is to be put on trial."

Aletheia was the first to speak. "We will have to review our plans. Rescuing a man imprisoned in a cell is difficult, but certainly feasible. Extracting an individual under close supervision during a major murder trial is a different matter. He will be guarded at all times. Any attempt by us to use force will invite a response from the entire Praesidium security establishment. I'm afraid the outcome would not be in doubt."

"Are you suggesting we abort the mission?" enquired Rambler.

"That is not an option," the Storyteller interrupted. "We must devise a different strategy. And remember, Adam is the key. You can set the course for a ship, but not the wind that drives it."

No one felt the urge to respond to the Storyteller's enigmatic intervention, but Eve was grateful for his emphasis on Adam's importance.

"If we can't use force what can we do?" asked Numpty, disappointed.

"We need a plan that utilises our strengths and exploits the Praesidium's weaknesses," said the Storyteller.

"We are secure within this laboratory," said Andrew, beginning to build a list of the questors' advantages. "The Praesidium knows nothing of its existence. We are at risk outside, but we have a safe bolthole. We know pretty much everything that's going on everywhere in the PCC. We not only have the monitoring facilities of the Praesidium at our disposal, we also have the scanning capabilities of the paradox device. We have the element of surprise. We can be sure Kit is innocent, so it should be possible to prove it."

Andrew tailed off. He had run out of ideas.

"You have omitted our greatest strength," said Aletheia, her blue-grey eyes almost smoking. "We are on the side of good. They are on the side of evil."

33. Confusion

That evening, Adam returned to his apartment confused. His meeting with Eve had left him disconcerted. Something had gone wrong between them – not in a trivial sense, but in a fundamental way. He knew for certain that if he was to save his marriage, it was he who would have to make most, if not all, of the effort.

Also, Eve had been right about Kit. The blind man had been in the PCC all along. Why had Minofel not told him? He and Kit had last met in Geneva, where Adam had made it clear to Kit that he was enjoying his new, supercharged career. Minofel had nothing to worry about, so why hadn't he told him?

Something had gone seriously wrong at the top of the Praesidium. John Noble had been murdered on the very day the Praesidium Chairman had congratulated him on completing his induction programme, promising him a senior position on the Praesidium board.

To top it all, Kit had been charged with John Noble's murder.

Adam poured himself a double whisky. He sat down in his favourite armchair and frowned. He still felt confident in himself. It wasn't that he was losing his grip; it was more that the situation was degenerating into chaos because of factors beyond his control.

"You look well," said Miss Tomic. She was as smartly dressed as ever, but she looked different. She looked older.

"Hello, stranger," said Adam. "You've been keeping out of the way the last few days. Are you all right?"

"I'm fine," Miss Tomic said, without conviction.

"Sit down and tell me what's the matter," said Adam. "And have a drink," he added, pouring her a double whisky, which she accepted.

"Our conversation on the roof did not go down too well with Minofel," Miss Tomic announced. "He has decided to punish me."

"To punish you?" Adam repeated. "What right has he to punish you?"

Miss Tomic smiled. "You really don't understand, do you? He has every right. From the moment my mother put me in his care, he has had every right. Just as you will find that if you cross him, he has every right to punish you."

"Your mother put you in his care?" Adam queried. "You'll be telling me about an imp and three wishes in a minute. What do you mean – your mother put you in his care?"

"It's not important. What matters is that I am free," Miss Tomic sighed. "I am tired, but I am free. I need to explain something to you. When you lost your daughter, you went through a bad time. Your grief almost destroyed you. At one point, you concluded that there was nothing more to you than your memories and your grief. You doubted your own existence. You began to think you had no self, that you were simply a vehicle for experience and the memories of experience. I can tell you that is not so. There is something that knows what it is to experience the experience, that ponders the experience, that above all can make sense of the experience. This something knows the difference between right and wrong, not as an absolute moral principle, but as the only way to understand a particular set of experiences. Let's call this thing the soul of man. It's what makes us human. I don't know the provenance of David Minofel but I know he is evil, and I know that the Praesidium, which retains his services, is desperate to destroy man's soul."

"Wait!" Adam interrupted. "I'm happy to agree that man has a core to his being, and I don't object to calling that core a soul, but how can you say the Praesidium is trying to destroy that soul? The Praesidium's only objectives are to enable man to recognise his nature and fulfil his potential."

"Man is an evolving entity," Miss Tomic replied. "Would you try to persuade a caterpillar that it is only a caterpillar, that it must always be a caterpillar and that it would be against its nature to become a butterfly?"

Adam smiled. "I had no idea you were a romantic."

"I'm not joking," Miss Tomic responded emphatically. "David Minofel led you down an increasingly evil path in Geneva as preparation for your induction programme here. Yes, here you have seen how depraved, fanatical and corrupt man can be. Yes, you've seen the forces of obstruction and negativity that hold man back. But there is more to man than this. When you set out on your quest that led to the Fourth Beginning you knew this was so. The Praesidium hired Minofel to excise that aspiration from your soul. But that aspiration is your soul. If you let him excise it, you will be as good as dead. Yes, you will be rich. Yes, you will be powerful. But you will be soulless and never be free."

"You should meet my wife," said Adam. "You seem to be in complete agreement with her about my moral state."

"What are you going to do about the blind man?" Miss Tomic changed the subject.

"Do about him? What can I do about him? I'm sure he didn't kill the Chairman, so I assume he will be found innocent. I didn't even know he was here."

"Simon Goodfellow," Miss Tomic replied, saying the name with obvious distaste, "is the man who abused Kit. He drove a knife through Kit's hand on a whim. He had him beaten and starved. Kit's abuser is now the Praesidium Chairman and Kit's main accuser. You know Kit is a good man. What chance do you think he has?"

"I'll do anything I can to help," said Adam, "but that's probably not very much. I'm not sure that I'm a board member. I don't know whether John Noble's invitation still stands. And even if I am on the board, I don't see how I could influence – or would want to influence – a trial."

The two of them sat in silence for a few minutes.

Adam was trying to sort out in his mind what he had learned from Eve and Miss Tomic, and what it meant in terms of how he should now act. Of course, in Geneva he had done things the world called bad, although as he'd learned in the induction programme, such behaviour was common among mankind. Indeed, in extreme form it was the key to success for the enlightened individual. After all, it was only common sense to do what had to be done. It was weakness to abandon one's goals because of spurious moral scruples. He wouldn't be where he was today had he not decided that Spinetti had to die. You could call it murder, but really it was simply the inevitable outcome of completing the project. Given that he had had no alternative, it was scarcely fair to confuse the issue by introducing inappropriate moral considerations.

Miss Tomic's suggestion that Minofel's purpose was to corrupt him was bizarre. Minofel was a business consultant; he wasn't the destroyer of souls. It was true he had given Adam a new perspective on life. He had extinguished Adam's desire to seek the truth, and replaced it with the belief that you should take this life by the scruff of its neck and shake it until it did what you want. There was a kind of truth in that, a more practical and rewarding truth than anything the pursuit of some elusive ultimate truth could offer.

After all, what had they really gained from the quest? The Fourth Beginning had ended almost before it had begun. For Adam, the quest had been an informative and challenging experience, but its only lasting effect had been the loss of fifteen years of his life while in hell at Cadnam – years which, happily, Minofel had now restored. Of course, David hadn't really given him back the fifteen years, but he had inspired and liberated Adam, opening up new possibilities, which certainly made him *feel* fifteen years younger. True, his skin was tighter and some of the wrinkles had softened, but that was because he felt more self-assured, more relaxed.

No, whatever his female critics said, he was in good shape. The one thing that worried him was the news about Kit. He liked Kit, although he had to admit that in Geneva they seemed to have drifted apart a little. Nevertheless, Adam knew Kit was a good man. If Kit had really been imprisoned in the PCC and beaten and starved, then something was wrong. If you wanted to use Miss Tomic's turn of phrase, Kit had a soul, a good soul. He was at the centre of himself, at ease with his being. There was no sound reason why anyone should abuse such a man.

oooOooo

Miss Tomic, who looked as though she had aged at least ten years, was exhausted. Minofel had been displeased with her attempt to subvert Adam. He had invited her to consider how lucky she had been – a beautiful woman with a brilliant mind, blessed with unremitting good health. It was a rare, perhaps unique, combination. All her life, she had been well cared for.

Her mother, a nervous and superstitious woman, had put her daughter in the care of Minofel as soon as her husband, Miss Tomic's father, died. David Minofel had looked after her, but it had dawned on her, as she grew up, that he was grooming her for his own purposes. It had taken her years to realise that she was just a tool in his tool box, a weapon in his armoury. If he wanted a favour from someone, he would use Miss Tomic to elicit it. That might involve serving a good dinner, offering companionship and intelligent conversation or engaging in skilful and enthusiastic copulation.

She had always known the harm she was doing. Indeed, Minofel seemed to take a perverse pride in knowing that his bright and beautiful plaything had a conscience. It was as though in the conflicted emotions that Minofel's demands generated in her there was a particular delight for him in seeing something so fine defile itself.

But then Miss Tomic had met Adam. In Adam she saw an ordinary man, and she had wondered why Minofel had singled him out. Most of Minofel's targets were outstanding in some way; they were very rich, or very clever, or very violent. Adam was none of these things. So Miss Tomic read his file. She followed his path on the way to the Fourth Beginning. She saw his weaknesses and his strengths; his generosity and his meanness; his love for Eve and his grief at the loss of his daughter; his quest for meaning; his curious mind. And then she understood why he had been chosen. He was a threat to Minofel.

Until then, she had thought David Minofel was invincible, all powerful. The moment she realised he was vulnerable, she began to plan her bid for freedom. She knew exactly what her freedom would cost her: Minofel would strip her of all her advantages. He would, if he could, take her beauty, her mind and her health from her. That was his way – implacable revenge against any who crossed him. But still, she would have her freedom. She would think her own thoughts. She would assert her right to be herself.

oooOooo

"I probably shan't see you again," Miss Gorgeous Tomic said quietly to Adam. "I'm afraid David Minofel has not finished with me, not yet. When he reviews what I've told you this evening, as he surely will, he will be bitterly disappointed that I haven't learned my lesson. So I shall say goodbye. But remember what I have told you. Believe me, it's worth years of experience."

34. A pre-trial consultation

"How you manage this trial is likely to determine your own future, and quite possibly that of the Praesidium," said David Minofel.

Simon Goodfellow and David Minofel had arranged to meet in the Praesidium's No. 1 Courtroom early in the morning. The sun, although still low in the sky, was sending shafts of light through the high courtroom windows. The courtroom was not large, nor did it need to be. It was rarely used, and even when it was occupied it generally attracted only small audiences. Although the Praesidium took pride in its ability to promote decadence, extremism, corruption, obfuscation and negativity in the world of man, within the Praesidium PCC few crimes were committed and fewer still brought to trial. The rare serious offence was generally dealt with by the board, outside the judicial process.

Simon was seated in the judge's chair. As acting Chairman of the board he was the most senior judicial authority in the Praesidium. Given the appalling nature of the crime, it was appropriate that he should take the judge's seat. Simon himself was elated at his self-engineered promotion and erotically stimulated by the thought that the man he would condemn to death was not only considered a possible Emergent (whose elimination would surely be a feather in the new Chairman's cap), but also entirely innocent of the crime for which he was going to die.

In general, Simon always claimed full responsibility for his successes, but even he had to admit that Minofel had, on this occasion, made a significant contribution. After all, it was Minofel's plan to blame the death of John Noble on the Emergent, and it was Minofel's man, Jedwell Boon, who had disposed of the body, thus ensuring the blind man would be blamed for the murder. Indeed, if Minofel hadn't helped, Simon might well have wished to despatch the Chairman, but he would not have had the means to do it without running a serious risk of detection.

There was, of course, a loose end: Kathrin. Although paralysed at the time, she had witnessed the killing of Noble. Simon didn't for a minute regret performing the murder in front of Kathrin. It had given him exquisite pleasure to see her, helpless and utterly distraught, watch the man she loved being put down. But this little self-indulgence had left Simon with a problem. The simplest solution was to continue his enjoyment of her and then kill her. Minofel's summons to the court room, very early in the morning, had interrupted Simon as he was about to introduce Kathrin to the darker and, for her, possibly fatal aspects of his sexual predilections. Killing her would be the simplest, cleanest solution. On the other hand, there was a case for caution. Killing a junior secretary from one of the administrative departments was one thing; defiling and murdering the wife of the Technical Director was quite another. He decided to postpone a decision until the trial was over. It shouldn't take more than a day or two at most. It was, after all, an open-and-shut case.

David Minofel was relaxing in the front row of the seats allocated for the audience. It gave him a perfect view of the judge's podium, the witness box and the desks for the prosecution and defence lawyers.

"Who will be acting as defence lawyer?" Minofel asked casually.

Simon was surprised. This was not a case in which the facts were disputed. "I thought we would dispense with prosecution and defence lawyers. After the accused's confession, I planned to deliver an excoriating summing-up, then move on to sentencing."

"Is that wise?" asked Minofel. "I thought you were going to proceed by the book. You must appoint a prosecutor and provide the accused with a defence lawyer. Otherwise, the High Council may question the validity of the judgement. I have someone in mind who will make the perfect prosecutor."

Simon took Minofel's point that the trial should follow due process. "Whom do you suggest?"

With the faintest hint of a smile, Minofel said, "Why Adam Smith, of course! He knows the blind man. He knows his strengths and weaknesses. More importantly, in Adam's old life, he and Kit were friends. Indeed, Adam felt a special bond with the blind man and admired him greatly. As you know, we at Slievins are always cautious about welcoming newcomers into the higher reaches of the organisation. The final test is what we call the 'great betrayal'. To be sure of all such candidates, we invite them to commit an act of betrayal that will sever their links with the past, a betrayal that will guarantee there can be no going back. If Adam successfully prosecutes Kit Turner, Adam will be ours irremediably."

"Excellent," said Simon. "A perfect solution for both Slievins and the Praesidium. It was always my intention that Adam should play a full part in the blind man's destruction. It may be more difficult to find a suitable defence spokesman. No one of substance will be keen to defend the murderer of our much-loved former Chairman. That could be a problem. We need to conclude the trial speedily. Members of the board are concerned that I am bringing a possible Emergent into the heart of the Praesidium. The sooner it's ended, the better."

"But the man is not an Emergent," said Minofel sharply. "You've had him in your tender care for weeks, and you have assured me that despite considerable provocation he has shown no signs whatsoever of Emergent qualities, unless you consider dumb and passive acceptance of abuse, torture and hunger oblique evidence of Emergent power."

"I'm certain he is not an Emergent," Simon assured his mentor.

"Then find a defence lawyer," said Minofel, in a tone that suggested the subject was closed.

35. Technical speculations and practical plans

The Praesidium security staff were finding the duty of monitoring the laboratory allocated to Andrew Rimzil exceedingly tedious. As they reported to the Head of Security, Rimzil spent all his time checking and running tests, and rechecking data sets.

Meanwhile, in the questors' laboratory, safe from the prying eyes of the Praesidium security staff, Andrew Rimzil and Prune Leach were discussing a purely theoretical application for the paradox device. It was Prune who had made the suggestion.

"You say that the whole of the Praesidium's energy comes from this Crucible of Eternal Light. Why can't the paradox device tap into that energy and draw it off? Given the infinite possibilities encompassed by the paradox device, it can use all the energy you throw at it. We could simply drain the energy that maintains the entire PCC."

"Nice thought," Andrew replied. "But at the first sign of an interruption in their power supply, House Services and Security would throw everything at finding the leak. This laboratory is cloaked, but the cloaking would not withstand a scan using the full power of the Crucible. They would find us, and that would be the end of it."

Andrew and Prune were silent for a minute. Then Andrew said "Unless …"

Prune's twinkling blue eyes brightened. He loved Andrew's "unlesses". When Andrew said "unless" in that tone, it almost always meant that he had found a way around a seemingly insuperable obstacle.

"Unless we recycle the energy, rather than drain it off. The Eternal Light provides an inexhaustible supply of energy, without generating any heat. I think it does this by converting negative energy into positive energy. It might be possible to use the paradox device to set up a loop, which would allow us to drain all the energy from the Eternal Light, convert it into negative energy, then feed it back into the Eternal Light for reconversion. We wouldn't be depleting the Eternal Light at all. The Praesidium would have no idea what we were doing."

"But how would that help?" asked Prune.

"It would mean we would control the energy," said Andrew. "If it worked, the paradox device would become the source of the Eternal Light. If we stopped feeding the negative energy back into the Light, it would weaken. And, as our ultimate weapon, if we drew off and converted all the energy, then returned all that negative energy in a single burst, I'm pretty sure the Eternal Light would die. All its positive energy would be cancelled out by all the negative energy."

Prune scratched his head. "So we wouldn't take the energy. We would just add a final loop to the process, a loop we controlled," he said uncertainly. "We could give it a go, I suppose."

"Why not?" said Andrew happily. "It won't do any harm. The Praesidium security people won't notice anything – and you never know, it might work."

oooOooo

While Andrew and Prune were chatting, the others were discussing the death of the Chairman and Kit's impending trial.

"If only we knew what actually happened, it would be easier to decide how to proceed," said Rambler.

"Can't argue with that," said Eve. "If Kit didn't kill the Chairman, someone else did. We need to know who, and then we need to prove it."

Andrew overheard Eve's last remark. "I might be able to help with the first bit," he said. "While Prune and I have been chatting, I've been running the data from last night. I just noticed a couple of anomalies, so I've called up the visual recordings. I've been tracking Jedwell Boon since I arrived here. No particular reason, except I can't track David Minofel at all. Don't know why, but he doesn't show up on scans. So I thought that tracking Jedwell would be the next best thing. After all, he's Minofel's man about town, so to speak. Anyway, we have visuals of Jedwell taking what I'm pretty sure is John Noble's body from an apartment in the accommodation block. The apartment belongs to Simon Goodfellow. We have another visual of him placing the body in Kit's cell in the detention centre."

"Good God, man!" said Eve. "Why didn't you say?"

"I thought I just did," said Andrew, a little put out.

"That's it," said Numpty. "Kit is innocent. The murder took place in Goodfellow's apartment. Kit couldn't have done it. Most likely, Goodfellow or one of his people did the killing."

"There's a problem," said Eve. "We don't have clear evidence of who killed the Chairman, only that Jedwell carried a body from an apartment to Kit's cell. And, of course, as far as the Praesidium is concerned, we don't exist, and neither does our evidence. Even if we revealed ourselves and gave them the evidence, I'm pretty sure they would declare it inadmissible."

"There's more," said Andrew. "This just in …" he added, aping a newscaster. "This morning, Jedwell went back to the apartment and escorted a woman from the premises. She looked dishevelled and distraught."

"From the apartment where we think the killing may have taken place?" asked Eve.

"The same," said Andrew.

"Who was the woman?"

"The wife of the Technical Director, Manfred Bloch," said Andrew.

"What was the Technical Director's wife doing in the new Chairman's apartment?" wondered Rambler.

"More to the point," said Eve, "what was she doing in the apartment where we believe the previous Chairman was murdered just a few hours earlier? Either she's part of it, or at the very least she knows what happened."

"Then we must talk to her," said Numpty.

The questors discussed who should seek out Kathrin. Eve was keen to continue her dialogue with Adam. If he knew, as he must, about Kit, then surely he would now take seriously the rest of what she had told him.

With Eve assigning herself to Adam, Aletheia volunteered to talk to Kathrin. The group thought it might be best if a woman undertook the delicate task of finding out why, among other things, Kathrin appeared to have spent the night with her husband's rival and enemy.

The matter was settled when a message was put out over the Praesidium loudspeaker system. It was Simon Goodfellow's voice.

"Fellow citizens of the Westminster PCC, as you know, this is a sad day for all of us. Last night, in an act of unspeakable evil, our Chairman was murdered. A suspect has been arrested, and in view of the compelling evidence in this case he is to be brought to trial immediately. A prosecutor has been appointed. All we now need is a spokesperson for the defence. We all understand the reluctance of the obvious choices – members of the board or senior managers – to undertake such a role, but I am determined, as your new Chairman, to follow due process. However heinous the crime and however damning the evidence, the accused has the right to a competent defence. In these circumstances, I am taking the unusual step of calling for volunteers. Let me assure the successful candidate that he or she will not be stigmatised for taking on this onerous task. Indeed, whoever defends the blind man will receive our thanks and respect for helping us to resolve this matter according to the Praesidium's much-valued and cherished judicial principles. Anyone who feels they can help in this matter should make themselves known to the courthouse officials immediately. Assuming a satisfactory defence counsel has been appointed, the trial will begin tomorrow."

"I must be the one to defend Kit," said Aletheia, in a soft but firm voice that would brook no argument. "Before I left Prometheus in his cave in the Caucasus, he told me that my primary task was to support Adam and Eve. He also said that if there was any threat to the blind man, I must protect him with my life. Yes, even if it means risking my immortality."

There was nothing more to be said. Rambler and Nephew Numpty undertook the task of seeking out Kathrin. It was agreed that as soon as they had anything to report, they would head directly to the courthouse to brief Aletheia. Eve would again visit Adam, whom Andrew, using the scanning function of the paradox device, had located in his apartment in the accommodation block. Prune and Andrew himself would work on the dark energy loop idea – or "deli" for short – as a backup in case of as yet unforeseen emergencies, and also because once Andrew and Prune had conceived an idea that excited them, nothing on earth could stop them from exploring it.

36. Appointment of the defence counsel

Following Andrew's directions, Aletheia made her way directly to the courtroom, where she announced that she wished to represent the blind man in the trial.

"You can't bring a sword into the courtroom," said the dour female court official. "Indeed, except for ceremonial purposes, you can't carry a sword anywhere."

Aletheia smiled. "I am unfamiliar with your traditions here," she said, handing over her sword. "I shall, of course, comply with your customs, however odd they seem to me."

The court official was bemused by Aletheia's turn of phrase, but mollified by her immediate compliance with the no-swords rule.

"Are you qualified to act as defence counsel?" she asked.

"Eminently so," Aletheia replied. "I seek the truth. Since my client is innocent, the truth will set him free."

"Hold on," said the woman. "He's not your client yet. We need to go through the formalities." She activated her computer screen, then made the preparations for recording Aletheia's details and registering her as a candidate look as onerous as possible. "Name?" she demanded finally.

"My name is Aletheia."

"Is that your first name or your second name?"

"I am also known as Veritas," said Aletheia helpfully.

"So it's Aletheia Veritas." The woman typed the name on to the form.

"Father?"

"That's a little tricky," Aletheia replied. "I consider Prometheus my father, though he made me out of clay, rather than seeding a woman. On the other hand, Zeus asserted normal, albeit divine, paternity, but his claim was false."

"Just give me the name of your father, dear," said the official.

"Prometheus," said Aletheia.

"I assume his second name is Veritas."

Aletheia nodded her assent. Evidently the woman felt everyone should have a second name.

"Occupation?"

"Mine or my father's?" Aletheia asked.

"Yours, dear." The woman sighed.

"I've spent most of my life successfully arbitrating disputes. In the end, the truth will out. I have considerable international experience."

"Where did you qualify?" the woman asked a little impatiently.

"Olympus," said Aletheia. The woman wrote "Olympus" in the university box.

"And where did you first practise?"

"I did most of my practising in Greece and the Caucasus. After that, I moved on to Rome, and then, as I say, the rest of the world. I spent quite a bit of time on the island of Lesbos, but that was part business, part pleasure."

"You seem rather young to have had so much international experience," said the official.

"I'm a fast learner. Not quite as fast as Pheme, but always hot on her heels. In any case, I'm not as young as I look."

Although the reference to Pheme meant nothing, the official seemed satisfied. Her administrative task completed, she allowed her official mask to slip. The girl in front of her was strikingly beautiful, with fine fair hair, blue-green eyes and a presence that was simultaneously attractive and authoritative.

"To be honest," the official confided, "we haven't had many applicants. In fact, to tell you the truth, you're the only one so far. The new Chairman has said that defending a man guilty of such a dreadful crime won't, in any way, harm the defender's career prospects, but we've all taken that with a pinch of salt. Whoever is appointed will always be remembered as the one who was on the wrong side in the biggest trial in the Praesidium's history. But I don't want to put you off. I'm sure you'll be fine. Besides, you could always go back to the Caucasus or wherever. Normally, I'd have to ask for proof of qualifications – you know, degree certificates, that kind of thing – but I've been told it's not necessary on this occasion. Off the record, they don't really want a first-class counsel. It would just slow things down."

"I fear then that I may be over-qualified," said Aletheia with an impish smile.

"Oh no, dear," said the official. "You seem to me to be just right."

"That's terrific," said Aletheia, using one of the idiomatic phrases she had added to her vocabulary before teleporting to the twenty-first century. "So, do you think I'll get the job?"

The official smiled. "With the benefit of my recommendation, I don't think there's any doubt about it." There was something very winning about this enthusiastic young woman. "You seem well-suited to the task, and you have the distinct advantage that you are the only applicant."

"If I am to be defence counsel," said Aletheia, now speaking in a serious voice, "there is something you could do to help me. I am familiar with the judicial process in many countries. I have worked in cases conducted under common law, civil law and religious law. I personally favour common law systems, although when Hammurabi knocked together his code I could see some advantages to a more top-down approach, and no one can lightly dismiss Justinian's *Corpus Juris Civilis*. I have little sympathy with judicial processes based on religious law. They tend to be far too whimsical, and have clearly been formulated predominantly by men, not gods. In any case, the idea that the gods might be a good source of justice has always struck me as totally bizarre. No one who has met or had dealings with Zeus could possibly recommend him as an authority on the law. The whole point about being a god is that you are a law unto yourself. As for the Abrahamic faiths, their rather silly, arbitrary rules about what you can do, and when and what you can eat and drink clearly disqualify them as serious contenders in the 'who's got the best legal system?' competition."

Aletheia paused. The official was entirely mesmerised. This beautiful young woman was surveying the world's judicial systems and talking about them with magisterial authority. The official, who had spent all her working life struggling with tedious administrative tasks in the lower reaches of the legal profession, glimpsed for the first time what the law was all about.

"Sorry, I digress," Aletheia said, beaming at her enthralled audience. "What I would find really useful is a brief summary of the rules under which court cases are conducted in the Praesidium. I can bone up on the basic types of law and any idiosyncrasies this afternoon so that I'm fully primed for the case. The trial will begin tomorrow?"

"Yes," said the woman. "It will begin tomorrow because I can report we have found our defence counsel. And yes, there is a printed summary of Praesidium court procedures and case law. I will give you a copy, but I have to tell you that it runs to almost two thousand pages."

"That's great," said Aletheia. "I'm a fast reader."

37. Serious words

Eve caught Adam as he was preparing to leave his apartment. When he opened the door and saw her, he considered welcoming her with a kiss, but remembering her final remark at their last meeting he decided against it.

"It's really good to see you," he said lamely.

"Obviously you've heard the news. Are you beginning to understand?"

"I understand someone has killed John Noble, and I understand Kit has been charged with his murder."

"You know that's nonsense. Kit wouldn't kill anyone."

"Are you so sure? I seem to recall there was a rumour he knocked Nick Peters off Mount Strobilos."

"Even if he did, he probably didn't mean to knock him off the mountain, and Peters didn't die anyway," said Eve

"I don't think Kit knew that when he hit him," Adam replied.

"Come on, Adam, you know Kit is innocent."

"I don't know anything of the sort. I do know there is to be a trial following due process. If Kit is innocent, I'm sure he will be exonerated."

"I very much doubt they understand due process. And I suspect that if they've charged Kit, they intend to find him guilty. Don't you understand that this place is founded on corruption? It is rotten through and through. These are the people who stopped the Fourth Beginning, whose minions at Cadnam killed Gwoat, who put you through hell and took fifteen years off your life. Wake up, Adam. You're not here because you're a high flyer. You're here because they're afraid you might one day actually get off the ground."

"Are you jealous?" Adam asked. "We've never competed in our careers. Are you upset because my career has taken off?"

Eve shook her head in disbelief. "I don't know what they've done to you."

"They've taught me that you can shape your own destiny if you learn to think clearly. They've taught me to set targets and then do whatever is necessary to achieve them. And they've taught me that to lead mankind you have to understand human nature. You have to take it for what it is, not pretend it is nobler, kinder or more generous than it is. That's not to say man is bad – just that he's human."

"That's a creed any dictator or sociopath could easily subscribe to," Eve replied. She decided to make one last appeal. "When we set out with the Storyteller on the quest, we wanted answers, answers to real questions. I wanted to know why Bella had died. You wanted to know if your life had any meaning. We went on a fantastic journey. We saw the creation of the universe. We saw the birth of life. We saw the emergence of human consciousness. And then we initiated the Fourth Beginning. Do you remember what that felt like? You and I were closer then than we had ever been. We unleashed something so powerful that we knew it would change the world. I don't mean it was just going to make our planet a better place – I mean it was going to change reality, just as the three Beginnings we witnessed had changed reality. We didn't know what the Fourth Beginning was, but we knew for sure it was good – magnificently, astronomically, universally good. And then it was aborted.

"When Kit came to our house weeks ago he wanted to talk to you. He warned me that we were in danger, that those who had stopped the Fourth Beginning wouldn't rest until they knew we could never again threaten them. Because that's what we did. The Fourth Beginning meant the end for them and they had no intention of being ended.

"As soon as I told Kit about Minofel and your appointment at ZeD, he said that he suspected you were in the hands of our enemies. The burglary was a set-up – the burglars themselves were part of the plot. Of course, we had to trust a man who had saved us from disaster. We should have seen what was going on from the start. We should also have seen what he wanted us to become. The first thing Minofel did was make us accessories to murder. It was all so easy. As you say, he set a target, then did what was necessary to achieve it. And he understood human nature. He knew that I wanted the rapist dead. He knew that you felt ashamed you hadn't been able to protect me. So he made the whole horrible incident go away. The only price we had to pay was guilt. He executed a man, and we went along with it.

"From then on, you were hooked. I don't know what you did in Geneva, apart from destroy the company, but I'm absolutely certain that Minofel engineered situations in which your moral sense was cut to pieces simply by 'doing what had to be done'. He was softening you up for this place."

Adam couldn't listen to any more. "Eve, Eve, where is all this coming from? David Minofel is a headhunter, a partner in the Slievins consultancy. Slievins has been around for ages, and has the highest reputation. I checked them out. I was headhunted, and I've done really well under David's tutelage. Geneva was a mess, but I've come out of it smelling of roses. As a result, I've been given access to a highly sophisticated, technologically advanced organisation that has its hands on all the levers of power in human society. I've found a truth – not the vague, abstract, woolly kind of truth, but real information on how things work and how to make things happen. Don't you see? They've offered me an appointment on the board of the Praesidium. That means our financial worries are over. I can look after you and our baby. I can afford an army of guards to protect you. I can give you anything and everything you want."

"All I want is the man I married back," said Eve sadly. "And I've lost him."

Now Adam shook his head. "You haven't lost me. I love you. I haven't changed. I've grown. Soon I will leave here and come back to be with you in Harrow. I don't know what my new job will involve, but I'll insist that I'm based at home."

"And what about Kit?" Eve asked. "He's on trial for murder, a murder he didn't commit. Are you going to leave him to the tender mercies of men like this Simon Goodfellow and David Minofel?"

Adam looked embarrassed.

"What?" Eve said when Adam failed to answer.

"The trial will soon be over, and if he's innocent, I'm sure he will be found not guilty. I was on my way out when you arrived. I've just heard they've appointed a defender, so the trial can go ahead tomorrow. I must go now. I've been appointed prosecutor and I have to prepare myself."

38. The long spoon

Adam had set aside the afternoon for a meeting with David Minofel who had suggested that a pre-trial consultation would be useful, following Adam's appointment as prosecutor. He had booked one of the smaller meeting rooms in the Praesidium's main building.

David greeted Adam effusively. "There are so many reasons to congratulate you that I don't know where to begin. It is unprecedented for anyone who has only just completed the induction programme to be invited to join the board."

"I wouldn't be too sure about that," said Adam. "It's far from certain the new Chairman will confirm my appointment."

Minofel grinned. "It's absolutely certain. I made it a condition of his elevation to the Chairman's post. What's more, there is still a possibility you could take the deputy chairmanship. I'm delighted for you of course, but I'm also delighted for myself. Slievins' partners judge each other, and themselves, by the success of those we choose. You have done me proud, as well as yourself."

Adam grinned. "Without the opportunities you opened up for me I wouldn't have succeeded, so it's credit and congratulations all round."

They shook hands warmly.

"Now, Adam," said Minofel, in his most serious voice, "this phase of your arrangement with Slievins is coming to an end. In future, I will be seeing less of you. I am still your mentor, since the chooser of a chosen one remains that chosen one's mentor. But I am confident you will now need much less, how shall I say, supervision in developing your career.

"So let me give you this last piece of advice. You are a man who seeks the truth. Here, with me, you have found it. There are really only two philosophies in life. There is the philosophy promulgated by religionists, moralists and ideologues who urge man to deny his true nature and subscribe to alien, and generally counter-productive, codes of behaviour. They invariably invite man to subordinate himself to a higher cause, a process which, funnily enough, always involves the transfer of power from the individual to those, usually priests or politicians, who promote the higher cause.

"Then there is the Praesidium's philosophy, which recognises man for what he is and defines the greatest good as whatever enables man to fulfil himself as he is. Man is essentially a selfish creature. The great gift of human consciousness, which you observed arising in the primitive Albert when you accompanied the Storyteller on your quest, was the creation of the self. Every man and woman is a miracle in that they are discreet, perfect examples of beings who can be satisfied only by selfish gratification. I say again, man is a selfish creature. That's not because man is sinful. It's not because man is a fallen creature. It's because it's inherent in man's predicament. It is because he is a self, coincident with a body that is entirely separate from all the rest of existence. It is because that self and that body are his only means of relating to the world. Above all, it's because it's true.

"Of course, individuals can be generous. They are capable of love. They are even capable of self-sacrifice. But even these are acts of selfishness – they satisfy the self, sometimes even when the only way to satisfy the self is to destroy it.

"In short, Adam, man is a selfish bugger. He is avaricious, corrupt, envious, greedy, lustful, and full of fear. He wears the clothes of a decent, upright citizen, but beneath those clothes, he is a whimpering soul, desperate for help that never comes, struggling throughout his contemptible life, terrified by the inevitability of the coming miasma of sickness and death.

"From this fundamental, elementary realisation stems the possibility of freedom. Embrace your inner self. I know that in your grief for the death of Bella you even began to doubt whether you had a self. You thought you might merely be a vehicle for grief – just the sum of your bitter memories. You will never have such thoughts again. You have learned just how powerful your self can be when unhampered by any kind of morality. Morality is the drug that makes man weak and dependent. And always remember, the weak shall inherit nothing but earth. They will crawl upon the ground, and when the rains of sorrow fall on them, as they fall on all men, they will wallow helplessly in the mud. That is not the way. Life is here to be beaten into shape. Do what needs to be done. Do unto others long before they do unto you. It doesn't matter if someone has to die, if tens, hundreds or thousands have to die. The number of the chosen is few. The number of whimpering souls is many, and there are plenty more where they came from. They say that every life has value. It doesn't. Most people merely take up space. They feed and breed. They spend their lives in an endless pursuit of self-gratification. They consume the planet's resources, but they completely fail to add value. They are not the ones who stand up, who stand out, who make the world what it is. They add nothing to the history of mankind. They take a free ticket on the train of life, remain seated throughout the journey and alight at their destination station, Oblivion, without even looking out at, much less having any effect on, the land through which the train has passed. It is as though they had never been. No, it *is* that they have never been. As we say at Slievins, other people are simply the means to our end.

"Now, tomorrow you will face a final test. Your friend Kit Turner, the blind man, is to go on trial and you are to prosecute him. He has to die. You must take responsibility for his death. Why? Because it will consolidate your position in the Praesidium, it will enhance your chances of taking the Deputy Chairman's role and it will be the most difficult thing you have ever done. It will be difficult because he is your friend. It will be difficult because you think you have seen something special in the blind man, something fine. Above all, it will be difficult because he is innocent of the charge against him."

Out of respect for his mentor, Adam had listened carefully to Minofel's sermon, but to be honest, towards the end he had started to lose focus – so much so that he almost missed Minofel's final revelation.

"What did you say?" Adam blurted out.

"You heard me," David Minofel replied. "You must ensure Kit Turner is condemned to death not despite, but because of, his innocence. It would scarcely be a test if he was guilty."

"But if it can be proved he is innocent, surely he must go free?" Adam persisted.

"There will be no proof he is innocent," said Minofel. "All the evidence will point to his guilt. So your task will be easy. But it is important that you know, despite the evidence, that he did not kill John Noble. Tomorrow you will confirm what I already know. You are truly a Slievins man."

39. Preliminary trial proceedings

The following day, a Thursday, the courtroom was full. Although the trial had been organised at short notice, most members of the board were present. Only Manfred Bloch and the Head of Internal Discipline were absent.

Manfred was absent because the previous day Silas Drahan, Head of Security, had noticed one or two almost imperceptible blips in the power supply from the Crucible of Eternal Light. Simon Goodfellow had ordered Bloch to conduct a thorough investigation. Any irregularity in the power flow, however seemingly insignificant, was always a cause for concern. Security was involved, but ultimate responsibility for the reliability of the power supply lay with the Technical Director.

While this problem with the supply added to Manfred's many other technical problems, chief of which was his prickly relationship with Andrew Rimzil, at least one worry had been resolved. The previous day, Kathrin had turned up at their home. He was much relieved that his fears about her disappearance had proved unfounded, although he was far from happy about the condition in which she had returned to him. Kathrin had seemed very upset, almost traumatised. He had asked where she'd been and what was wrong, but she had been unable, or unwilling, to answer. She kept saying she would tell him everything after she had rested. And then she had fallen asleep fully dressed. Given her highly disturbed state, he thought it best to let her rest. He had planned to talk to her in the morning, but the problem with the power supply had come up and he had left early, before she woke, to begin his investigation.

The other absentee from the courtroom was Gustave Houry, the Head of Internal Discipline. He had been despatched on a secret mission by Simon Goodfellow.

Back in the courtroom, there was a buzz of anticipation and expectation among those who had managed to find a seat. The occasion was sad and solemn, but major court cases in the Praesidium PCC were rare. A trial of someone for the assassination of a sitting president was unprecedented, hence the excitement.

Simon Goodfellow, attired in the black gown of a senior judge, waited until ten minutes past the appointed time before making his entrance. He wanted to create a powerful impression. This was his first public appearance since assuming the chairmanship. He strode boldly through the courtroom and mounted the judge's dais. He glared at the audience until they fell silent. The only noise that could be heard was the faint hum of the air-conditioning plant.

The clerk of the court, Mr Justin Ice, said in a loud voice, "The Praesidium court is now in session."

The position of clerk of the court was, in effect, a sinecure. Ice had served as John Noble's secretary until his retirement three years earlier. He had been a loyal supporter, and latterly friend, of the late Chairman. On Ice's retirement, Noble had appointed him to his current, largely honorary, position. As court cases were rare, Ice, who had no formal legal training, was relatively inexperienced in court proceedings, but being a conscientious administrator, he had made an effort to familiarise himself with court rules, customs and etiquette. Even so, he was, to be honest, a little over-awed by the situation. This was going to be the biggest court case in recent years, if not in the entire history of the Praesidium. And it was to be presided over by a new Chairman, a man with whom Ice had previously had little contact. What was more, the subject of the case was the cruel murder of his friend and patron, John Noble.

"Bring in the accused," commanded Simon Goodfellow.

A door at the side of the courtroom opened and Kit entered, a guard on either side. The guards escorted him to the front of the court, then manoeuvred him into position, facing the courtroom audience. He was pale and thin, but he kept a straight back, despite the partially healed lacerations from his beating. The intense magnetic resonance imaging head coil, which had been strapped to his head, made him look sinister, giving the impression that he was dangerous and possibly mentally deranged. The two guards remained by Kit's side, ready to perform a summary execution if there was any indication that the blind man was capable of exercising Emergent powers.

Simon glowered at the defendant, then looked over to Adam, who was seated at the prosecutor's desk. Adam felt intensely uncomfortable for several reasons. If we exclude his arraignment before God in the Garden of Eden at Hook, this was the first time he had been in a court. Despite feeling well outside his comfort zone, he was also to play a key role in proceedings. As a newly appointed, fast-tracked member of the Praesidium board, all eyes would be on him and, although he was the prosecutor and Kit the accused, he felt they were both there to be judged. Then, of course, there were the two major problems: first, that Kit was a friend whom Adam respected; and secondly, Adam knew that Kit was innocent. On consideration, "uncomfortable" inadequately described Adam's feelings.

Simon turned to the defending counsel's desk. He frowned. The desk was bare and there was no one sitting behind it.

"Where is the defending counsel? I was told a defending counsel had been appointed."

The main door at the back of the court swung open and the light from the glass windows of the PCC shone through. Silhouetted in the doorway was the striking figure of Aletheia – tall, graceful and powerful. Prometheus' finest creation strode through the courtroom and took her position behind the defending counsel's desk. There was a murmur of admiration and surprise.

"And you are?" Simon asked. He viewed the woman with a mixture of curiosity and, Simon being Simon, lust. She was the sort of female that Simon particularly enjoyed breaking – beautiful and strong.

"I am the defence counsel."

Simon considered pursuing his question, but being impatient to expedite the trial he decided against it.

"Very well," he said. Then he turned to Adam. "Read out the charge."

Adam rose and read from the sheet that Justin Ice had prepared on Goodfellow's instruction.

"The defendant is charged with the murder of John Noble, Praesidium Chairman, by means unknown …"

Aletheia stood up and interrupted Adam. "I beg the court's indulgence, but I must ask for a recess. I was given this case only yesterday. I have not yet had the chance to meet the defendant, much less prepare his defence." She remained standing and waited for the judge's response.

"There is no need for a recess, my dear," said Simon in his most patronising voice. "The case against the defendant is overwhelming, and while I don't doubt for a minute your competence as a barrister, even the best legal brain would find it impossible to mount a credible defence, however long the court allowed him or her to try."

"I have two problems with your response," said Aletheia firmly. There was a gasp from those packed on to the courtroom benches. "First, it is inappropriate for a judge to determine the guilt of the defendant before the trial has begun. Secondly, and in this instance, perhaps more importantly, I think you will find that under the rules of procedure in the Praesidium handbook on court processes, the defence counsel must be allowed, and I quote, 'a reasonable period in which to prepare the case for the defence'. And, with further reference to the handbook, I formally request that the prosecution supply me with all the evidence they intend to introduce in their case against my client."

Aletheia remained standing after finishing her response.

Goodfellow was shocked and irritated. He turned to Justin Ice for support.

Justin Ice was not a brave man, and he would have given anything to have been able to support Goodfellow, to correct this upstart defence counsel. But he couldn't because clearly this Aletheia knew the rules. Even if he sided with Goodfellow, she would simply read the rules to the court.

This was not how Goodfellow had intended matters to proceed. Inside he was raging, but he decided to put a good face on it.

"Of course we will allow a reasonable period for you to consult with your client. I assume the handbook does not define the term 'reasonable', so I will allow you twenty-four hours. There really is very little for you to get your head around." Then he gathered his papers and said, "We will convene again tomorrow at the same time and hopefully progress beyond reading out the charge."

"May I ask the judge to instruct the prosecution to hand over their evidence?" Aletheia persisted, entirely uncowed by the judge's irritation.

Goodfellow gave the deepest of sighs, indicating that his patience had been tested to its limit. "Yes," was all he said.

Kit turned his head towards Aletheia and smiled. She smiled back. Both of them knew that however things turned out, they were going to be the best of friends.

40. A death in the family

Gustave Houry had rushed to Simon Goodfellow's house first thing that morning before the new Chairman set out for the court. As Head of Internal Discipline, the matter was strictly speaking outside his remit. He should really have reported the news to Security first. But this information was too urgent to go through official channels.

He had caught Goodfellow eating breakfast.

"What is it?" Simon had asked. This was not a good time for an unscheduled meeting.

"We have been infiltrated," Gustave said breathlessly.

"Infiltrated? By what?"

"Not by what? By whom? Adam's wife, Eve, has visited her husband twice. On the second occasion I had her followed. There's a nest of infiltrators in the Praesidium's main building."

"Where in the main building?" Simon demanded.

"On the ground floor, where Rimzil has his laboratory."

Simon was unimpressed. "We are monitoring his laboratory twenty-four hours a day. If there was anything amiss, Bloch would have informed me."

"That's what I thought, but Rimzil has set up a virtual laboratory, a perfect replica of the real laboratory, and he's cloaked the replica lab. We've been monitoring the real laboratory. Meanwhile, in the virtual lab, he and his guests have been able to do whatever they want."

"That's not possible," said Simon, before adding, "is it?"

"I'm afraid it is. There are at least five people in the virtual laboratory, people who shouldn't even know about the existence of the PCC, let alone be living in it. One of them is Eve, Adam's wife. I don't know the others, although I think one of them is a colleague of Rimzil."

"But how did they get here without us knowing?" asked Simon. He was still sceptical.

"I can't be sure, but I think it has something to do with the paradox device. I suspect Rimzil has used it to create and cloak the virtual laboratory, and to import the infiltrators. I'm guessing here, but I can't think of any other explanation."

"But surely the Technical Director – or Security, or someone else – would have noticed something of what was going on. You say that Rimzil and these insurgents have been living in this virtual laboratory. Did no one notice that there was no one in the actual lab, the one we've been monitoring?" Now Simon Goodfellow was seriously worried.

"You'll have to ask the Technical Director. According to his logs, Rimzil has been present, or at least on view, in the real laboratory at all times, but we may have been watching a virtual clone, or a hologram …"

"Or a trick with smoke and mirrors!" Goodfellow interrupted angrily, "Surely Bloch noticed something?"

"I have no wish to speak ill of a board director," Houry trod carefully, "but Manfred Bloch has had problems in handling Rimzil. Rimzil is a brilliant man, far brighter than Manfred, and he treats his host like a lab assistant. Bloch doesn't know how to deal with him."

"I see," said Simon, making a note to include Bloch's managerial inadequacies in his critique of the Technical Director should Bloch ever decide to challenge or undermine him at the High Council.

"There's something else …" Feeling nervous, Gustave hesitated.

"Spit it out, man. I have to preside over a trial this morning and I need to leave in the next few minutes."

Gustave plucked up his courage and said, "Two of the infiltrators are on their way to the Blochs' home to talk to Kathrin, Bloch's wife."

Alarm bells rang in Simon's mind. "I thought Kathrin was missing," he said carefully. "I know Manfred has been fretting over her absence."

"Well, she's back home," said Gustave. "I know that for sure. Minofel's man, Jedwell Boon, must have found her somewhere. We have him on camera delivering her to the Blochs' house."

Now Simon was really worried. What the hell was going on? Had Minofel ordered Jedwell to release Kathrin? What game was he playing? It didn't make any sense. After all, Minofel was as implicated in Noble's death as anyone. He had made it possible. Surely Jedwell would not have acted without his master's approval?

"And why would the infiltrators want to talk to Bloch's wife?" he asked, looking hard into Gustave Houry's eyes in an attempt to assess how much he knew.

"I have no idea," Gustave replied. "But I think it may be connected to the trial of the blind man." He had said all he dared to say. If Goodfellow thought he knew the truth about John Noble's untimely demise, he would be in as much danger as the infiltrators.

"I see," said Simon slowly. "Very well. I'm going to give you some orders which will seem strange to you. You may even be tempted to ask me why I am giving you such orders, but that would be a mistake. I will judge you entirely on your willingness to undertake the tasks I'm setting you and your competence in accomplishing them. Do I make myself clear?"

Gustave Houry nodded.

Goodfellow straightened the judge's gown that he had just put on. "Go to Manfred Bloch's house. Kill the infiltrators. And kill Bloch's wife."

oooOooo

Gustave Houry left Simon Goodfellow's presence with mixed feelings. He was astute enough to realise that he was in the middle of a series of events that would either make or break his career, and quite possibly determine his lifespan. If all went to plan, he would be generously rewarded, his future assured. If he failed, it would be a disaster for many at the top of the Praesidium, and he suspected that he was likely to be the first casualty.

By making use of the Praesidium's ubiquitous auditory monitoring system, he had heard enough of the conversation between Rambler and Numpty, while they were on their way to Kathrin's home, to know the infiltrators were convinced of the blind man's innocence. They were certain that Kathrin would be able to help them in proving it. It seemed that Andrew Rimzil had visual evidence to prove that John Noble's body had been moved from an apartment in the accommodation block to the blind man's cell.

Gustave had checked the Praesidium tapes and found nothing, which meant that someone had tampered with them because, according to Rambler and Numpty, the evidence on Rimzil's own monitoring system was perfectly clear.

oooOooo

While Gustave was reporting to Goodfellow and receiving his instructions, Rambler and Numpty were with Kathrin in her sitting room. Kathrin had slept soundly throughout the night and woken a little crumpled, but much refreshed. At first she had been unwilling to receive visitors, especially strangers, but when Rambler, who clearly posed a threat to no one, had explained their purpose, she had welcomed them into her home.

Once inside, Rambler and Numpty listened intently to every word Kathrin said. She told them everything. Rambler made copious notes, while Numpty made various sympathetic noises as Kathrin revealed the full horror of what she had been through.

When she finished, Rambler and Numpty both thanked her for her frankness and invited her to join them in the sanctuary of Andrew Rimzil's cloaked laboratory.

"When this Goodfellow realises you're no longer captive in his home, he will have to deal with you," said Numpty. "You're the only witness to him killing the Chairman."

"It's kind of you but I think I'm probably safer here. When Goodfellow discovers you and your friends are here, he will use all the resources of the Praesidium to destroy you and no one can stop him."

"Surely you could stop him, if you had the chance to testify at the trial. If you testify, you can save our friend Kit and destroy Goodfellow," suggested Rambler.

"He will not allow me to testify," Kathrin replied. "Even if I reached the court, he would begin by trashing my reputation – not, I admit, a particularly difficult task. He would then take pleasure in destroying my marriage. Finally, I fear he would find it all too easy to persuade the court to disregard my testimony as an adulteress and proven deceiver who loved the victim and despised the man she is now falsely accusing. Goodfellow has his hands on the levers of power. Believe me, he will systematically abuse his position – and anyone who stands in his way."

"We could protect you if you testify," Numpty pleaded. "Kit is a good man. We really need your help."

"You could perhaps ask Jedwell Boon to testify," said Kathrin thoughtfully. "He took John Noble's body from Goodfellow's apartment. His testimony would be as good, if not better, than mine."

"Except that Jedwell Boon is David Minofel's man, isn't he?" Rambler objected. "In any case, he would have to implicate himself in Noble's murder if he was the one who disposed of the body."

"That's true," said Kathrin, "but he also rescued me. He came back to Goodfellow's apartment and brought me here. He asked for nothing. I don't know, but he might help. I can't, for the reasons I've given."

Rambler stood up. "If that is your decision, so be it. You have given us enough to mount a fairly solid defence of our friend. For that, we thank you. We will find Jedwell Boon and see what he says."

Rambler expected Numpty to join him, but he remained seated. "Uncle, you go. You can tell the others what Kathrin has told us. With Andrew's evidence, we have a good case. I will stay here for now. It's obvious that this Simon Goodfellow will want to dispose of Kathrin, as indeed he would have done in his apartment had she not been rescued. I will keep her safe."

"Again, you are too kind," said Kathrin. "But I am safe here. Even Goodfellow would not dare to harm me in my home, the home of the Technical Director."

"Nevertheless, I will stay for a while," said Numpty. He turned to his uncle. "When you have the chance, ask Aletheia what we should do to protect Kathrin. She will know what's best. I will stay here till I hear from you."

"Are you sure?" asked Rambler. Although he agreed with Kathrin that it was unlikely that Goodfellow would dare to harm her in her own home, he felt uneasy about leaving his nephew in what could become a dangerous situation.

"I'm sure," said Numpty firmly. "There's nothing I can do to help while I'm holed up in Andrew's sanctuary. Besides, Aletheia, you and the others are better placed than I to attend the court hearing and save Kit. I can be of more use here."

"Very well, my boy," said Rambler. "But please take care."

With that Rambler, clutching his notebook, left the Blochs' residence and headed straight for the Praesidium's main building and the safety of Andrew's replica lab.

Halfway there, his path crossed that of a slim, wiry man with closely cropped hair and a lop-sided mouth delineated by thin lips. Both men were preoccupied with their own thoughts, so neither noticed the other. Thus, while Rambler made his way back from Kathrin's house, Gustave Houry made his way towards it.

oooOooo

When Houry reached Kathrin's house he rang the bell. Numpty answered the door.

"Mrs Bloch is not receiving visitors," he said formally and firmly.

"She will receive this visitor," said Gustave with equal determination. "I have a message from her husband and I won't allow a total stranger, who has no authority, to prevent me from delivering a private message from a member of the board to his wife."

Although he felt a little disconcerted, Numpty stood his ground. But Houry had a job to do, a job best done quickly. Numpty didn't see the blow coming. Houry chopped Numpty's temple with the hard edge of his hand and the lad crumpled.

Houry made his way into the kitchen where Kathrin was making coffee for her young protector. She turned. When she saw it was the Head of Internal Discipline, her face paled. She knew him as one of Goodfellow's henchmen.

Without a word, Houry drew a long knife and walked steadily towards her. "Nothing personal," he said.

He was about to deliver a fatal stab when a small bronze of a swordfish hit him on the back of his head. Numpty had recovered and thrown the bronze ornament, the first heavy object that came to hand, across the room. His aim was good. It was not a serious impact, but it knocked Gustave Houry to his knees. He turned as he pulled himself up.

"Obviously, I didn't hit you hard enough," he said, with a sneer. "I won't make the same mistake again."

Numpty had drawn the knife Aletheia had given him. It was shorter than Houry's blade but better than nothing. "If you leave now," said Numpty, "I will let you go."

"You will let me go," Houry laughed. "*I will let you go,*" he said, mimicking Numpty, as he lunged at him.

Numpty had completed only one lesson in swordsmanship with Aletheia, but he knew enough to sidestep the clumsy thrust. He also knew he must strike quickly, while his opponent was off balance. The problem was that he had never stabbed anyone before, and he was surprised by how difficult it was proving to be. Fortunately, as Houry recovered from his failed attack, he turned and impaled himself on Numpty's outstretched knife. Numpty had delivered a blow to Houry's stomach – not a fatal wound, to be sure, but certainly a painful and debilitating one.

Numpty's initial instinct was to help the man. It was silly, but Numpty was no killer. He put his arm round the man to steady him, leaving his knife where it had lodged for fear of causing further pain or increased bleeding if he withdrew it. He had seriously injured a fellow human being, and although he knew he had done the right thing he felt sorry for his victim.

Just as he was suggesting that the man sit down, Houry rammed his own knife directly into Numpty's chest, puncturing the lad's heart.

The lad scarcely had time to grunt before he died.

A moment later, Kathrin struck the back of Houry's head with the bronze statuette that Numpty had thrown at him, but she had the good sense to use the point of the swordfish as a spike. She drove the spike as hard as she could into Gustave Houry's brain. It was only four inches long, but four inches was long enough.

oooOooo

In the virtual lab, Luke awoke abruptly from the comfort of the dog bed Eve had provided. He stared upward for a moment, blinked once or twice, then let out a howl of anguish that came from the deepest part of his soul.

The Storyteller walked over to the dog and comforted him. "It was never without risk," he minded to Luke. "You cannot involve yourself in stories of good and evil without putting your life on the line. The boy is dead. Your friend is dead. It is dreadful that Numpty has died. It will devastate his uncle. But he has died a good death, a heroic death, defending and saving the life of a woman."

The Storyteller informed the others of the manner of Numpty's passing.

"Is there nothing you can do?" asked the distraught dog. He and Numpty had formed a close relationship during the quest for the Fourth Beginning. Numpty had risked his life to save him. Both of them had derived benefits from the initiation of the Beginning, which its abrupt termination had not diminished; both had enjoyed heightened mental acuity, which had brought them even closer together.

"I can do nothing," said the Storyteller, answering Luke and addressing the others. "It is not for me to intervene, however much I might wish to do so. You, and what you do, will determine how this story plays out. But I will admit I am full of foreboding. The forces ranged against you are as bad as any you can imagine. Simon Goodfellow now controls the Praesidium, and none will challenge him. He is an evil and sadistic man. I pity anyone who attracts his attention. But worse than Goodfellow is David Minofel. He and his creatures, the Monitaurs, represent a truly terrifying and daunting prospect."

"Enough," minded Luke. "Let me grieve for Numpty. Leave me in peace."

"I'm sorry," the Storyteller responded. "You are right. We need some time to grieve – but not too long. We must act soon, or I fear there will be more to grieve for, and fewer to do the grieving."

oooOooo

When Rambler reached the "real" laboratory, he was eager to tell the others what they had learned from Kathrin. They now knew who had killed John Noble, as well as the manner of his death. He turned the handle on the left side of the laboratory door and entered.

As soon as he stepped through the door he knew something was wrong. It was as though the very air was weighing heavily on the questors. Eve went to Rambler's side and put her arm round him.

"Oh no," he said, slumping to the ground. No one needed to tell him. He began to sob, slowly at first, as though the pain had to travel from somewhere deep inside him, but once the channel for his grief had opened up, the sobbing became uncontrollable. Andrew and Prune abandoned their bench, where they had been trying to lose themselves in their work, but there was nothing they could say or do. They just looked on helplessly.

"I'm sure it was quick, very quick," Eve whispered into Rambler's ear. "He didn't suffer."

"It was a noble death," said Aletheia who had just returned from the courtroom. "Ήταν ένας καλός άνθρωπος (he was a good man). He led a good life. He died a good death. There is no better fate available to mortals."

"It is not right," Rambler said eventually. "It is against nature. I should have gone before him. Oh, my dear nephew! What shall I do? Where shall I be without you?"

"You will live on to honour his memory," said Aletheia firmly. "And your love for him, and his for you, is embedded in reality. I have seen much and I know this – empires come and go. The face of the Sphinx will be blown away eventually by the wind and sand. Even the Parthenon will fall into ruins. Yet love cannot be touched by the passage of days or years or centuries. Love lives forever in its own eternal present."

Aletheia allowed the questors a minute of silence to dwell on their sadness, and then she asked Rambler to tell them what he had learned.

To his surprise, Aletheia's words had comforted him and he was able to pull himself together. Without needing to refer to his notebook he told them everything.

"If Kathrin will not testify, we must seek out this Jedwell Boon," said Aletheia. "I can present a defence for Kit based on the truth, but it will not win the day unless I have proof."

41. Client relations

When Simon Goodfellow left the courtroom following Aletheia's intervention, he made straight for the apartment that was always allocated to David Minofel whenever he chose to stay overnight in the Praesidium complex.

On entering the apartment, Simon was surprised to see that Minofel was in the middle of packing. He had a large suitcase open on the bed and there was a closed briefcase on the floor. On the coffee table there was a hat box.

"You're leaving," said Simon, stating the obvious.

"Oh yes, I'm leaving," said Minofel.

"Well, perhaps before you go," said Simon, his voice bubbling with anger, "you would be kind enough to explain why you told your man Boon to remove Kathrin from my apartment and take her back to Bloch's house."

"I didn't," said Minofel.

"Are you telling me that he removed the woman on his own initiative?"

"I can't think of any other explanation, can you?" Minofel replied.

Simon was entirely flummoxed. "Do you realise what your Jedwell has done? He has put the whole plan in jeopardy. Kathrin witnessed Noble's death. She could destroy us both."

"That's why I'm leaving," said Minofel complacently. "Timing is everything."

"But you can't just leave," Goodfellow shouted. "How could you let Boon do this? Don't you control your own people?"

"Obviously not well enough," Minofel replied, with a smile. "You can control people in many ways. You can use rewards or punishment, hope or fear, or any combination of those emotional drivers. But at the end of the day there's something in people that can rebel, something that enables them to say 'no, no more'. That's the problem with people. Not that I'm complaining – it's that spark of rebellion that keeps Slievins in business. You wouldn't need our help if it weren't for that spark."

"You won't stay in business for long if you cut and run when the going gets tough, especially when you are responsible for the problem."

"Don't worry about the Slievins business model," Minofel replied, still smiling. "It's stood the test of time. For as long as men need managing, the managers will need Slievins. We always manage to manage the managers. That's our motto. Or one of them anyway."

"You are under contract," said Goodfellow. "You have to help me sort this out."

Minofel stopped smiling. "My contract required me to ensure the questors never again tried to initiate a Beginning. Given the state Adam is in, and the fact that the rest of the questors are running around like headless chickens trying to save the blind man from execution, I think you will agree that the requirements of that contract have been fulfilled.

"And, yes, there was a second contract," Minofel continued, "to deal with the possibility that the blind man was an Emergent. You have assured me he is not. But in the best traditions of Slievins, and on the time-honoured principle of belt and braces, I've enabled you to put him on trial for murder so that you can destroy him and his reputation in a single hanging. So don't talk to me about contractual obligations. As ever, Slievins has done its client proud."

Simon Goodfellow looked into Minofel's eyes. They were cold. There was no sign of anger, no sign of sympathy, and certainly no indication he was prepared to compromise.

"Very well," said Simon. "I will handle the situation myself in my own way. I will show you how to deal with the problems you have created but obviously cannot solve. By now, Kathrin will be dead. It will be difficult to explain her death but, given where she died, I'm hoping to put the blame on Bloch, suggesting a fit of jealous rage after she revealed her affair with me. As for your contracts, you can keep the fees you've been paid, but I'll not pay you a penny more. You need to learn that there is more to client relations than simply fulfilling the letter of the contract. There is also the spirit."

Now Minofel laughed. "I've always found that relying on the spirit of things is an unrewarding strategy. I will tell you what is going to happen. I am leaving and I am taking the Monitaurs with me. You probably haven't been told this, but they belong to Slievins. When your founder, Nastafilu Verdicel, began to build his empire, he made a pact with the forbears of Slievins: they would give him temporal power, and in return he would run the affairs of men along Slievins' lines. It was then that we gave the Praesidium the services of the Monitaurs. That pact has survived for centuries. The Praesidium is kept in power, free to do as it pleases, so long as what it does is true to Slievins' principles. The pact is still strong, but you have put your own power at risk. So I will take the Monitaurs, and Slievins will discuss with the Praesidium's High Council where they would now be best deployed. Don't be angry. You asked me once what you could do to thank me for all the help I gave you in seizing the chairmanship. Well, now you know. I will take the Monitaurs as a down payment, and if you fail to hold on to your prize, I will return to take the Crucible of Eternal Light for good measure. Slievins has always envied, perhaps even resented, the Praesidium's hold on the Crucible. We have always believed it would be safer and more productive with us than with you. If it comes to it, the Crucible of Eternal Light will more than cover any outstanding fees." At this point, Minofel closed his suitcase. "I am leaving now."

Goodfellow was about to remonstrate with the practitioner, but Minofel frowned and Simon thought better of it.

"In one instance, I will concede that things have not gone as they should. My man Jedwell has, after years of faithful service, let me down – let me down rather badly. I suppose I saw signs he was going off the rails, so to speak, on a London tube train on the way to Harrow. When the train stopped at Wembley, he decided to go off-piste and save a maiden in distress. I do not hold his failure to keep the blind man captive in my home in Geneva against him. Kit Turner is more difficult to manage than you imagine. But certainly Boon's failure to chastise Miss Tomic effectively when she took it upon herself to warn Adam – that was inexcusable, and I admit I should have acted then. His rescuing of Kathrin was a disgrace and unforgivable. Again, I should have acted sooner. I do find it interesting that all his mistakes have involved protection of the fairer sex. I hadn't realised it but despite the rather brutal assignments he has happily undertaken for me, Jedwell must have been a romantic all along. I suspect this tendency is connected with the untimely death of his mother. Anyway, no harm done. If you eliminate Kathrin, the problem is solved. I can assure you that Jedwell Boon will not obstruct your plans in future."

"Kathrin is already eliminated," said Goodfellow. "I, at least, can rely on my own staff to do as they are told."

"It might be worth your while checking that one out," said Minofel, grinning. "I fear your man Houry may have proved a tad less reliable than you think."

With that, he picked up his suitcase and his briefcase and walked to the door.

"You've forgotten your hat box," said Goodfellow.

"That's a parting gift from me to you," said Minofel as he left the apartment. "I hope you like it."

Simon went over to the coffee table and pulled the ribbon, which was tied beautifully around the box in an elaborate bow. He had the feeling he knew what form the gift would take. He lifted the lid. He was right. There, staring up at him with glazed, lifeless eyes, was the round, shiny bald head of Jedwell Boon.

42. The trial begins in earnest

When everyone was present, the sitting judge, Simon Goodfellow, acting Chairman of the Praesidium, asked that the charge against the accused be read out.

Justin Ice, clerk of the court, stood up.

"The accused, one Kit Turner, did, these three days past, persuade the former, and now deceased, Chairman of the Praesidium, John Noble, to visit him in secret in his cell in the detention centre. There, by means not yet determined, he did kill John Noble."

"How do you plead?" enquired the judge.

Kit said nothing.

"How do you plead?" the judge repeated, with some irritation.

Still Kit said nothing.

"Are you deaf as well as blind?" Goodfellow demanded. "For the last time, how do you plead?"

"He pleads not guilty." Aletheia said. Her voice was soft and low, yet her words reached every corner of the crowded courtroom.

"Very well," said Goodfellow. It was irregular. The defendant should have entered his plea himself. But given this Aletheia was his appointed counsel, her plea on his behalf was acceptable. "Then I invite the prosecution to present the evidence."

Adam hesitated. He had not slept well since his last talk with David Minofel. Minofel had made it clear that the trial would be a farce. Kit was innocent, but he was to be found guilty. Why had Minofel told him Kit was innocent? Of course, Adam was already convinced of Kit's innocence, but why had Minofel felt the need to confirm that Kit was innocent and that he would be found guilty. Surely there were better ways of testing his loyalty to Slievins. He thought back to the day when Miss Tomic had told him the letter he was taking to Spinetti contained a bribe.

"A blind and deaf defendant against a dumb prosecutor," quipped Goodfellow. "I should perhaps remind the court that this man is on trial for a capital offence. This is hardball, not pinball."

At last Adam spoke. "John Noble's body was found inside the cell of the defendant. It is not known why the deceased visited the defendant, nor is it known why or how the deceased died, but he was a man in his prime, with no history of illness. Assuming there was foul play, the most likely suspect must be the defendant."

Adam sat down.

Simon Goodfellow frowned. "Given the evidence against the defendant is overwhelming, that must be the weakest presentation of a prosecution case I have ever heard. I suggest you try harder."

Adam knew he had to prosecute the case if he wanted to establish himself on the Praesidium board, but he was desperate to give the defence counsel openings to challenge the evidence. He was trying to wriggle in a space with no wriggle room and Goodfellow would not allow it. Adam could hear Minofel's voice inside his head, saying, "We at Slievins always do what needs to be done. Only those who shed the shackles of spurious and alien moralities can truly be strong. What does it matter if someone has to die, if ten or thousands have to die."

Adam spoke again.

"It is clear beyond reasonable doubt that John Noble was murdered. At the board meeting earlier that day he had taken decisions of strategic importance to the future of the Praesidium. He showed no signs of ill health or mental instability at that time. The following morning his body was found in the locked cell of the accused. The cell is in the detention centre which, for obvious reasons, is well guarded. Access to it is restricted. If John Noble was murdered, it would seem to be beyond reasonable doubt that Kit Turner murdered him."

That was it. He had done it. He sat down. For no reason he could think of, he murmured "God forgive me".

"Good," said the judge.

Aletheia did not wait to be invited to present the defence. She stood up, her blue-green eyes blazing. She addressed the judge.

"Did you not say a moment ago 'given that the evidence against the defendant is overwhelming'? That alone is enough to disbar you."

There was a ripple of astonishment around the courtroom. The Praesidium had over the centuries modernised itself in the technical sphere, but it remained a strictly hierarchical and patriarchal organisation. Young women – however attractive, articulate or charismatic – did not address members of the Praesidium board in this manner.

Simon Goodfellow himself was taken aback.

"But I have no wish to see the judge disbarred," Aletheia continued, "because I want this trial to proceed. I intend to prove that the evidence against my client is purely circumstantial, that the prosecution has offered no motive and no means, and that my client is entirely innocent."

Despite the provocation, Simon decided to give Aletheia her head. After all, for the trial to carry weight with the High Council it had to be fair. The accused must be afforded a proper defence. But he also decided that at the earliest opportunity this arrogant upstart must be punished for her impudence. He would take her and break her. He would maim her and tame her. He would enjoy and destroy her. He would employ the entire armoury of devices at his disposal to heighten pleasure and pain, his pleasure and her pain.

"It is certain John Noble is dead," said Aletheia, "but there is no proof he was murdered. Even if he was murdered, the prosecution offers no explanation as to how a blind man, debilitated by weeks of abuse and hunger, could have overcome a man who was in his prime – powerful, sighted, fit and well. What's more, the prosecution has failed to ascribe to my client any motive for the commission of this crime. Given the circumstances, surely my client would have appealed to John Noble for mercy rather than kill him in his cell, thereby ensuring his own conviction and execution."

"Thank you for presenting your defence," Goodfellow interrupted. "I think it would be helpful if the prosecution cross-examined the accused. During the cross-examination, the prosecutor may be able to elicit some answers to the questions the defence counsel has posed."

Aletheia gave way.

Reluctantly Adam stood up. "How do you explain the presence of John Noble in your cell?" he asked.

Kit said nothing.

Adam tried again. "Why did the Praesidium Chairman come to your cell?"

Kit remained silent.

"Did you kill John Noble, the Chairman of the Praesidium?"

Kit refused to answer.

"No, he did not," said Aletheia firmly.

"Yet he will not answer the question himself," noted the judge. "He did not plead not guilty, and he does not deny he killed John Noble. His silence on these questions cannot be without significance."

"I am his defence counsel and I speak on his behalf. The defendant is not under any obligation to answer for himself."

Justin Ice was mentally checking through the rules and regulations governing courtroom procedures; although it was unprecedented for a defendant to refuse to answer all questions, there was nothing to prevent an accused from relying entirely on his defence counsel.

Simon Goodfellow looked to Ice for some comment but Ice just shook his head.

"I think perhaps a review of court procedures will be in order when I am confirmed as Chairman," Goodfellow remarked to the clerk of the court.

"I should like to resume my defence of the accused," said Aletheia. "The prosecution mentioned the board meeting attended by John Noble on the day of his death. The prosecution also referred to the taking of 'decisions of strategic importance to the future of the Praesidium'. What were these decisions?"

Goodfellow stepped in at once. "The proceedings of board meetings are confidential and, in any case, irrelevant. They could have no bearing on what the Chairman did hours later – or on his murder."

"Nevertheless, the prosecution introduced the board meeting in his evidence to prove that John Noble was sound in mind and body. Since this is a capital case, I must press for details of the meeting and the nature of the decisions that could affect the future of the Praesidium."

There was no way Goodfellow would have his abortive coup and subsequent dismissal paraded before the court. "And I must deny your request. The confidentiality of board meeting deliberations is sacrosanct and is not to be set aside, however serious the case."

"Very well," Aletheia continued, unabashed. She turned and faced the audience. "The prosecution's case is based on circumstantial evidence. Some of you may think the evidence compelling …"

Goodfellow interrupted. "You are not trying to persuade the people here. I am the judge. There is no jury, in either a formal or informal sense. I am the one you need to persuade. And you are right – I do find the evidence compelling." He needed to throw this extraordinarily self-confident advocate off balance. In fact, he wanted to close the case down as quickly as possible.

"Since you do not dispute the evidence is circumstantial, I should like to offer you an alternative account of the events of that night. John Noble did not visit Kit, the blind man. Why would he? No, he visited someone else – someone of his own rank, someone who had a good reason to do John Noble harm. That person killed John Noble, then had the body carried from his apartment to the blind man's cell, where it was left for whoever found the body to draw the obvious, but wrong, conclusion."

Goodfellow laughed. "Excellent. If this court had an inexhaustible supply of time and patience, we could explore other possibilities, including perhaps the intervention of fairies or aliens from Alpha Centauri. But sadly, both the court's time and my patience are limited."

"Then let me put a little more flesh on my alternative scenario," said Aletheia. "John Noble went to the aforementioned colleague's apartment under duress, where he was injected with a substance that paralysed him. He was then suffocated with a plastic bag. Once dead, this unnamed colleague summoned one of his lackeys and instructed the lackey to place the body in Kit Turner's cell. Is that better?"

"I don't think that takes us any further," said Goodfellow cautiously.

"Oh, but it does," Aletheia insisted. "Because it's testable."

"And how is it testable?" asked Simon Goodfellow.

"Because if my scenario is correct, there will be an almost imperceptible mark in the side of John Noble's neck, low down on the right side, where the paralysing agent was injected."

43. Good news, bad news

"It works. It bloody works," said Prune. "We've got ourselves a deli." Prune Leach was referring to the dark energy loop idea that he and Andrew had been working on.

As Andrew had said, the idea was idiotic or, if not idiotic, certainly paradoxical. They assumed the energy that sustained the Eternal Light was the dark energy that permeated the universe. Somehow, the Eternal Light was able to turn the dark energy into positive energy. Using the paradox device, Andrew and Prune had found a way to siphon off all the energy from the Eternal Light, turning it back into dark energy, then feeding it back into the Eternal Light for reconversion. It meant that before the Praesidium got to use the energy of the Eternal Light, it passed through the paradox device. And that meant that Andrew and Prune, tucked away in Andrew's parallel laboratory, had control of all the energy the Praesidium needed to sustain itself.

There was something else, something that Andrew had observed but could not explain. There seemed to be some kind of rapport between the paradox device and the Eternal Light. "It's like a love match," Andrew tried to explain to Prune. "They seem to be made for each other, an inexhaustible supply of energy feeding a device capable of realising an infinite number of possibilities."

That was the good news.

The bad news was that despite using Andrew's scanner and then physically searching the Praesidium's main building, at great risk of arrest, Eve and Rambler had found no trace of Jedwell Boon. Without Jedwell Boon, there was no witness to substantiate the truth and prove Kit's innocence. Unless, of course, they could persuade Kathrin to change her mind, assuming Goodfellow had not made a second, and this time successful, attempt on her life.

The other bad news was that Security now knew of their bolthole. Andrew's shield was holding, but Security was probing the defences of the parallel laboratory. Fortunately, Security needed energy to break through Andrew's cloaking, just as Andrew's cloaking needed energy to sustain itself, and with the benefit of deli the questors had as much energy at their disposal – in fact, exactly as much energy – as the Praesidium. Security was desperately trying to work out what to do. If the questors could match them joule for joule, they could end up in cataclysmic deadlock, consuming all the energy the Eternal Light could produce. And that wouldn't do at all.

Now that Security knew of the existence of the parallel laboratory, Andrew no longer had to maintain the fiction of his presence in the real lab. Andrew had not found it particularly difficult to be in two places at once, but it had made the others feel slightly uneasy and he was pleased to resolve the issue.

"So, what are we going to do now?" asked Prune Leach. "Aletheia is battling for Kit in the Praesidium court. Are we going to sit here twiddling our thumbs?"

"Aletheia asked us to seek out Jedwell Boon," observed Rambler, "and we have tried, but he is nowhere to be found. There is nothing else we can do that will help."

Eve felt sick. She kept thinking that if it was true that babies are affected by their mother's mental state during pregnancy, the little one she was carrying was going to be full of doubts, fears and worries.

"Without the evidence of a witness," she said, "Aletheia will probably fail. Goodfellow will find Kit guilty. And we know what that means. And what about Adam? Are we simply going to give up on him? Am I going to give up on him? He's been corrupted by Minofel and Slievins. But that doesn't mean he's irredeemable, does it? He's the father of this child. In any case, we should at least give Aletheia some moral support."

"If we leave here we will be arrested," said Rambler. "Given the dubious integrity of the Praesidium's judicial system, I fear that if we are arrested, we will meet the same fate as Kit. For myself, I don't really care. They have taken my nephew from me. They are welcome to my life. But Eve, you must think of your baby."

The questors fell silent. None of them liked the idea of just waiting while Aletheia did all the heavy lifting, but Rambler had a point: it wouldn't help Aletheia, or Kit, if they found themselves in a Praesidium cell.

"There is a way," said Andrew, "but it will take a fair amount of chutzpah, and it's not without risks. Two of us could go to the court to give moral support to Aletheia and Kit. I suggest that Eve and I go. When they try to arrest us, Prune here can shut down the deli for an instant. We know how sensitive everyone here is to any interruption in the power supply. We will tell Security that the next blip will be longer if we are not taken to the courtroom immediately. They probably won't agree straight away, but by the second or third blip, they should get the message."

"What do we do if they say they will kill you unless we surrender?" asked Rambler.

"That's the risk, or one of them," said Andrew. "If they do that, start voiding the dark energy back into space. Don't let them get hold of the paradox device, whatever happens to us. But I don't think that's how Simon Goodfellow will play the game. He wants to be confirmed as Chairman. That's why he's allowing Kit to be tried, rather than quietly despatching him in his cell. He won't want to order a massacre of more interlopers – interlopers who have successfully breached Praesidium security and interfered with the Eternal Light. There's something else. This isn't just about destroying Kit. It isn't just about preventing us from trying to initiate a Beginning either. This is all about corrupting Adam as an end in itself. The key is Minofel. I think he and Slievins run the show. I also think that while the Praesidium runs the affairs of men, Minofel and Slievins run the Praesidium. I think Minofel knows Kit is his enemy and he can do nothing about that, except destroy him. But Adam is open to persuasion. This has all been about bringing Adam over to Minofel's side."

"You see this as some archetypal battle between good and evil for the soul of man?" suggested Rambler.

"Sounds like archetypal bollocks to me," said Prune. "Don't take too much notice of Andrew. He's been coming up with strange ideas ever since he split himself in half. He even thinks there's some kind of love affair going on between the paradox device and the Eternal Light. I've got a theory. If you split yourself in two, there's a risk you become a halfwit. That said, I like your plan," he addressed Andrew, "except for the part about who goes to court. While I've got serious doubts about your more outlandish speculations, I'll admit that you are far better than me at controlling the paradox device. And we need the best man at the controls of the only thing we have in our favour."

44. The trial resumes

When the court reconvened, Eve and Prune Leach arrived early and grabbed front row seats in the audience. All had gone as Andrew had predicted. The second blip in the power supply had elicited an urgent message from the acting Chairman to bring the two questors to court.

"The court is in session. Judge Goodfellow presiding," announced Justin Ice.

Kit, wearing his intense magnetic resonance imaging head coil, was brought in by his guards. The coil was tightly fitted and left a mark on Kit's forehead.

When the court had settled down, Goodfellow announced, "We shall begin with the results of the examinations of John Noble's body."

Dr Eli Sandmore, the Praesidium's Chief Medical Officer, took the stand. Dr Sandmore was a large imposing figure, exuding a spurious authority that impressed the naïve. "In the company of the defence counsel I examined the body of our late, much-lamented Chairman. I have to report that the body shows no signs of foul play. The likely cause of death was heart failure, which as we well know can strike at any time, even a seemingly fit man. Whether this heart attack was a natural occurrence or induced by the exercise of some malign power I cannot say. Furthermore, I found nothing to support the defence counsel's assertion that the Chairman had been injected with some kind of paralysing substance. There was an indentation on the Chairman's neck in the position specified by the defence counsel, but it was impossible to tell whether it was a mark left by an injection, or an indentation caused by some other agent, for example, a bee sting or, indeed, scarring left by the extrusion of a comedo – in layman's terms, a blackhead."

"Thank you," said Goodfellow. "Although the results of the examination are inconclusive, I think we will consider the matter settled. We can fairly say that there is no clear evidence to corroborate the defence counsel's bizarre and entirely fanciful version of events."

"What!" exclaimed Aletheia. "You cannot be serious."

The clerk of the court intervened. "You cannot address this court in such a discourteous manner." So far, Justin Ice hadn't been very helpful to the acting Chairman and thought an intervention at this point would find favour with the judge.

"Quite so," the judge said. "But we must give this attractive young firebrand some latitude, if only because the sight of her in full flow is enough to stir the loins of the most anaemic of men."

Aletheia ignored Goodfellow's patronising sexism. "There can be few in the medical profession who cannot distinguish between a puncture of the skin by a hypodermic needle and a bee sting. I gave the court a true account of how John Noble died, and I told the court precisely where it would find the evidence to corroborate my version of events. Even the good doctor Sandmore concedes that my account was consistent with what he found. Strangely, his conclusion is not consistent with his findings. I must therefore question either the doctor's competence, or his impartiality."

There were murmurs of approval and admiration from some in the courtroom. The audience had assumed the case against the blind man was incontrovertible and, therefore, that the trial would follow an entirely predictable course, ending with an entirely predictable outcome. But this striking, vibrant defence counsel was giving the proceedings an entirely new and entertaining dimension. Goodfellow decided he had given the girl enough latitude. She had to be reined in, disciplined. The very thought of how he would restrain and then discipline her after the trial in the privacy of his apartment distracted him for a moment, but then he pulled himself together and called for silence.

"I thought the Chief Medical Officer's testimony might be insufficient to convince this young woman. Therefore, in the interests of justice – for justice must not only be done, it must be seen to be done – I ordered a second doctor to provide a completely independent second opinion. The court will now hear the testimony of Dr Theon Diss. Most of you will know of Dr Diss as the Senior Medical Officer of the Praesidium's High Council. Unfortunately, because of more pressing engagements, Dr Diss cannot be here himself today, but he has provided an affidavit, which Mr Justin Ice will now read to the court."

Ice stood up, coughed and read out: "*Having thoroughly examined the body of the deceased, John Noble, and the report prepared by Dr Eli Sandmore, I, Dr Theon Diss, can unreservedly endorse the conclusions in Dr Sandmore's comprehensive and thorough report, in particular, his determination that the mark on the deceased's neck is not indisputably evidence of an injection by a hypodermic needle."*

Simon Goodfellow thanked Ice and added, "We really must leave this matter now. It has taken up too much of the court's time. The testimony of two of the Praesidium's most eminent doctors should be sufficient to satisfy us all – even the defence counsel. After all, justice delayed is justice denied, and I think in this case we all want to see justice applied as quickly as possible."

"Excuse me," said Aletheia.

"No," snapped Goodfellow. "Enough. Failure to accept the findings of the investigation is an insult to our expert witnesses, and therefore unacceptable to this court."

"I am not challenging their findings, I'm endorsing them," said Aletheia.

Goodfellow frowned. What game was she playing?

"In his expert testimony, I believe Dr Sandmore observed that the body showed no signs of foul play. If that is the case, why does the prosecution assume it was murder? Where is the proof? Might John Noble not have died of natural causes?"

Simon Goodfellow looked at Aletheia with mixed emotions. She had a point. No one had considered this line of defence. Dr Sandmore had said, "The likely cause of death was heart failure, which as we well know can strike at any time, even a seemingly fit man." But this was ridiculous. Of course Noble had been murdered. He knew it. Aletheia knew it. The blind man knew it. Minofel knew it. Adam knew it. Jedwell and Kathrin had known it. Anyone who knew anything knew it.

And yet Aletheia had a point. Indeed, the court had just spent the last half hour eliminating the one piece of physical evidence supporting the case for foul play.

"This would be a good time for a brief adjournment," Simon Goodfellow declared. "We will reconvene in half an hour."

oooOooo

Simon withdrew to the judge's chambers. He was not happy. This trial was his first public appearance as Praesidium Chairman (albeit only acting Chairman at present), and he had hoped for a speedy hearing, a severe but justified punishment, and for the whole matter to be despatched with the type of ruthless efficiency he intended to be the hallmark of his tenure in office.

Instead, the prosecution was diffident, the defence counsel determined and agile, and the clerk of the court well-meaning but ineffectual. And David Minofel, who had virtually set up the murder of John Noble and put the blind man in the frame, had scuttled off, leaving his client to sort things out.

Other matters were troubling Goodfellow: where was Gustave Houry? No one had heard from him since he had been sent to deal with Kathrin. He was probably having some difficulty in the disposal of her body. Body disposal, like personnel elimination, was usually handled by Security, not Internal Discipline, so Houry was operating outside his comfort zone. Still, he should have reported back by now.

And what was Manfred Bloch doing? He'd been tasked with investigating the blips in the power supply. First he had sent Goodfellow a message saying there was nothing wrong. A few hours later, he had sent a second message, saying he thought there might be something seriously wrong. According to his staff, Bloch had been working on the problem with several senior engineers for the last thirty-six hours without a break but had not yet found a solution to the as yet undefined problem.

Yet, clearly there was a problem. The questors had used blips in the power transmission to persuade him to permit two of them to attend the trial. He had no idea how they had caused the blips, but if they had some means of interfering with the PCCs power supply, it was a matter of extreme urgency that Bloch find the problem and put a stop to it.

As for this Aletheia, what could he say? Where had she come from? He'd not seen her before anywhere in the Westminster PCC. Of course, she might have been working in one of the obscure administration departments of House Services, but he couldn't believe someone of her presence and mental acuity, not to mention her striking physical attractions, would have spent long hours happily checking the domestic staff's expense receipts or running inventories in the accommodation block laundry.

To be clear, none of these issues caused Simon Goodfellow serious concerns. As Praesidium Chairman, he had his hands on all the levers of power. Each PCC was an autocracy. He had absolute authority. If he wanted to execute the blind man, he simply had to order it. Indeed, he could have the entire board executed if he so wished. He had never understood John Noble's lackadaisical management style. No, with the exception of the problem Manfred Bloch was wrestling with, Simon had nothing at all to worry about.

Nevertheless, to ensure confirmation of his appointment as Chairman, the trial had to be brought to a satisfactory conclusion. Aletheia's latest tactic required a different approach. Goodfellow summoned Adam.

When Adam entered the judge's chambers, Goodfellow greeted him by saying, "To be frank, I'm a little disappointed with your performance so far. I was wondering if I could persuade you to take a more active, more enthusiastic, part in the proceedings."

Adam grunted. He was very uncomfortable in the role he was being forced to play, and the Chairman's sarcasm was extremely irritating. "It's not impossible," he replied, "that my enthusiasm for prosecution is being hampered by a well-founded conviction that the defendant is entirely innocent."

If Adam had hoped for some concession, for some understanding of the moral dilemma with which he was wrestling, he was disappointed. "What the hell has that got to do with anything?" Goodfellow almost snarled at him. "Your job is to prosecute the blind man. My job is to sentence him. And Silas Drahan, Head of Security, will have the pleasure of executing him. After all, killing a Praesidium Chairman is just about the worst thing anyone can do."

"And I suppose the fact the Kit didn't do it is irrelevant!" said Adam.

"Not entirely," Goodfellow returned, "because your job is to prove he did – a job possibly made a tad more difficult by the defendant's innocence."

"And how am I to do that?" asked Adam.

"You're really not very good at this, are you?" sneered Goodfellow. "I'm beginning to wonder what Minofel saw in you. Let's be clear on our roles in this affair – you're the prosecutor and I'm the judge."

"Pity it isn't the other way round!" snapped Adam.

"Your chances of a seat on the board are beginning to fade away, my friend," warned Goodfellow. "I suggest you concentrate on the facts. Noble was found dead in the blind man's locked cell. That's a good start. Aletheia has now suggested Noble died of natural causes. Apart from the puncture in his neck, which our expert witnesses have dealt with, there is no evidence of foul play. So we have to prove a man has been murdered without any indication of physical violence. Now, how do you think we can do that?"

"Poison," said Adam, "probably injected in the neck, but not by Kit, because he had limited access to noxious substances, if we exclude the food he's been fed."

Goodfellow ignored the remark. "No, we have a much more exciting explanation – mind control, exercised by a suspected Emergent."

"What's an Emergent?" Adam asked. He recalled Oliver Nates's slip of the tongue.

Simon Goodfellow hesitated. He was going to have to explain what an Emergent could do without reawakening Adam's memories of the quest or reigniting any residual aspirations he might still retain for initiating a Beginning.

"There are some people, Adam, who can fool others into believing they have some kind of unnatural power. Most people are gullible, easily deceived – even eager to believe in nonsense. Although Emergents are invariably charlatans, they can exercise influence over the way people think, even what they see and do. They exploit people's credulity for their own ends. The clever ones disguise their selfish purposes, at least in the early stages of their deceit, but in the end they take advantage of their victims. Don't misunderstand me – we have no objection to the deceit or the exploitation. The problem is the type of ideas they promote. In order to take advantage of their victims, they tend to encourage people to deny their own nature, to follow false and impractical forms of morality, to wander off into utopian fantasies. Emergents are harmful because they encourage false hopes and unnatural aspirations. Kit Turner is one such. You have spent time with him, and I'm sure there have been instances where you have been surprised at something he has said or done, something that seemed out of the ordinary, even remarkable.

"We have been monitoring Turner for weeks. You will have seen that in court he wears a head coil with numerous sensors attached to his head. Emergents are capable of unusual brain activity. We believe this is how they affect what people think, see and do. The sensors measure this activity and give us early warning of any attempt by the subject to use his powers."

Although Adam had always felt there was something remarkable about Kit, he found it impossible to attribute malign motives to his friend. "I've known Kit Turner a long time and we've been through a lot together. There's nothing sinister or malevolent about him."

Goodfellow smiled. "He wouldn't be an Emergent if the people he duped thought he was harmful. Anyway, further discussion of the methods of Emergents is pointless. We have tested Turner thoroughly and concluded that he has no Emergent powers. Nevertheless, the suspicion that he might be an Emergent is what we need to focus on now. John Noble visited Turner in his cell. Why? The Chairman of the Praesidium board had no reason to visit an insignificant guest in our assessment block. He went because Turner summoned him using his Emergent powers. Noble then died in Turner's cell, yet there are no marks of violence. How did the Chairman die? He died because Turner used his powers of mind control to engender a heart attack, or some other similarly cataclysmic episode. Turner's Emergent powers satisfactorily explain the two questions that need to be answered. Why was Noble in his cell? And how did Noble die? With those answers, and the incontrovertible facts of where the body was found, it will be clear that Turner is guilty. Even the redoubtable Aletheia will have to concede defeat."

"Wait a minute," said Adam. "You just said you tested Kit and that he has no Emergent powers."

Goodfellow was losing patience. "We really don't have time for this. This afternoon you will outline the Emergent scenario to the court, then call on Silas Drahan, Head of Security, to provide evidence of Turner's Emergent powers. We should be able to wrap this case up by the end of today."

And with that, he dismissed Adam.

oooOooo

When Adam had gone Goodfellow summoned Silas Drahan.

Drahan was Simon Goodfellow's most reliable supporter. Goodfellow had discovered, years before, that Drahan, of Polish and Estonian extraction, was a man after his own heart. He liked order. In particular, he liked imposing it on others. Drahan had never been close to John Noble, but it was Noble who had recognised his talent and appointed him Head of Security.

"Yes, sir, how can I help?" asked Drahan. He stood in Goodfellow's presence, waiting for instructions.

"I need to brief you on your part in this afternoon's proceedings," said Goodfellow.

Drahan listened carefully. His cold grey eyes, sharp and alert, were focused on Goodfellow throughout. Simon could not help thinking that it was a good thing they were on the same side. Silas Drahan was an intimidating figure, above average height, powerfully built, with a heavy facial bone structure. His forehead hung over his eyes, giving him a slightly primitive and threatening look. Not a man to be argued with. Happily, Simon and Silas had a natural rapport. They had the same approach to their work, and enjoyed similar types of pleasure in their leisure time.

"Can you remember everything?" Goodfellow asked at the end of the briefing. "Do you have any questions?"

"Only this," said Drahan, with a grimace that approximated to a grin. "What are you going to do with Aletheia after the trial?"

They both laughed.

"Whatever I choose to do, I promise you can have whatever is left when I've finished with her," said Goodfellow.

"With all due respect," Drahan replied, "knowing you, what's left probably won't be worth having."

45. The trial concludes

When the trial resumed, everyone was curious to know what line the prosecution would take. They didn't have long to wait: Adam followed instructions and introduced the factor of Emergent powers.

"The defendant has been held here for the last few weeks on suspicion of being an Emergent," Adam announced.

He was surprised at the reaction. There were gasps of astonishment and fear from many in the audience. Emergents were the only real threat to the existence of the Praesidium and its staff. They were exceedingly rare, but even the slightest suspicion that an Emergent was active caused alarm. Bringing one into the PCC, into the heart of the Praesidium, struck many as foolhardy and shocking.

"It is the prosecution's argument that the only explanation for the facts in this case is that the defendant used his Emergent powers to lure John Noble to his cell and then to terminate his life."

"What the prosecutor lacks in eloquence," said the judge acidly, "he makes up for with brevity."

"The prosecution calls Silas Drahan, Head of Security, to the stand," Adam added. He had fulfilled his role. As he sat down, he looked at Eve. She had watched his performance with tears in her eyes.

Silas strode to the stand. "Over the last few weeks, Security and Internal Discipline have been examining and monitoring the defendant with the purpose of determining the extent to which he is capable of exercising Emergent powers. We have clear proof that he is capable of mind control. We have had sworn evidence from David Minofel, the practitioner hired by the former Chairman, that the defendant took control of the mind of Jedwell Boon, the practitioner's factotum, persuading Boon on several occasions to disobey his master and execute the defendant's bidding. On one occasion, the defendant rendered Boon, a powerful man, too weak to raise a salt cellar from the table. On other occasions, the defendant compelled Boon to act out of character, again disobeying or disregarding his master and jeopardising a mission. The defendant also persuaded an assistant to the practitioner, a Miss Tomic, a woman almost a daughter to the practitioner, to betray the trust between them and attempt to suborn one of David Minofel's protégées. We conclude from this evidence that the Emergent powers of the defendant are entirely consistent with the prosecution's contention that the blind man lured John Noble to his cell and then, using mind control over his body, murdered him."

Aletheia rose to intervene, but Silas indicated he had not completed his evidence and that he would brook no interruption.

"As final proof, I wish to submit some readings from our wireless monitoring of the defendant's brain activity. On the night of the murder, there were two spikes in the defendant's alpha wave activity. The first coincided with our estimate of the period during which John Noble was making his way to the defendant's cell. The second spike came some twenty minutes later, after Noble entered the cell. We can only assume the defendant summoned Noble to make some demand of him. When John Noble refused, the defendant, out of anger or spite, demonstrated his Emergent powers by snuffing out the life of the Praesidium's Chairman."

Before Aletheia could speak, Simon Goodfellow took a moment to thank Silas Drahan for his exemplary testimony. He then addressed Aletheia.

"As the judge in this case, I have been determined that this should be a fair trial, and I have allowed you some latitude in presenting the defence. I am prepared to extend that latitude further still, but I must warn you that there are limits. I suggest you try to emulate the most striking feature of the prosecutor's submission – that is, its brevity."

Aletheia rose. She had been hoping that, against the odds, either Jedwell Boon or Kathrin would appear and testify to what had happened, but it was now clear that she would have to argue simply on the evidence before the court. "We have two versions of events. The first version asserts that John Noble was murdered – not in Kit Turner's cell, but elsewhere – and that the body was then placed in Kit Turner's cell by the murderer or his accomplice. The second version, as you have just heard, involves the employment of unnatural powers to lure the Chairman to the defendant's cell and then to kill him. You might well think that both versions are improbable but, based on the known facts, this court must decide which is most likely to be true. Given that my client has no motive for killing the Chairman, that the prosecution offers no testable evidence to support the charge against my client, and that I know my version to be true, the conclusion is obvious."

Aletheia sat down.

Judge Goodfellow began his summing-up. "It will come as no surprise to those who have followed the evidence in this case that my conclusions differ from those of the defence counsel. The facts are that the body of the Chairman was found in the locked cell of the defendant. No one other than the defendant was present in the cell. The defence counsel dismisses the evidence of the last witness, including the spikes in the alpha wave chart, out of hand ..."

"Anyone can produce a timeline chart with two spikes in it," Aletheia interjected.

"You go too far," roared the judge. "You show contempt for all our expert witnesses, and now you impugn the integrity of one of our most trusted board members. Who the hell do you think you are, young woman? You seem to have interpreted my leniency towards you as weakness. Do not do so again."

"There is no proof against, and no motive for, my client," Aletheia continued, unabashed. "Quite apart from the inherent improbability of my client being able to exercise unnatural mental powers over others – for which, incidentally, there is no evidence other than highly dubious speculative and anecdotal trivia – my client could have no possible motive for killing the Chairman. The suggestion that he killed the Chairman because the Chairman refused an unspecified request is pathetic. You see before you a good man. Does he seem like a man who would kill another out of anger or spite?"

"And what motive do you have," asked the judge, with a sneer, "for your putative murderer of the Chairman, the one who is supposed to have placed the body in Turner's cell?"

That was a question Simon Goodfellow should never have asked of Aletheia. There was a dreadful silence, a silence that grew in strength until it became almost unbearable.

Goodfellow looked into Aletheia's eyes, his face at first impassive. Then, as he realised what she intended to say, his eyes blazed with rage. In the darkest, deepest corner of his mind he emitted an unheard howl of rage. Aletheia looked at Eve and saw that she had fear clearly scrawled across her face. Adam looked at Aletheia, who looked back at him with contempt. Kit looked up for the first time in the proceedings and turned towards Aletheia. He nodded, accepting that she had no choice. She answered the judge's question.

"The motive of a vain and evil man who had just failed to oust the Chairman from his position on the board. A man who knew that the only way to recover the situation was to murder him. There is your motive, and I accuse you, Simon Goodfellow, of John Noble's murder."

46. The sentence

Once the uproar had subsided, Judge Goodfellow spoke.

"This time you have gone too far, far too far. Your disrespect for the testimony of Doctors Sandmore and Diss was impolite and distasteful. Your insinuation that our Head of Security would fabricate evidence was outrageous. I warned you, and what was your response? You accuse me of the crime for which this blind man faces trial. What are you trying to achieve? You are scarcely serving the interest of your client by alienating witnesses and accusing the judge. I can only assume you are seeking notoriety, regardless of the cost. Well, notoriety is yours, but the cost will be high. Arrest her."

Two security officials, who had been stationed in the court as backup for those guarding Kit, stepped forward to seize Aletheia. Aletheia looked over to Kit. He looked back, shook his head and minded to her two words: "Not yet." Aletheia allowed herself to be taken down without a struggle.

With Aletheia removed, Goodfellow immediately resumed his summing-up. "The court has been meticulous in following procedure and, as all have seen, has allowed the defence counsel unprecedented latitude, a latitude which sadly has been grossly abused. Nevertheless, this has been a scrupulously fair trial. It remains only for me to give my judgement and pass sentence."

Simon paused to allow everyone to prepare themselves for the verdict. Then, in his most authoritative voice, he declared, "I find the accused, Kit Turner, guilty of the murder of the late and much-lamented Chairman of the Praesidium, John Noble. Murder of any senior member of the Praesidium is a capital offence. In this instance there can be no doubt what the punishment must be. The defendant will be taken from this place to his cell. From there, tomorrow morning, he will be taken to the place of execution, there to be hanged by the neck until dead. We abandoned public executions many years ago, but on this occasion, because the crime is so heinous and because it has touched everyone who knew and loved John Noble, I propose to make an exception and revive the practice. The execution will take place in the square outside the Praesidium's main building at eleven o'clock tomorrow morning."

47. Thoughts that do lie too deep

On the evening of the day the trial ended, Adam returned to his apartment with his mind in turmoil. He had done everything the Praesidium had asked of him. He had even betrayed his friend.

He settled into an armchair in his apartment and poured a whisky. Of course, he hadn't really betrayed Kit because Goodfellow was going to find Kit guilty, with or without Adam's co-operation. So, what Adam did hadn't mattered – didn't matter.

Except it did matter. It mattered because Adam had not fought for the life of his friend. It was a fight he could not have won, but he had a nagging feeling that he should have fought anyway.

On the other hand, if he had fought and lost, what damage would he have done to others? At the very least he would have ended his career, a career that promised so much. His chance to exercise real power, to fulfil the Praesidium's objectives, to make, rather than seek and fail to find, the truth – all would have been lost. At worst, the Praesidium might have simply decided to eliminate him. After all, they had invested heavily in developing him, and if that investment had been a waste of resources, they might well have decided it was best to cut their losses.

If they eliminated him, why would they hesitate to take down the others? The questors had put themselves in harm's way by infiltrating the Westminster PCC. It made no sense to let any of them return to their own world now that they knew of the PCC's existence.

So if fighting for Kit made no sense, why did Adam feel sick to the core of his being?

He decided to go up on to the roof of the apartment. He needed fresh air. He poured himself another whisky, walked out on to the balcony and made his way up to the roof. It was a clear night. He breathed deeply. Suddenly, he felt utterly exhausted. He sat on the seat beneath the pergola, downed the whisky and fell asleep.

Dreams are a mystery. Some people think they foretell the future; others that they are the mind's way of making sense of it all. Most dreams fade away as soon as we awake, as though they exist in another world to which we have only fleeting access. Occasionally, a dream is so vivid, or so traumatic, that it survives into the daylight and we attempt to apply rational analysis to tease out its significance, almost always unsuccessfully.

Adam's dream was different.

He was standing in a large hall. It was not the Praesidium courtroom, much less God's Hall of Justice in the Garden of Eden at Hook. It was a large featureless space, enclosed within large featureless walls. At one end, on a dais, sat the three members of the tribunal. In the middle was Aletheia. On her right was Kit and on her left was Numpty. All three were silent, waiting for Adam to speak.

"Why am I here?" he asked.

The members of the tribunal talked among themselves for a moment and then Numpty spoke. "Do you mean why are you standing here before us? Or do you mean why do you exist?"

Adam showed some irritation. Numpty was being silly again. "I mean why am I standing here before you?" he snapped.

"Numpty's questions were not silly," said Aletheia, "and the answer to both questions is this – you are here to be judged."

Adam laughed. He felt the hair bristle on the back of his neck. "I really don't think any one of you is in a position to judge me. I'm not on trial."

"Yes, you are," said Aletheia. "That's what this is all about. You are charged with multiple crimes. Kit is on the panel because you have wronged him most grievously, Numpty is here because he is the most honest and bravest of us all, and I am here because I am the goddess of truth."

"And what am I charged with?" Adam asked.

"That is for you to say," Aletheia replied.

Adam laughed again. "So I'm supposed to lay charges against myself."

Then he stopped laughing. He felt a panic attack coming on, just as he had in his darkest moments following Bella's death. After his daughter had been killed in a storm, he had questioned everything, including his own existence. Was he anything more than the grief and pain he felt? Once again he was having to look inside himself.

Numpty spoke. "I've felt that too. I've wondered if there is anything more to me than the memories I accumulate as I live my life. But after some discussions with Luke, I have concluded there must be an 'I' to ponder those memories, to understand their significance and to make sense of my existence. It is therefore perfectly possible for you to lay charges against yourself. Indeed, there is no one better placed to undertake the task. You are to be both prosecutor and defence counsel."

"'After some discussions with Luke!' After some discussions with my dog? What are you talking about?" Adam decided Numpty had lost it once and for all.

"Let's stick to the point," Aletheia intervened. "What do you charge yourself with and how do you plead?"

"I can't answer that. I won't answer that," said Adam. "Why should I?"

"We are not here to punish you, Adam," said Aletheia. "We are here to assuage your guilt. You do feel guilty, don't you?"

Adam was confused.

"You need to dig down inside you," Numpty suggested. "Surely there you will find the cause of your guilt."

"I haven't said I feel guilty," said Adam.

"Avarice, blackmail, murder – do any of those ring a bell?" Aletheia asked.

Adam began to squirm.

"That's your soul feeling a bit sick," said Numpty. "Speaking as an inveterate osmotic gouger, I know just how you feel. The deeper you dig into the darkness the worse you will feel. All the dank, dark dirt closes in on you. Then just when you think you will suffocate, when you are sure you are about to cease to exist, only then are you finally sure you do exist and, with luck, a blade of hope pops out of the earth."

"I'm sure I exist," said Adam, pulling himself together. "As for guilt, I have done no more than was necessary."

"Then how about betrayal?" enquired Aletheia. "Was betrayal necessary?"

Kit intervened before Adam could answer. "There was nothing Adam could do. I was going to be found guilty and condemned to death, whatever he did. There was no point in Adam losing everything in an heroic, but futile, gesture."

"Is that what *you* think, Adam?" asked Aletheia.

Adam felt tears begin to form in his eyes. If Kit had not intervened, he would have said exactly what Kit said, and he would have justified himself. But hearing Kit defend him was too much.

"Sorry," Adam choked on the word. "I'm so sorry."

Kit stepped down from the dais and moved to embrace Adam, to comfort him. Adam laid his head on the offered shoulder and sobbed, his eyes closed.

oooOooo

"It's a little too late for that, don't you think?" said a voice next to Adam's ear.

Adam reluctantly pulled back. The dais was gone. The walls were gone. He was nowhere. He was nowhere – and he was in the arms of David Minofel.

"You need to sleep," said Minofel. "You are so tired. You need to sleep."

Adam was about to tell Minofel that he was already asleep, that all this was a dream, but suddenly he felt exhausted. Minofel laid him down, and Adam slept.

When he awoke he was lying on the ferny floor of a dark forest. Tall trees brooded over him, like menacing sentinels. High above him the canopy of branches and leaves was so dense it obscured the night sky.

"Where am I?" he asked. But there was no one to answer.

He stood up and peered into the gloom – nothing but tall trees wherever he looked. He was rooted to the spot; there was no reason to move in any one direction.

Suddenly, a wind began to blow and the leaves in the tree tops began to whisper. Adam tried to make out what they were saying. It was difficult because there were so many voices, but after a minute or so he realised they were all saying just one word: "Confess. Confess. Confess."

Adam fell to his knees and words poured out of his mouth:

> There is a world, the depth of which I am afraid,
> where truth lies huddled in a dream
> and threatens to invade my mind
> with all terrors of mankind –
> worlds of forests, shuffling leaves,
> children playing endlessly,
> murdered by such hands as these
> beneath the roots of giant trees.

The wind ceased. There was silence. There was darkness. There was nothing. Adam felt himself fragmenting, shattered by a primal fear.

Then someone took his hand. In a black and empty universe, he felt an overwhelming sense of comfort. He was reforming. A woman's voice asked, "Now do you understand?"

Adam awoke, and awoke, and awoke.

48. A surprising reaction

Manfred Bloch returned home after two days of continuous work, half in the control room of his Technical Division and the other half down in the chamber containing the Crucible of Eternal Light.

Bloch was a highly competent and experienced engineer, but what he had discovered unnerved him. Somehow, the flow of energy generated by the Eternal Light had been adjusted to allow the possibility of external interference in the control systems. There was nothing wrong with the power supply; it was flowing normally. The control room systems were all working perfectly. The only problem – and it had taken Bloch's team hours to discover it – was that their control of the system now seemed to require the co-operation, the acquiescence, of the Eternal Light itself. As an engineer, Manfred found the concept difficult to comprehend, and the best combination of words he had been able to devise to describe the situation was "consensual control". It seemed the Praesidium had complete control of the Eternal Light, just as long as the Eternal Light was happy to allow it.

Manfred decided to have a shower and a good long think before reporting his findings to Simon Goodfellow. If he found it difficult to explain the concept of "consensual control" to his fellow engineers – and he did – Goodfellow would certainly find it impossible to grasp, and would probably be inclined to conclude his senior engineer had taken leave of his senses.

Manfred also badly needed to talk to Kathrin. When he'd left her she was sleeping, but before she had drifted off, it was clear she was upset, possibly even traumatised. Manfred knew his wife had her own life, and needed space and time for herself, but he loved her and, whether they were together or apart, if anyone upset Kathrin, they would have to answer to him.

When he reached his home, he found the main door double locked and the alarm set. He called Kathrin on the intercom. No one answered. He used his key to unlock the door and entered the code to deactivate the alarm. The code was rejected. He entered the code a second time. Again, it was rejected. After thirty seconds the alarm went off. Manfred, confused and irritated, was shaking his head when Kathrin appeared, holding a gun.

"What's going on?" he asked.

Kathrin dropped the gun, ran to him, and threw herself into his arms. He held her.

"Shut the door," she said. "Shut it and lock it."

He did as she asked.

"The code doesn't work," he said, referring to the incessant ringing of the alarm.

Kathrin punched in some numbers and the alarm stopped.

"What's going on? Did you change the code?"

Kathrin took her husband by the arm and led him into the sitting room.

"Kathrin, talk to me," Manfred pleaded. "What is the matter?"

She sat down on the settee and he sat beside her. "I will tell you everything, but you must promise to help me, and forgive me," she said.

"Of course," said Manfred.

"No, I can't ask you to forgive me. I have no right. You must decide when I have finished. But promise to let me finish, and please remember that whatever I have done I have always loved you, and I always will."

"Please tell me what is going on. Why are you so upset?"

So Kathrin took her husband's hand and told him all. He paled when she told him of her deep attachment to John Noble, and shook when she confessed to her affair with Goodfellow. Given how much he disliked Goodfellow, the affair seemed calculated to cause him maximum pain, ameliorated only a little by the fact that she had embarked on her relationship with the Deputy Chairman solely in order to destroy him.

It was when she told Manfred how John Noble died, how she had been forced to witness the murder, how Goodfellow had defiled her on the night of the murder, that Manfred Bloch found a channel wide enough to accommodate his emotions. Goodfellow would answer for his crimes; Manfred would have his revenge. It would be his gift, and his absolution, for Kathrin.

Then Kathrin told him about the visit of Gustave Houry, how Houry had killed Numpty, and that she had killed Houry. "Simon wants me dead," she sobbed. "He knows I can destroy him. He sent Houry. He will send others. That's why I locked the door and changed the code. Nowhere is safe."

"Where are the bodies?" asked Manfred.

"They're in the guest bathroom. I had to drag them there myself."

"We will leave them there for now. We need to bring Goodfellow to justice before he does any more damage."

"Can you forgive me?" Kathrin asked.

"This is not the time to talk of forgiveness," said Manfred. "But this I will say, as you said to me – I have always loved you, and I always will."

There was a loud ringing at the door. Kathrin started.

"Don't worry, that will be the alarm people. Once the alarm is activated they have to attend, even if the alarm is cancelled."

Manfred opened the door.

Four guards from Security forced him back into the house. Two guards secured Manfred. The other two seized Kathrin.

"What is this?" demanded Manfred. "How dare you! Leave my wife alone. I am the Technical Director. I am a board member of the Praesidium."

"You are under arrest for collusion in the murder of John Noble," said the guard in charge. "By order of the new Chairman."

oooOooo

Manfred and Kathrin were taken to the detention centre, where they were put in separate cells. Neither was given any further explanation for their arrest. Manfred demanded to see Silas Drahan, Head of Security. An hour later, Drahan entered Manfred's cell.

"What is the meaning of this?" demanded Manfred.

"The charge is that as soon as Simon Goodfellow failed in his bid for the chairmanship, you realised that the only obstacle to your accession to the top job was John Noble. You knew that Kit Turner was extremely dangerous and that he was determined to destroy the Praesidium by means of his Emergent powers. You therefore devised a plan to persuade Noble to visit the blind man. You told Noble that he needed to see for himself what the Emergent was capable of. You offered the blind man his freedom if you became Chairman. We all know how the meeting ended."

"But that is a pack of lies," said Manfred Bloch.

"You asked why you are here and I am telling you. Whether the charge is true is, as you must know, irrelevant. The matter is unlikely to go to trial. Simon will almost certainly decide to deal with you out of the public gaze."

"And what do you think the High Council will say when they discover the new Chairman has murdered this Praesidium's Technical Director?"

"He will argue that in this instance it was better to deal with the matter privately. It would irreparably damage the reputation of the board if it were known that a board member had used an Emergent to engineer the death of a sitting Chairman. So look on the bright side. You will not be shamed in court. You and Kathrin will die in an appalling accident. Your good name will remain untarnished."

"So why have we been arrested?" asked Manfred.

"It takes a little time to arrange a convincing accident, and our new Chairman was worried that if you and Kathrin were free you might decide to promulgate the most atrocious slanders against him."

"You mean we might assert that the disgusting little pervert murdered John Noble himself?" said Manfred.

"Quite," said Drahan. "The only word I would quibble with is 'little' – Simon is of at least average height."

When Manfred remained silent, Silas Drahan made to leave.

"There is one thing you should tell your master," said Manfred. "Tell him I have identified the problem with the power supply."

"I will," said Silas. "I'm sure he will be grateful."

"You misunderstand me," said Manfred. "Tell him I have identified the problem. I haven't solved it."

49. Preparing for the endgame

When Eve and Prune Leach returned from the trial that evening, the mood in Andrew Rimzil's laboratory was sombre.

There was no need for them to recount what had happened. Rambler, the Storyteller and Luke had watched the court proceedings on Andrew's monitoring system. Andrew had been at the controls of the paradox device, ready to take any action that was necessary. Once or twice he'd been tempted to intervene, but Kit had insisted Andrew should use the paradox device only as a last resort.

That evening they sat and talked. The main topic, of course, was Kit. If the questors did nothing, Kit faced a hanging the following morning. Using the enhanced paradox device, Andrew could remove Kit from the Praesidium's clutches in the twinkling of an eye, or even quicker. If Andrew gave the device a few simple commands, Kit could be out of his Praesidium cell and back in the Smiths' house in Harrow – or, indeed, anywhere else that he might want to be. But throughout his ordeal, Kit had remained adamant: he wanted to stay where he was; he *had* to stay where he was.

Why? Because of Adam? Or because of Kit's desire to reactivate the Fourth Beginning? Or, as Kit explained it, because of both. Kit knew that Adam was key to any effort to reactivate a Beginning – and so did Slievins. That was why David Minofel had selected Adam and groomed him. That was why Adam had been brought to the Praesidium PCC for further training. Slievins was determined to make sure that Adam would never again even consider embarking on another quest.

Adam had hankered after the truth. They had given him the truth. It wasn't the truth he had wanted or expected. It was a hard, unrelenting, unforgiving truth, the truth of a deconstructionist: the whole is simply the sum of its parts. Man is nasty, brutish, greedy, lustful, vain and corruptible; his aspirations to be better than he is are a perversion of his true nature. Such aspirations cause anxiety, guilt and a host of mental disorders – above all, they diminish him.

Of course, Slievins' truth had an upside. It offered a kind of freedom for those bold enough to seize it, and with that freedom, a chance for untold wealth and unlimited power. Slievins people ruled the world. The Praesidium was man's greatest achievement. It was an entity created by man, for man, to enable man to fulfil himself. With the power of the Eternal Light and the help of the Monitaurs, the Praesidium kept man on track. Life was a zero-sum game. There was suffering for the many so there could be joy for the few, poverty for the generations so there could be riches for the elite, death for the masses to facilitate truly fulfilled lives for the chosen.

In short, Slievins and the Praesidium had stripped Adam of any moral sense – or, as Kit had put it, they had destroyed him as a human being.

"So, what are we going to do about Kit?" asked Prune. The conversation had been wide-ranging but failed to produce a plan of action.

"And what about Aletheia?" added Eve.

"I've a feeling Aletheia can look after herself," Andrew said, answering Eve's question. "I could see on the scanner that she had half a mind to resist arrest. I'm pretty sure Kit asked her to restrain herself. I don't know what she is capable of, but if I were Goodfellow, I would tread carefully. After all, she is the daughter of Prometheus."

"Which brings us back to Kit," said Prune.

"Well, we are not going to let them hang him," said Andrew firmly. "I don't care what Kit has told us. If it comes to it, I will remove him. I will have a lock on him as soon as he appears in the square outside the main building, and I'll take him out of there before they can do him any more harm."

"He said we should do nothing without his approval," Eve reminded them.

"I know," said Andrew. "But we can't let them kill him. What good would it do? None. It would only show that Kit could stick to his principles, whatever the cost, but no one in the Praesidium would know or care. Let's face it, they have a rather different value system."

"So why has he put up with what they've already done to him?" Eve asked. "You saw the state he was in. He's lost weight. He's in pain. They've starved and beaten him. What's the point?"

"I think he's trying to save Adam," said Rambler. "Funnily enough, I think Kit and the Praesidium are playing the same game. Adam is the prize."

"Well, if you're right," said Andrew, "we can't let Kit lose his life over a game – a game I'm sorry to say, Eve, he is almost certain to lose."

The matter was settled. As a last resort, Andrew would use the paradox device to save Kit.

The questors' main concern was the fate of Kit, but Eve was not yet prepared to give up all hope for Adam. She had known Adam longer than any of the others, and although she would have been the first to admit he was far from perfect she would not believe he had been corrupted beyond redemption. He was the father of the child she carried, a child that would need its father. When they had initiated the Fourth Beginning, they had achieved a union that was more joyous and complete than she had imagined possible. No, she would not give up on Adam yet.

50. The day of execution

The following morning was a crisp, clear sunny day in the Praesidium PCC. In normal circumstances, the weather in the PCC matched the weather in central London, but that day, on Goodfellow's orders, the Praesidium's weather had been tweaked in order to lift everyone's spirits, as bright, light days with a warm gentle breeze tend to do.

Eve set out early before the other questors awoke. She dressed and slipped out of Andrew's still shielded laboratory and into the corridor that led to the main reception hall. Despite the early hour, there were some people about. Service staff were making their way to work while others were returning at the end of their shifts. The reception desk in the hall was staffed twenty-four hours a day, every day.

Eve left the reception hall and headed for the bridge that led to the accommodation block. She stood on the moving walkway, giving herself a chance to rehearse, once again, what she would say to Adam. She would remind him of what they had shared together, the good times and the bad; she would tell him of her hopes for the child she carried and the role she prayed he would play; she would tell him that Kit was a good man and a good friend, and that no half-decent human being would connive in his destruction. She would prove that Kit was innocent.

When she reached the door to Adam's apartment it was still very early. She hesitated before pressing the buzzer. Adam was probably asleep, but what she had to say couldn't wait.

When Adam opened the door, he was shaved, showered, and fully dressed.

"Eve," he said unnecessarily.

"May I come in?"

"Of course," said Adam. "You've no idea how pleased I am to see you."

"Why?" said Eve, surprised.

"There's a problem," Adam replied. "There's a really big problem. Kit is innocent and I have to prevent this hanging. I'm a board member – at least, I think I am – so I have some influence, but if I try to go up against Simon Goodfellow I'm likely to end up in the same position as Kit."

Eve threw her arms round Adam and burst into tears.

"What's the matter?" asked an astonished Adam.

Between sobs, Eve explained that she and the others had thought they had lost him.

"Thanks for the vote of confidence," said Adam.

"You prosecuted Kit. You've gone along with everything Minofel and the Praesidium have asked of you. What else did you expect?"

"You're right," Adam said, conceding the point. "And when we have time, we will need to talk. I've done some things – many things – that will shock you, things that seemed perfectly reasonable at the time. Things, I suspect, that neither you nor the law will forgive. But I'm not going to add the killing of my friend to my list of offences. I will make a stand this morning, but we have to be careful, and I will need help."

Eve was about to explain Andrew's plan to save Kit when the door to Adam's apartment burst open. Four security guards entered, followed by Silas Drahan and Simon Goodfellow himself.

"Will you never give up?" Simon Goodfellow enquired of Eve. "If Adam wanted your company I'm sure he would have found time to visit you. I'll make allowances for your condition. It is not uncommon for women at your stage in a pregnancy to develop a certain mental flaccidity, so I shall treat you with kindness and courtesy, but we have a busy morning ahead of us. We have a ceremony at which Adam has his part to play. We really don't have time for emotional outbursts or uxorial tantrums. My apartment is not far from here. You will be taken there. My staff will ensure your comfort. Adam and I will visit you there as soon as the ceremony is over."

"Ceremony!" Eve exploded. "You call the hanging of an innocent man for a crime you committed a 'ceremony'?"

"Be careful, my dear," Goodfellow warned. "The last young lady to make such an appalling and groundless accusation was treated with less consideration, less kindness and courtesy than I have offered you. You are Adam's wife and deserve respect. But with respect come responsibilities. I suggest you go quietly to my apartment and wait for us there."

Two guards stepped forward, one on either side of Eve, and ushered her to the door. She looked at Adam. He indicated she should comply.

"Sorry about that," said Goodfellow when Eve had left. "Not what you need before such an important occasion. But we must all make allowances for the ladies, eh!"

"Time for us to go," said Silas Drahan. He was wearing his full ceremonial uniform, to which was attached an impressive array of medals for outstanding service to the Praesidium.

oooOooo

There was something of a carnival spirit in the square outside the main Praesidium building. Flags were flying. The Communications Department, a subdivision of Internal Discipline, had found a stock of balloons in the department's storeroom, purchased for the celebration of John Noble's appointment as Chairman some fifteen years earlier. They had decided to issue them free of charge to all Praesidium staff. Given the department was operating despite the strange absence of its leader, Gustave Houry, this surprise initiative was a feather in the cap for Gustave's deputy.

The same department had arranged for stalls providing tea, coffee, sandwiches and bars of chocolate to be set up on all four sides of the square, to serve the needs of the milling crowd.

One or two of the more entrepreneurial staff from House Services had set up charcoal braziers to provide hot food, such as burgers in buns and shish kebabs in pitta bread, a dietary option proving more popular than the sandwiches. Security had wanted to close down these unlicensed food stalls, but Goodfellow intervened, saying there could be "an exception to the rule on this most exceptional of days".

The provision of alcoholic beverages had been considered but rejected after consultation with Silas Drahan. Quite apart from security concerns, Drahan had suggested that eleven in the morning was a little too early to start drinking.

The mood of the crowd was mixed but essentially positive. All the junior staff were delighted to have a break from their repetitive administrative tasks. Those at the level of middle management had more conflicted emotions. The break was welcome, but the work still had to be done. The actual execution would be over quickly enough, but there would be too much excitement in the crowd for staff to be expected to troop back to their offices, settle down and work in the afternoon.

In the middle of the square stood the newly erected gallows. To indicate the seriousness of the occasion and the finality of the punishment, the platform on which the gallows stood had been draped in black, in contrast to the brightly coloured bunting, flags and balloons among the spectators who, unlike the blind man, were able to look forward to a happy, sunny afternoon.

"You have done well, " said Goodfellow to Drahan. "And at such short notice."

"It's not a problem," Drahan assured Goodfellow. "Gustave's deputy has stepped up to the plate and done an excellent job."

Simon noted Drahan's implied criticism of Houry, evidence of the continuing rivalry between the Heads of Security and Internal Discipline for his favour. "You need friction to generate fire," was one of Simon's favourite sayings.

"I want your men to bring Aletheia from her cell and seat her at my side," said Goodfellow.

"You wish to have the defence counsel witness the outcome of her impeccable defence?" Drahan enquired, with a laugh.

"Of course," Goodfellow replied. "I have lots of plans for the delectable Aletheia. I feel I have so much to teach her. My first lesson will be that there is a high price to pay for attempting to thwart me. In this instance, it will be someone else who pays the price, but even so I think the blind man's execution will cost her more than a little."

Goodfellow and Drahan walked through the crowds. It was a good opportunity for the new Chairman to meet those over whom he now exercised absolute power. Simon hoped that his presence among the people at the execution of the man who had cruelly murdered his predecessor would garner approval. Not that approval and praise mattered a jot when the lives of everyone depended on his goodwill, but there was undoubtedly something gratifying about the sycophantic antics of the oppressed when in the presence of their oppressor.

Thirteen seats had been set up in front of the gallows platform for board members and special guests. All the members of the board, including Adam, were present – except, of course, for the Head of Internal Discipline. The Monitaurs – in human form, of course – had also been invited to witness the execution, in recognition of the work they had all done on Adam. Drahan issued orders for an extra chair to accommodate Aletheia. By ten thirty, those who had been allocated seats had taken them. Aletheia was brought in under guard and seated next to Goodfellow.

"I realise this will be upsetting for you," said Goodfellow, as though preparing a recalcitrant child for punishment, "but it is for your own good. You did your best to defend your client, but in the end the evidence was against you. That's how things work. Now he must suffer the consequences."

Aletheia looked around the square. She took in the scene at a glance. It was a beautiful sunny day. The people were animated, chatting to friends and work colleagues, drinking their tea or coffee, enjoying their snacks and waiting with curiosity and excitement for the main event. Flags and balloons contributed to the picture of a happy, animated country fair.

"How many of these people know that Kit is innocent?" she asked.

Simon frowned. "Oh dear. It seems that despite your legal training you haven't really grasped how the judicial process works. Kit is not innocent. Yesterday, he was found guilty, after due process."

"Yes," said Aletheia, unabashed, "but nevertheless he is innocent. I know he is innocent. You know he is innocent. Who else knows?"

"Why do you ask?" said Goodfellow, irritated, but also curious.

"I ask because the truth is important to me," said Aletheia. "In the end, truth conquers all."

"I thought that was love, not truth," scoffed Goodfellow. "Not my kind of love, I hasten to add, which explores the deeper, darker recesses of the soul by gouging into the orifices of the body and peeling away the cosmetic skin and the pinguid, oleaginous flesh. No, not that kind of love! I mean the other kind of love – the vacuous, sentimental nonsense of religions and romance, propagated by cynical deceivers to calm the fears of an ignorant population, who are quite rightly terrified by the appalling nature of the human predicament."

Aletheia was not impressed. "You do realise that you are mentally sick? And you also realise that I cannot allow you to execute Kit."

"If anyone is delusional, my dear, I think it much more likely to be you than me. In a few minutes, the condemned man will mount the scaffold. I take no pleasure in this man's death – it's far too straightforward and abrupt for my taste – but die he must. He has been found guilty of the most heinous crime and must face the consequences."

As Simon Goodfellow spoke, Kit emerged from the entrance of the Praesidium's main building escorted by two security guards. A palpable wave of excitement swept across the square. The intense magnetic resonance imaging head coil had been removed, but the marks where the sensors had been attached were clearly visible. The guards guided Kit towards the platform and helped him up on to the scaffold, almost carrying him up the steps. The murmur of the crowd rose, and then subsided into silence.

Silas Drahan got up from his seat and turned to address the assembly.

"This man, Kit Turner, came here as a guest, but he had plans to destroy us and all we have worked for. He abused our hospitality. He lured our Chairman into his presence, then killed him. He hoped that in the ensuing grief and confusion he could attack the pulsing heart of the Praesidium, the Eternal Light. He claims to have worked alone, but we believe he is part of a wider terrorist conspiracy. Security is exploring all possibilities, and will ensure the safety of the Praesidium and all who are loyal to it."

The accusation of conspiracy and a threatened attack on the Praesidium's power source had been concocted by Silas Drahan himself. As he had explained to Simon Goodfellow, it would do no harm to persuade everyone in the Praesidium that the blind man had been a threat to all of them. This was not the execution of a murderer; this was the elimination of a serious threat to the PCC itself.

Ironically, his fabrication was not too far from the truth. In the questors' laboratory, Andrew, Prune, Rambler and the Storyteller were watching closely the proceedings in the square. Luke was lying in the bed Eve had provided. To the casual observer, he seemed asleep, but in fact he was reaching out to Kit to comfort him as best he could. Andrew was seated at the paradox device. He had locked on to Kit from the moment he had appeared. If need be, he could remove Kit instantaneously. In the corner of Andrew's scanning screen was a red dot. Activating the red dot took Andrew into a simple routine that enabled him to constrict or block the energy loop that fed the Eternal Light.

Silas Drahan addressed the crowd. "It is customary to offer the condemned man an opportunity to express his final thoughts, but this particular felon has refused to speak throughout his trial. We can therefore reasonably dispense with this formality and proceed directly to the execution."

He nodded to the executioner, who had taken a position next to the gallows.

Adam stood up.

Immediately, Goodfellow addressed him. "Be careful what you say, Adam. You risk losing everything. And I mean, everything – everything you have hoped for, everything you have worked for, and everything you hold dear."

"This will not stand," Adam called out to the assembly. "This man, Kit Turner, is a good man and he is innocent of any crime. There is no one here less guilty than he." Adam turned, walked over to the platform, and climbed the steps. He stood beside Kit. "I have chosen. I am with him."

A confused hum came from the crowd.

Before Goodfellow could speak, Drahan barked an order to the guards who had escorted Kit to the gallows. "Arrest that man."

"On what charge?" Aletheia demanded.

Drahan turned towards Aletheia and snarled, "Interfering in a judicial process will do for now. Later, I favour accessory to murder. Accessory after the fact – and for all we know a conspirator before."

"Take that man down," ordered Goodfellow, pointing to Adam and addressing the guards. "And get on with the execution," he addressed the executioner.

Goodfellow was angry. What should have been a simple salutary lesson in the consequences of crime was fast becoming a farce.

Aletheia walked to the platform and climbed up to join Adam and Kit.

"I also testify to this man's innocence," said Aletheia. "I speak the truth. Let any who deny it beware."

There were now six people beside the gallows: Kit, Adam, Aletheia, the two guards and the executioner. Goodfellow could see that with only two guards immediately available, removing Adam and Aletheia could be problematical if they resisted. It would, in any case, take time and risk making this serious and sombre ceremony appear ridiculous. Adam's assertion of Kit's innocence and Aletheia's endorsement of his words didn't help matters.

"Hang the man now," Goodfellow commanded. Only quick incisive action could redeem the situation.

The executioner understood what was required. He shoved Kit into position over the trap door and placed the rope around his neck. As he did so, Kit turned his head. Aletheia looked into Kit's sightless eyes, then closed her own and smiled. Although no one in the square noticed it, there was also a brief interruption in the Praesidium's power supply, followed by a measurable surge.

What then happened fulfilled Simon Goodfellow's worst fears. After weeks of abuse and torture, beatings and starvation, this blind man, who was about to die, had shown no signs of Emergent powers. Even when charged with a capital offence and put on trial, he had said nothing in his defence. He had seemed broken. And now, without a word, he demonstrated that, all the while, he had actually been deceiving his tormentor. He made a fool of the man who'd set out to destroy him. Goodfellow felt utterly dismayed.

Kit simply disappeared.

For a moment there was a stunned silence, and then it began: a roar of astonishment intermingled with fear.

Drahan could see that Goodfellow was flummoxed. "Clear the square," he shouted. "Clear the square now. Take Adam and Aletheia to the Security Complex."

oooOooo

In the laboratory, Rambler, Prune and the Storyteller were staring at the screen, intently watching the events in the Praesidium square. All three gasped.

"Where's Kit?" asked Prune. "Andrew, what did you do?"

Andrew was feverishly running a scan of the paradox device.

"Andrew," said Prune, now with some urgency, "what did you do?"

"I didn't do anything," said Andrew. "I was ready to extricate Kit. I had a lock on him from the moment he set foot in the square. When Adam and Aletheia took a stand, I thought things had gone far enough so I activated the teleport function, but nothing happened. I had the feeling the paradox device had taken over. It seemed to know what I intended and had decided it was probably better at getting the timing right than I was."

"What does that mean?" asked Prune, both irritated and confused.

"More to the point, where's Kit?" asked Rambler. "Why isn't he here?"

"I don't know," said Andrew.

"What do you mean you don't know?" said Prune. "You can't teleport someone somewhere without knowing where."

"I'm scanning the paradox device. The device is not being very helpful. It says Kit decided where he wanted to go. That's it. No further information available."

"Isn't that a little worrying?" asked Rambler. "I mean, don't you control the device?"

"Not completely, evidently," said Andrew. "I have a feeling that either the device is developing a personality, or someone – not me – is somehow melding with the device. I did tell all of you that we should use the device cautiously because no one knows what its limits are, not with any certainty. And since we've linked it to the Eternal Light through the power loop, it has developed some degree of independence."

"Developed a personality ... human machine interface ... possible mind melding ... some degree of independence?" muttered Rambler, scribbling in his notebook.

Prune Leach was simply muttering.

51. Diabolical discussion

When the square was cleared, Simon Goodfellow and Silas Drahan made their way towards Drahan's office in the Security Complex. When they entered, they were surprised to find David Minofel seated in an armchair provided for guests, browsing through the latest edition of the Praesidium's house magazine.

"The best laid schemes o' mice an' men gang oft agley," said Minofel with a chuckle.

"What are you doing here?" asked Goodfellow. "You bailed out as soon as you thought things might get difficult."

"Get difficult!" Minofel repeated. "All hail, master of euphemism!"

"What do you want?" demanded Silas Drahan.

"I thought you had established that the blind man was not an Emergent," Minofel said, serious now. "I warned you to be careful, but your arrogance blinded you to the risks."

"Where is the blind man?" Drahan pressed. "And how did he disappear?"

"I have no idea where he is," Minofel replied. "Except that he is now out of our reach and more dangerous than ever. How he performed his truly impressive disappearing act I cannot tell. You can never know what a true Emergent can do – that's one of the problems. All we know for sure is that if the time is right and the circumstances are propitious, they can trigger a Beginning.

"But this was never about Kit Turner. It was always about Adam Smith. After all I did in London and Geneva, after all my Monitaurs did here, you lost him. Somehow, Kit Turner and Eve beat the combined strength of Slievins and the Praesidium. This will go to the highest level. Of course, I'm surprised and disappointed. But for you the consequences will be rather more serious. This Westminster PCC is at risk. I am here to take the Monitaurs to safety. Their work here is done, and Slievins always protects its own."

"So, we can no longer count on you for help?" said Goodfellow, fear and outrage intermingled in his voice.

"You have Eve under guard in your apartment. You now have Aletheia and Adam, as well as Manfred Bloch and Kathrin, imprisoned in cells in this complex. So you have some bargaining counters to negotiate with Andrew Rimzil and Prune Leach. You can disregard Rambler and the Storyteller – they are of no consequence. If you play your cards carefully and concentrate on destroying the others without allowing yourselves to be distracted or diverted, you will have at least a chance of surviving. Your biggest problem will be Aletheia, the Titan's greatest work. She and Prometheus have always had a soft spot for humanity. She's into the truth thing, and her entirely misplaced belief in the truth makes her strong. She is a formidable enemy. I shall watch the outcome with interest, but I shall watch from afar."

oooOooo

With that, David Minofel left Drahan's office and made his way to the chamber containing the Crucible of Eternal Light. Miss Tomic, who had aged by at least fifteen years since Minofel had pronounced her punishment, was waiting.

"Is everything ready?" he asked.

She nodded and opened a case containing four phials of concentrated liquid, one yellow, one red, one blue and one grey.

"Are they fully charged?"

Again, Miss Tomic nodded.

"You're not very talkative," observed David Minofel. "It's almost as though you resent your accelerated ageing. But it's all your fault. 'How sharper than a serpent's tooth it is to have a thankless child!' All you had to do was do as you were told. That was always the deal. It's all I ever asked. I even gave you a second chance – or at least Jedwell did. Never mind. Look on the bright side. Working out your notice in my employment will not take long. Indeed, it will be over pretty quickly – you have about one day for each year of your previously allotted span." He chuckled.

"Has it ever crossed your mind to consider," Miss Tomic said, speaking slowly and deliberately, "just how irritating others find all your smiles, your laughs and your chuckles?"

oooOooo

"We need a plan," said Goodfellow to Drahan. "And we need drastic measures. You must get rid of Kathrin and Bloch. As for Adam, I've not yet given up all hope. I still think I may be able to blackmail him, or coerce him, into seeing sense. Just make sure you keep Aletheia under control. Evidently, Minofel sees her as the greatest threat. I'm not sure why he fears her, but I'm prepared to take him at his word. He seemed to lose heart as soon as he learned she was coming here. And now he's buggered off."

"And what will you be doing?" asked Silas Drahan.

"I'm going to my apartment. I will deal with Eve. As soon as I've finished there I will join you here, and we can resolve the Aletheia problem together."

52. Problem resolution

Goodfellow left the Security Complex and set off for his apartment. Silas Drahan remained in his office and began to ponder whether to use a gun or a knife. He could, of course, simply have ordered the guards to despatch the captives, but the fewer the number of witnesses, the smaller the chance that anyone would ever raise a charge of extra-judicial killing. It was unlikely, but you never knew what someone with a grudge might do, and you could never be too careful. While the Praesidium was more than happy to promote indiscriminate carnage in the world of man, within the organisation itself there was a general preference for the rule of law.

There was another reason that Silas Drahan had decided to undertake the job himself. Before joining the Praesidium he had enjoyed a distinguished career in the Polish mafia, where his speciality was using his dogs, a pair of brutalised Dobermans, to savage victims until they begged to die. He would then cut out their hearts and feed them, still warm and sometimes, though rarely, still beating, to his dogs. Since joining the Security cadre of the Westminster PCC he had made speedy progress up the chain of command, but each promotion took him further away from the work he loved. This current situation presented Silas with a rare opportunity to, once again, get down and dirty.

First, he chose a long curved knife from the armoury of weapons he had brought with him from his days in Katowice. Just then he noticed Aletheia's sword, which had been confiscated when she applied at the court to be Kit's defence counsel. The sword had been brought to Security for storage, and when Silas had seen it he decided to add it to his own collection. He replaced the curved knife and took the sword. It was a fine piece of workmanship. Of course it was. It had been fashioned by the crippled son of Hera, Hephaestus, who had reluctantly chained Prometheus to the Caucasian rock. Later, when Prometheus had been released by Herakles, Hephaestus offered Prometheus the sword, the finest he had ever forged, by way of apology. This was the sword Prometheus had given to Aletheia. What more appropriate weapon could he use, thought Silas, to despatch Kathrin and her husband, and later Aletheia herself, than the very weapon Aletheia had impudently and imprudently brought to the Praesidium?

From his office it was a short walk along the corridor, then one floor down in the lift to the cells. He had ordered his guards to use Cells C1 to C4 to hold the detainees in solitary confinement.

He was therefore surprised when he found all four prisoners in Cell C4. He was about to turn back. He had no wish to tackle all four together, given that at least three of them could be expected to put up significant resistance. As he turned to go back for reinforcements, he heard Aletheia invite him to join them in Cell C4. The gate of the cell swung open.

"Why are you not locked in your cells?" asked Drahan.

"That's a question you should be asking your guards," suggested Aletheia. "They're in the adjacent cells – C1, 2 and 3. Although I fear they are unlikely to answer your questions satisfactorily, or at all – or ever," she added helpfully.

Aletheia stepped out of Cell C4. "That's a fine sword you hold," she said. "Not dissimilar to the one I brought with me."

Drahan was on his guard. He brought the sword forward, ready to thrust or slash.

Aletheia laughed. "I hope you're not thinking of threatening me with my own sword."

"Why not?" enquired Drahan.

"Because the sword was made by a god for a Titan, then given to an immortal. You, a mortal, cannot use it against a god, a Titan, or an immortal. It will destroy you."

Silas Drahan felt disconcerted. What was she blathering on about? Gods, Titans, immortals. Was she playing mind games? Well, he could play mind games too. "At this moment, Simon Goodfellow is with Eve. So, Adam, if you ever want to see her again, I suggest you persuade this foolish girl to step back into the cell."

"What is Eve doing with Goodfellow?" asked a distraught Adam.

"More to the point, what is Simon doing to Eve?" said Drahan. Then, answering Adam's question, he said, "She was arrested on leaving your apartment after her third attempt to persuade you to betray the Praesidium."

"If she is harmed ..." Adam began.

"The sooner you and the girl get back in the cell the sooner I can make sure Eve is safe. You know what Goodfellow is like, so I suggest you comply quickly."

Adam was disturbed rather than compliant, and Aletheia showed no sign of backing down. Drahan reviewed the situation. She said the sword couldn't harm her. He looked down at the blade. It was a fine weapon, but not endowed with magical properties. It would cut her as surely as it would cut anyone.

Before he could look up and decide where on Aletheia's body to plunge the blade, there was a mesmerising blur of colour. Even Adam, who had a perfect view of the action, had no idea what happened. All he saw was a momentary haze. When the haze cleared, he found he was facing the still-standing, but now headless, body of Drahan. Blood was pulsing from the severed neck. Some feet away lay Drahan's head, staring up at the corridor ceiling with a look of blank surprise. Slowly, Drahan's body sagged to the floor.

"Does anyone have a cloth, by any chance, so I can clean my blade?" Aletheia asked demurely.

"You could use this," said Kathrin, offering Aletheia her headscarf. Happily Adam had blocked her view of the beheading.

"That must be a blade of the finest steel," observed Manfred Bloch, whose youth had given him a certain appreciation for this kind of metalwork. On his left cheek he bore a fine, pale duelling scar.

"I'm just glad you're on our side," muttered Adam.

"We should leave here now," said Aletheia. "They have only a skeleton staff on duty because of the day's festivities, but at some point someone will raise the alarm."

"I have to go to save Eve," said Adam. "I have to go now."

"Wait." Aletheia took Adam's arm. "Think. This is the end game. We need to plan our next moves carefully. Manfred Bloch, you must convene an emergency meeting of the board. Take Kathrin with you. She will testify that Goodfellow murdered John Noble. She was a witness and will be believed. As the most senior board member after Goodfellow, you can take charge. Adam, you must go back to Andrew's lab and tell him to prepare for our departure. Time is of the essence. He will know what to do. I will go to Simon Goodfellow and bring Eve back."

"No," Adam objected. "I must go."

"Use your brain," said Aletheia. "If you go, he will threaten to kill Eve and you will do whatever he demands."

"And you won't? How does that help? I love my wife and she is carrying our child. She must not be harmed."

"We are wasting time," said Aletheia impatiently, handing her sword to Adam. "I will go to see Goodfellow. I will go unarmed. He will let me into his apartment. Once I am in the apartment, I will be able to decide on a course of action. Don't worry, Adam, I know what I need to do. If Eve is unharmed when I arrive, I promise no harm will come to her thereafter. Now, stop arguing and let me go."

53. Meeting of the board

When Manfred and Kathrin reached the boardroom, they found there were only five other members present.

John Noble was dead. Simon Goodfellow had not been invited, and was, in any case, otherwise occupied. The Monitaurs had not responded. (Unbeknownst to all except Simon Goodfellow, they had been distilled and removed by Minofel to a place of safety.) Gustave Houry, the Head of Internal Discipline was missing and about to be confirmed dead by Kathrin. Manfred would report the death of Silas Drahan, adding the Head of Security to the growing death toll.

The only members in attendance were the Heads of Accounting, Human Resources, House Services, Planning, and Research. All five were in a state of fear and confusion. The extraordinary disappearance of the blind man had unnerved them. The rumour that Kit might have been an Emergent, previously scotched by Goodfellow, had taken on a new lease of life; the possibility that there might be a threat to the Praesidium itself from an Emergent inevitably caused panic. The absence of so many board members was a further cause of consternation.

Manfred took control.

"I will not pretend that what I have to say is easy to believe, but it is true."

"Excuse me," interrupted the Head of Human Resources, "but I was unaware your wife was a member of this board."

"She is here to submit testimony to the board," Bloch replied sharply.

The Head of Human Resources gave way and Manfred continued, "Simon Goodfellow murdered John Noble."

There were gasps of astonishment. One board member expressed the general scepticism.

"That can't be true," said the Head of House Services. "The blind man killed John."

"No, he didn't," Kathrin said, intervening. "Simon Goodfellow murdered John Noble in his apartment. David Minofel's man, Jedwell, placed the body in Kit Turner's cell."

"And how would you know this?" asked the Head of HR.

"I saw him do it," Kathrin replied simply.

The Head of HR was incredulous. "Simon killed our Chairman in front of a witness?"

"Then he sent Gustave Houry to kill my wife," added Manfred.

"And where is Gustave?" enquired the Head of HR.

"He's dead," said Manfred. "Look, much as I would like to provide you with all the details, we don't have time. We have a nest of subversives roaming around the Westminster PCC. Adam has re-joined the questors, and they are holed up in a virtual laboratory on the ground floor, constructed by Rimzil using his paradox device. We need to capture Adam, if at all possible, and kill the others. Aletheia is on her way to see Simon Goodfellow. He's holding Adam's wife, Eve, in his apartment. Aletheia is hoping to rescue Eve and re-join the questors. Then they all plan to make their escape. It will not go well for us if they succeed. The High Council is going to take a pretty dim view of Goodfellow's conduct, but the Council will be more tolerant of evil than bungling incompetence. If, at the end of the day, the Council sees that we have failed to eliminate a possible Emergent, and failed to corrupt a leading questor, despite paying a practitioner enough to exhaust the whole of this year's budget, they may well conclude that we don't deserve any budget at all next year."

"What are we to do with Simon Goodfellow?" asked the Head of Planning. "Assuming he makes short work of the Aletheia woman."

"Assuming you're right, I propose to strip him of all his honours and charge him with murder of John Noble. But I have seen this Aletheia in action. You will have noticed the absence of the Head of Security. Well, so has he. She decapitated him."

"Do you mean she killed Silas Drahan?" asked the Head of Planning.

"Just so," said Manfred. "And given the demise of Silas Drahan, I propose to take over Security."

Bloch waited for the assent of the other board members.

"Good. I will ask my people in the Technical Division to use any means to break the electronic shield protecting Rimzil's parallel laboratory. In the meantime, I will wait outside the laboratory with a team of security officers to deal with Aletheia and Eve, if they make it back. I suggest that as a temporary measure House Services should take over Internal Discipline. Let's get something right. I think that covers everything. Let's go."

oooOooo

When Adam reached the lab, he found Andrew and Prune engaged in a speculative discussion about the evolution of the paradox device. Rambler and the Storyteller were debating whether Kit's disappearance should be seen, in narrative terms, as a technological triumph or a good, old-fashioned miracle. The Storyteller favoured the *deus ex machina* explanation.

Luke looked as though he was asleep but was actually relaying detailed minutes of the emergency board meeting, convened by Manfred Bloch, to Aletheia. When Luke had finished, Aletheia thanked him for the briefing. "Least I could do," minded Luke back. "It's also the most I could do, stuck in here. To be honest, I'm fed up with being confined to barracks. I'd like to stretch my legs."

Adam interrupted all three conversations. "Aletheia has gone to Simon Goodfellow's apartment. He's holding Eve. Is there anything we can do to help Aletheia?"

"We can try to scan Goodfellow's apartment," suggested Andrew. He took his seat in front of the paradox device and activated the monitor. "That's odd," he said. "It just said 'No'".

"What?" said Adam and Prune in unison.

"A machine can't say 'No'," Adam objected. "Do you mean it can't do it."

"No, that's not what I mean," said Andrew slowly. "It's perfectly capable of scanning Goodfellow's apartment, but Aletheia thinks it best that we spend our time preparing to leave."

"Who's asking Aletheia?" enquired a bemused Prune.

"Apparently, the paradox device," Andrew replied.

54. "I would some god ..."

When Aletheia reached the door of Simon Goodfellow's apartment, she found a guard outside.

"I have come to see the Chairman," she announced.

The guard looked her up and down. She was wearing a simple tunic without pockets. He could see she was unarmed. "I will let him know," said the guard.

When Aletheia entered the apartment, Goodfellow came to greet her.

"This must be my lucky day – two beautiful women making their way to my apartment on the same day."

"Only one came willingly," said Aletheia sharply. "Eve, I think, was coerced."

"Come now, my dear," Simon beamed. "No nitpicking. We're not in court now. May I offer you a drink?"

"No, you may not. Those who accept your hospitality tend to end up insensible and defenceless."

"Defenceless, perhaps," Goodfellow conceded, "but not insensible. There would be little pleasure in inflicting pain on an insensible body. Not that I have any intention of inflicting pain on you. I was thinking more of pleasure, of prolonged and exquisite delight." His eyes ran over Aletheia's body, as though he was assessing a fine filly he was thinking of buying and riding.

"Just for the record," said Aletheia sharply, "my own predilections lie with the fairer sex – my own – so, were I to consider embarking on a relationship with a mortal, even if your own proclivities were less depraved, you would fail to pass the pre-qualification stage. Now, where is Eve?" Aletheia asked firmly.

"Oh you're good, you're very good," said Goodfellow. "There's so much more pleasure in taming a wild spirit. As for Eve, she is resting in a guest room," he assured her. "The baby is making its demands on her body."

"Rather different in kind from those you plan to make."

Goodfellow smiled. "I see my reputation extends even to strangers who visit the Praesidium." Then he added, "I should prefer to talk about the demands I might make on you. Indeed, if you are – how shall I put it – compliant, I might find it in me to leave Eve untouched."

"You might find it in you," Aletheia repeated. "You must be prescient."

"What does that mean?"

"It means foreknowledge of what is going to happen," Aletheia explained.

"I know what the word means, my dear," Goodfellow responded a little impatiently. "I meant what did you mean by saying I was prescient."

"When you abuse your victims, what do you feel?" Aletheia asked.

"I think you do me an injustice. There are no victims. My partners are always willing to explore the darker corridors of human sexuality, at least at first. What do I feel? I feel pride and I feel pleasure. I take pride in revealing to the uninitiated the paradox embedded in the pleasure/pain nexus. I take pleasure in my partner's pain, just as I expect them to take pleasure in my pleasure."

"If you believed that, you would be entirely deluded," said Aletheia, "but you are not deluded. You cannot play games with me. I am Aletheia. I am the goddess of truth."

Goodfellow laughed. "If anyone's deluded, I think it might be you. Humanity dispensed with gods and goddesses long ago."

"And the truth? Has humanity dispensed with the truth?"

"That's a tricky question," Goodfellow replied. "There are so many truths, or versions of the truth."

"No, there is only one truth," said Aletheia. "For example, you are a selfish, evil, sadistic man. That is the truth. You might prefer a different description of yourself, but it would be a lie."

Goodfellow refused to be provoked. "I didn't expect us to be debating philosophy on our first assignation. Should you not wait until you know me better before coming to a final judgement?"

"You don't understand," said Aletheia, with a hint of pity in her voice. "I already know you completely. When the Titan Prometheus made me, he breathed into me his powers of empathy and forethought. There is no corner of your twisted soul on which I cannot shine the light of understanding – and that is what we are going to do. What happens when you see the truth will be your responsibility, not mine."

Simon Goodfellow had no idea what Aletheia meant; it sounded like psychobabble. But he certainly understood what she was doing. Standing in front of him, she disrobed, sliding the top straps of her tunic from her shoulders and allowing it to slither to the ground. She stood before him, glorious in her form, her blue-green eyes blazing, her fair hair swept back. The naked truth.

At first, Goodfellow could not take his eyes off Aletheia, but then the brightness of the light on her white flesh began to hurt his eyes. This was no normal light. Suddenly everything went black. He shuddered; it was as though she had blinded him.

Against the black background, lights began to flicker until a picture formed. It was of his apartment, the room where he took his pleasure. He was there, watching an old film; it was as though someone had recorded his activities on ancient nitrate stock. There was a girl on the bed. She looked vaguely familiar, but not familiar enough for him to attach a name to her. She was crying, and she was bleeding.

"Please don't hurt me any more," she pleaded.

A grey, faceless figure knelt beside her. The girl screamed. Simon watched the grey man continue to abuse the girl. To his astonishment, his own body felt every cut of the knife, every tear of the flesh. The girl's body and his were one. He tried to cry out in pain. He tried to protest. But the grey man continued his grisly work, and now Simon was matching the girl, scream for scream, sob for sob. He felt the pain. He felt weak, vulnerable, terrified. He was being abused appallingly in every part of his body.

The film ended, the tail end of the nitrate stock flipping through the projector, over and over again. Goodfellow tried to reach out into the blackness to stop what was happening, but he could touch nothing, nor could he move.

Another film was loaded. This time the scene was his sitting room. Kathrin was there, paralysed; John Noble was on the floor beside her, his head in her lap. Goodfellow recognised the scene well enough, although he knew no one could have recorded it. But there was something wrong. He was not there; someone else was. It was the grey, faceless man. The grey man was placing a bag over John Noble's head. Suddenly, Simon himself couldn't breathe. Somewhere in the blackness, someone had placed a bag over his head. Each time Noble desperately sucked for air, Goodfellow sucked too, in perfect harmony. It became more and more difficult to breathe. Then he couldn't breathe at all; he knew he was dying. The film ended, and Goodfellow took a mighty gasp of breath.

This wasn't fair. Why should he himself have to feel what he had done to others? There was a profound misunderstanding. The perpetrator was not the victim. The master was not the slave.

In the darkness, Simon Goodfellow heard Aletheia's voice. She seemed far away, but he could hear what she said clearly enough. "This will go on until you have had enough. And when you have had enough, the grey man will come for you. Your end will be cruel, but when he has finished, it will be over. Do not ask him for mercy. That will simply make him more determined to prolong your agony. You see, there is no pity in his heart. And do not ask the grey man for forgiveness, because he has nothing to forgive. He is not punishing you. He does what he does for his own pleasure. He feels only what he feels, whereas now, and until you die, you feel, and will feel, only what your victims felt."

Each of Simon Goodfellow's acts of abuse was replayed before him in precise detail. Each time, he felt the searing pain he had inflicted on his victims. His screams and sobs had no effect on the grey man.

"Please stop this," Simon begged Aletheia in one of the brief interludes between scenes. His face was lined with pain, his torn flesh and broken body nothing more than a source of agony.

"There's nothing I can do," said Aletheia, "and that's the truth."

oooOooo

Aletheia, now dressed in her tunic once again, found Eve in the guest room, tethered to a post with a rope around her neck and bound hand and foot. Aletheia released and embraced her. "As you will see, you have nothing to fear from Simon Goodfellow," she said.

They walked from the guest room into the sitting room where Simon Goodfellow was now writhing on the floor.

Eve winced at the grotesque sight. "What's happening to him?"

"Nothing he doesn't deserve," said Aletheia.

"What have you done to him? Shouldn't we help him?" said Eve.

"You're a kind, good-hearted person," Aletheia replied. "That is why you cannot help him. I have done nothing to harm him. Whatever is happening to him is entirely self-inflicted."

They left the apartment.

"What happened to Kit?" Eve asked.

Aletheia smiled. "To everyone's surprise, he decided to move on just before they were going to hang him. He is where he wants to be. I will answer all your questions when we are safe. Now we need to return to the lab as quickly as possible."

55. The brutal truth

Aletheia and Eve hurried across the bridge that connected the accommodation block to the Praesidium's main building. On the moving walkway were clusters of people still talking about the remarkable and worrying disappearance of the suspected Emergent.

The two women reached the corridor leading to the lab without difficulty, but as they walked towards the lab door, they saw Manfred Bloch and half a dozen heavily armed security guards.

Manfred stepped forward to meet them. "I am hoping we can resolve the situation without bloodshed," he offered. "We want Adam. The rest of you can go."

"And why do you want Adam?" Eve asked.

"You must understand we have invested a great deal of time and effort in your husband. That time and effort involved costs – very high costs – which we have to justify to ourselves, and to those above us."

"You cannot have Adam," said Aletheia. "When he stood beside Kit Turner on the scaffold and spoke for him, you lost, and you know it."

"We think he may be salvageable," said Bloch. "We intend to try."

"I don't think so," said Aletheia firmly.

"Then my hopes for an amicable resolution are fading," said Manfred with a sigh. "We seem to have reached a stalemate. We have failed to break through the shield that Rimzil is using to isolate his laboratory. Even so, you cannot seriously expect to get the better of me and six armed guards. I see you have no weapon. So I will issue an ultimatum. Either Adam joins us here, in which case you and Eve are free to join the others and leave unharmed, or we will execute Eve and imprison you. That is my final offer."

Two guards stepped forward and seized Eve.

"By what right do you threaten to execute an innocent woman?" said Aletheia angrily. "I thought you would have learned your lesson."

"You may consult with your friends, but I want an answer," said Bloch. He knew the other questors wouldn't abandon Eve and

Aletheia. With a little luck, he might be able to seize them all, he thought. At the very least he would be able to prevent Adam from leaving. He looked expectantly at Aletheia.

"I think you and I should have a talk in private," Aletheia suggested.

Bloch frowned. "We have nothing to discuss. You have to make a decision."

"I've made my decision, but I should like to explain my thinking to you, in private, as a matter of courtesy."

Reluctantly, Bloch agreed. It was a waste of time, but if Aletheia needed a few minutes to come to terms with defeat, what was the harm. He had no reason to fear her. She was unarmed, and in any case he could take care of himself. He ordered the guards to stay where they were, to guard Eve and prevent anyone from entering or leaving the laboratory.

"We can talk in the reception hall," Aletheia suggested.

They settled in a corner of the area set aside for those waiting for an appointment.

"It's a fine building you have," said Aletheia, "so full of natural light. My home is a massive cave in the Caucasus. We have light there too, but it is not from the sun."

Manfred Bloch frowned. He had no idea what she meant by saying her home was a cave, so he simply asked, "You're from the Caucasus? I thought you were Greek from your name. Where were you born?"

"I was not born. I was created by the Titan Prometheus, and given immortality by the king of the gods, Zeus."

Suddenly, Manfred Bloch was afraid; he was obviously dealing with a lunatic. "I see," he said.

"No, you don't," said Aletheia. "You are having difficulty in grasping what I'm telling you. This is a worry because if you have a problem with my provenance, you'll find my prognosis for the Praesidium utterly incredible."

"Your prognosis for the Praesidium?" Bloch repeated.

"I am going to destroy this PCC," Aletheia announced. "I will give you six days to make arrangements. You may decide to evacuate, although it's certain that you will have difficulty in integrating back into the world you have done so much to harm. Or you may decide to take the more honourable course and go down with your ship.

Whatever you decide, I and my friends will be leaving you today."

"I see," said Manfred again. "Could you give me a clue as to how you propose to execute your plan?"

"Of course," Aletheia replied. "It is really important you understand what is going to happen. Only when you understand will you take the right decision. You know of the paradox device. You've been trying to persuade Andrew to make one for the Praesidium. You also know about, but cannot explain, an anomaly in the Praesidium's power supply which is derived from the Eternal Light. Well, through and with the paradox device, I have been able to take control of this PCC's power supply. I don't expect you to take my word for it."

"Good," said Manfred, whose patience was wearing thin, "because that is impossible."

"I will show you now," Aletheia replied.

As she spoke, the internal lights went out and an alarm rang through the reception hall, before stopping.

"There," she said.

"That was just a blip in the supply," Manfred replied, a little uncertainly. The failure of the internal lights was not immediately evident because the sun was filling the reception hall. "You see, the alarm has stopped."

"The alarm has stopped because not only have I cut off the main power supply, but I have also drained your reserves, so even your alarm system won't work."

Manfred Bloch could see that panic was building in the reception hall as staff and visitors found that nothing dependent on a power supply would work.

"What do you mean 'through and with the paradox device'?" asked Manfred, now shaken.

"Well, I'd like to say it's simple, but it isn't. I don't really understand it myself. Maybe Prometheus has had a hand in it. All I can say is that I have developed a kind of relationship with the paradox device, just as the paradox device has established some kind of relationship with the Eternal Light. The paradox device seems to be the key, and the link."

"I'm an engineer," said Bloch. "What you are saying is meaningless to me. You cannot have a relationship with a device, or with a power source."

"I will restore the power now," said Aletheia. "You don't have to understand. You just have to know."

"Even if everything you say is true," Manfred said, still incredulous, "how can you turn the power on and off while sitting here talking? You have no means of access to the controls of the paradox device."

"That's why I said 'with'. The device is with me, within me, as I am within it. It's all a paradox. It's a paradox that I, the goddess of truth from ancient times, should be here at all. It is a paradox that you, an ancient and wholly pernicious society, have survived in secret for thousands of years and are able to govern the affairs of men. And it's a paradox that a woman, a device, and a power source should form a symbiotic relationship able to bring the mighty Praesidium to its knees. It's all profoundly paradoxical, but it's also true."

"If you cut the power supply, this PCC will collapse," said Manfred, as though putting the horror of it into words would somehow deter Aletheia.

"Of course," Aletheia replied. "You have six days. After three days, the power from the Eternal Light will begin to diminish. By the sixth day, you will have insufficient power to maintain this Parallel Coincident Construct. On the seventh day, everything and everyone in it, will evaporate. So evacuate or die. This is my final judgement. You have done so much harm to mankind for so long. You have encouraged his weaknesses. You have inhibited his ambitions for improvement. You have obstructed every opportunity for a Beginning. I believe you do not fully understand the harm you have done, but that is irrelevant. It is over. It must stop. It will stop."

Manfred sat in the reception hall taking in what Aletheia had said. After years of faithful service his ambition to take over as Chairman of the PCC had been fulfilled. But his success was to be short-lived, and even assuming the Praesidium survived, his name would forever be associated with the destruction of the Westminster PCC. He had failed Nastafilu Verdicel and all his successors, defeated by a Caucasian goddess from ancient times who had established a perverse and inexplicable relationship with a computer system and a power supply. Tucking his knees in and putting his arms round them, he began to rock backwards and forwards on his seat.

"We must go now," said Aletheia. "You must tell the guards to release Eve. She and I will enter the laboratory and you will never see us again."

"And if I refuse?" asked Manfred weakly.

"The next time you consider refusal, I will take one day from the six days I have allowed you to make good your escape. After three refusals, you will find the Eternal Light is leaking power, and there will be only three days left. Remember, if you waste time, you, Kathrin, and everyone on this construct will be obliterated. And if you think that killing me will solve your problem, I have to tell you that if any harm comes to me, the paradox device will immediately feed dark energy back into the system, causing an abrupt and catastrophic power failure. Within minutes, this construct will begin to disintegrate. It's up to you."

Manfred was shaking his head. How could he evacuate the PCC in a few days? What about the other Praesidium PCCs around the world? They all depended on the energy from the Eternal Light. Did this delusional woman, with her incomprehensible symbiotic relationship, intend to annihilate all the PCCs? London had the privilege of guarding the power source for the entire Praesidium organisation. Was he going to have to inform members of the High Council that the London PCC had utterly failed; that their work, and probably their lives, were finished; that the Praesidium itself was doomed? It was too much to take in, too much of a burden for one man to carry.

"Do you have any idea what you are doing?" he asked.

"I am destroying you and all your works," Aletheia replied, "without regard for the lives that may be lost and the suffering entailed. I would have thought you would have approved. Isn't this entirely in accordance with the Praesidium's view of the true nature of man?"

"But I thought you were a goddess?"

"I am a goddess, the goddess of truth. But I was fashioned by Prometheus, the friend and admirer of man. Prometheus foresaw that man had a great destiny, a destiny which the Praesidium is committed to frustrating. You are, and always have been, an impediment to man's development. I am merely flushing the blockage away. Now, unless we go back to the laboratory immediately, I will start to feed dark energy back into the Eternal Light."

Manfred staggered to his feet. Aletheia took his arm to steady him. He shook her off. Together, they walked slowly through the reception hall and back along the corridor to Andrew Rimzil's laboratory.

oooOooo

When Eve and Aletheia were reunited with their friends, there was great rejoicing. They had succeeded in rescuing Adam, and Kit had escaped hanging.

But there was sadness and trepidation too. Rambler knew he would never fully recover from the loss of Numpty. His nephew had been a crucial part of his life and the source of so much satisfaction to him. Nurturing and educating Numpty had given Rambler's life purpose and value. More than that, Numpty had given Rambler love. He would always remember their years together: how Numpty had always been ready to learn; how he had questioned everything, listened carefully to the answers, and learned from them; how, after the Fourth Beginning, his mental acuity had undergone a step change, and he had become his uncle's equal. Above all, he would marvel at the courage his nephew had always shown when he stood up to the violent biker at Fleet services, when he had faced a dreadful death before the angelic host in God's domain at Hook, and when he had taken on Gustave Houry to protect Kathrin. Numpty had led a good life, which had ended with a good death. That, at least, was some comfort for the grieving Rambler.

As for Adam, he was at the end of one ordeal but at the beginning of another. Just as Minofel and the Praesidium had recast him in their image, he now had to look deep inside himself to determine who he truly was. As Aletheia had said, he must review what he had done and see it through the eyes of truth. Whether he could survive the process, whether he could ever redeem himself, was uncertain. He had done dreadful things – illegal and immoral things. He would have to discover whether there was more to him than the evil he had done. Numpty might have advised him to become an osmotic gouger, to delve into the depths of the evil that had absorbed him in the hope that, out of facing and understanding what he had become, eventually a brighter, cleaner, kinder Adam might emerge into the sun. The prognosis seemed poor, except that throughout his life he had held on to his love for Eve. He hoped that his love for her, and hers for him, might in the end help him to become a better man, if not a good one.

There was still the issue of reigniting the Beginning. Kit had sought out the questors in Harrow to persuade them to restart the Beginning aborted by the Praesidium. He had almost convinced them it was possible. That possibility would give Adam and Eve hope, but it was a hope they knew would never be realised without Kit. He was the only one with the strength, the will and the courage to lead them.

But Kit had disappeared and no one seemed to know where he had gone. Of course, they had all speculated about it: perhaps he'd just set off on his travels round the world once more; perhaps he had gone back to Hook, to see whether his spurious father was mellowing at all in his vicious, dictatorial kingdom; or perhaps he was gathering his strength for a final, definitive attempt to help mankind take the next step along the path that Prometheus had envisaged for his protégée so long ago.

Luke listened carefully to all their speculations. He was very tempted to put them out of their misery, but every time he was about to succumb, Kit would mind to him a simple message: "Now is not the time". In fact, the admonition was unnecessary since with Numpty gone and Andrew Rimzil preoccupied with the paradox device, the only one Luke could tell was the Storyteller. And the Storyteller was always loath to intervene.

There would be time for them all to ponder everything when they were back, safe and sound, in Harrow.

56. Job done

Aletheia walked into the Slievins offices in the City of London. She was wearing a dark trouser suit, a white shirt and highly polished black leather boots. The heels on her boots added two inches to her height, making her already tall figure even more imposing. Her fair hair was tied back into a ponytail. Her blue-green eyes exuded energy and purpose.

"I'm here to see David Minofel," she said to the receptionist.

The receptionist was typing a note into her computer. "Do you have an appointment?" she asked, without looking up; then she said, "Bugger!" Her screen had gone blank.

"Sorry," she said, now looking up, "but my computer's crashed."

"That is not the only thing that will crash if you don't learn some manners."

The girl now took in the powerful figure of the trouser-suited goddess of truth and immediately understood she was in the presence of someone who commanded respect.

"Do you have an appointment?" she repeated tentatively.

"If you mean is my name inscribed in your now defunct computer beside a specific time in your daily diary, then no, I do not have an appointment," Aletheia responded imperiously. "But, if you mean was my meeting this afternoon with David Minofel ordained from the beginning of time, or at least shortly after, then yes, I most certainly do have an appointment. I will add only this – unless you escort me to David Minofel's office immediately, I will put such a surge through your electrical circuits, the whole building will need rewiring."

"Your name?" asked the now cowed and terrified receptionist.

"I am Aletheia, goddess of truth, creation of Prometheus, true friend to mankind."

The receptionist called David Minofel's office. "There's a lady called Aletheia here for you."

After a moment, she disconnected and said, "He will see you now. I'll take you to his office."

Aletheia and the receptionist entered the empty lift. The receptionist, now in permanent apology mode, said, "Sorry, but it's the top floor," and then added, "I hope you're all right with heights."

"I doubt whether Minofel's office is quite as high as my home, the mighty cave on Mount Strobilos, where great eagles soar over the Caucasian plains," Aletheia replied.

The receptionist abandoned any attempt at small talk.

Minofel's office was at the top of a skyscraper, with excellent views of the City and central London. The office had a large antechamber to accommodate Minofel's personal assistant. At her desk, now approaching retirement age, was Miss Tomic.

Aletheia nodded briefly to her as she passed through.

"What an unexpected delight!" said David Minofel warily. He had quickly closed the wall cabinet containing his most prized possessions, the phials of blood samples taken from some of history's most notorious tyrants and criminals. "Just passing by?" he asked. "Is this for pleasure or business?"

"It's both," Aletheia replied, "my pleasure, your business."

"Well, sit down and let's explore both," said Minofel. "Can I get you something to drink?"

"No, thank you – unless that vending machine offers nectar."

"Very well," said Minofel. "What can I do for you?"

"By now you will be aware that I am destroying the Praesidium," Aletheia began in a matter-of-fact voice. "Within days, all the Parallel Coincident Constructs around the world will collapse."

"You overstate the situation a little," Minofel responded, "but you have certainly presented the Praesidium with some logistical problems and, incidentally, given Slievins an enormous amount of additional business. We have been retained to implement an emergency plan to provide alternative sources of energy for each PCC. Temporarily, we are going to draw on the electricity supply in each city, so we will have to find a way of concealing the drain on national grids, but with luck we will be able to maintain most of the PCCs until we can find an alternative, independent energy supply. Some we will lose, but it will be far from a complete wipeout. Our logistics people are working on a rather clever quick fix. By the way, in the longer term, we are talking of 'going green' – you know, solar energy. It's quite exciting."

"You never give up, do you?" Aletheia responded. "But this time you have lost. You will certainly lose some PCCs. You failed to take Adam. You failed to break the blind man. The questors will have the chance to regroup. And they will be stronger because they now know you can be beaten."

"Of course we never give up," said Minofel with a laugh. "It's business. And yes, this time we failed, but what the hell – every failure ensures more work for us. One of our mottos, which I have to say is disarmingly honest, is 'Succeed or fail, Slievins always wins'. As goddess of truth, that must be one you would approve of. Fortunately, our clients don't seem to understand the motto, which is just as well, eh? Again, it's business. Just business."

"Well, here's a little more business for you to deal with. I am taking Miss Tomic with me."

"Really!" Minofel was genuinely surprised. "I am aware of your sexual preferences, but didn't you see her on the way in? I would have thought something a little fresher would have been more to your taste."

"You never fail to disappoint," Aletheia responded. "I am taking Miss Tomic because she is one of ours, and you know it. She was so fine in mind and body, you couldn't resist the temptation to defile her. But did you never wonder why she was born so exceptionally intelligent and beautiful? Yes, she was tricked and trapped by you, then shamelessly used and abused by you. But, like Adam, you lost her, just as in the end you lost Jedwell Boon. Let's be frank – no matter how you tell it, you have come off worst in this encounter."

Minofel shrugged. "Not our most successful operation, I grant you. But the occasional failure is not without benefits. It keeps us on our toes and reminds the clients how important our work and our successes are. As for Miss Tomic, take her by all means. At the rate she's ageing, I doubt if she's got twenty-four hours left in her, and they will be the hours of physical and mental decline and decay. If you want to see her through the dribbling, babbling, leaking stages, you're very welcome."

Aletheia stood up. "It's the Praesidium that is dribbling, babbling and leaking at the moment. And that's the truth." She turned and walked out of Minofel's main office. In the outer office, she stopped by Miss Tomic's desk. "Leave everything," she said to Miss Tomic, "and come with me".

"Where are we going?" Gorgeous Tomic asked.

"We are going home," said Aletheia.

"I am not sure I can travel far. And it won't be worth the effort. I am getting old rather quickly, and will be dead soon."

"Why is this happening to you?"

Miss Tomic sighed. "Because it is David Minofel's wish and my punishment. I am decaying. He has the power, and he has told me I am dying. Therefore, I think I am."

"Don't worry," Aletheia assured her. "Our journey will take us far in space and time. As we separate you from Minofel's malign influence in distance, the ageing will stop, and as we leave him behind – or, more precisely, ahead – in time, the ageing process will reverse. I promise you that by the time you meet Prometheus, you will be as you were before Minofel punished you, but with an added bonus. Prometheus is a Titan. He has the power of the gods of ancient times, and he has promised me that he will give you immortality."

Already Miss Tomic felt the juices of youth starting to flow through her once again. The ache in her back was beginning to fade, the wrinkled skin on the back of her hands was becoming smoother and tauter, her sight was improving.

"How can I begin to thank you? Don't bother with immortality. Just feeling well again would be enough."

"No need for thanks," said Aletheia. "Prometheus will do all this for you because you deserve it, because it will please me and because he will greatly enjoy upsetting David Minofel."

oooOooo

At the Smiths' home in Harrow, Eve was taking an afternoon nap. Adam was in the garden mowing the lawn. Eve woke up when for no apparent reason Luke, who was asleep, barked once excitedly. Aletheia had just minded to him the news of Miss Tomic's change of fortune.

All in all, Luke decided, it had been a satisfactory outcome. Kit had been saved. Adam had taken the first step on the path to redemption. Eve and their unborn baby were safe. They had not destroyed the Praesidium, but they had certainly disrupted its operations. And if they ever decided to join battle with the Praesidium again, Luke reckoned that thanks to Rimzil's enhanced paradox device, the questors would have the edge. Of course he, like Rambler, missed Numpty dreadfully, but as he had explained to the Storyteller, dogs tend to see things differently from humans. "We're more like Vikings," Luke had explained. "If you live well and, most importantly, die well, then all's well."

The Storyteller had missed the point, replying, "I always thought the Vikings were humans."

"You people!" Luke had thought. Adventures and quests were all very well, but what quests were really all about, if you had any sense, were happy dreams in front of a crackling fire in a home full of love.

As Aletheia would say, "That is the truth."

oooOooo

In his flat in Maida Vale, Rambler was sitting at his desk. He was trying to write up his notes on recent events, putting particular emphasis on the possibilities of the putative eccentric, symbiotic relationship between Aletheia and Rimzil's paradox device.

He was trying to explore the potential for such an odd phenomenon but not succeeding very well. His mind kept returning to Numpty, to the good years he and his nephew had spent together, and how abruptly they had ended when Numpty had bravely and selflessly given his life in defence of Kathrin Bloch.

He recalled one of his last philosophical conversations with his nephew. They had discussed the question of the existence of the self. "*Cogito ergo sum*," Rambler had said, trying to assuage Numpty's existential doubts. And Numpty had responded with the concept of the osmotic gouger, one who seeks the truth by digging deep into the mysteries of life in the hope and expectation that a seed in the dark, dank soil below would grow into a beautiful flower in the sunlight above. This thought brought Rambler some comfort. "*Sum ergo cogito,* perhaps," he mused.

The doorbell rang. Rambler put down his pen, closed his current notebook, left his desk and made his way to the door of his flat. There had been few visitors since his return.

"Let's go," said Kit when Rambler opened the door. "We can give the others a bit of a break, but you and I have work to do."

www.ingramcontent.com/pod-product-compliance
Lightning Source LLC
Chambersburg PA
CBHW070421010526
44118CB00014B/1850